£12.50

CURRENT TRENDS IN BRITISH GERONTOLOGY

Current Trends in British Gerontology

Proceedings of the 1980 Conference of the
British Society of Gerontology

Edited by
REX TAYLOR
MRC Medical Sociology Unit,
Aberdeen

and

ANNE GILMORE
Department of Social Administration,
University of Glasgow

Gower

Published by
Gower Publishing Company Limited,
Gower House, Croft Road, Aldershot, Hampshire GU11 3HR, England.

 British Library Cataloguing in Publication Data

British Society of Gerontology. *Conference (1980: Aberdeen)*
Current trends in British gerontology.
1. Gerontology—Congresses
I. Title II. Taylor, Rex
III. Gilmore, Anne
612'.67   HQ1061

ISBN 0-566-00495-X

Reproduced from copy supplied
Printed and bound in Great Britain
by Billing and Sons Limited and Kemp Hall Bindery
Guildford, London, Oxford, Worcester

CONTENTS

5 Studies in Methodology

CONTRIBUTORS

Mark Abrams	Age Concern, Mitcham, Surrey.
Robert Anderson	Department of Agriculture, University of Aberdeen.
David Challis	Personal Social Services Research Unit, University of Kent.
Gerry Evans	Withington Hospital, Research Section, University of Manchester.
Eileen Fairhurst	Geigy Unit for Research in Ageing, University of Manchester.
Graeme Ford	MRC Medical Sociology Unit, Aberdeen.
Marie Gardiner	Department of Psychology, Gartnavel Royal Hospital, Glasgow.
Mary Gilhooly	MRC Medical Sociology Unit, Aberdeen.
Katie Gilhome-Herbst	The Mental Health Foundation, Wimpole Street, London.
Chris Gilleard	Department of Psychiatry, Royal Edinburgh Hospital, University of Edinburgh.
John G. Greene	Department of Psychology, Gartnavel Royal Hospital, Glasgow.
Ian Hanley	Department of Clinical Psychology, Royal Edinburgh Hospital.
Mike Hepworth	Department of Sociology, University of Aberdeen.
Peter Hildebrand	The Tavistock Clinic, London.
Beverley Hughes	Withington Hospital Research Section, University of Manchester.
Scott Kerr	Department of Psychology, University of Edinburgh.
Kathleen Kindness	Psychology Department, Royal Cornhill Hospital, Aberdeen.
Roger Lightup	Geigy Unit for Research in Ageing, University of Manchester.
Ronald Lyle	Department of Psychology, Stobhill Hospital, Glasgow.
Malcolm McFadyen	Department of Psychology, Royal Cornhill Hospital, Aberdeen.

Tony Prior   Department of Psychology, Royal Cornhill Hospital, Aberdeen.

Malcolm Reid   Department of Physical Education, University of Aberdeen.

Gilbert Smith   Department of Social Administration, University of Hull.

Nicky Smith   Department of Sociology, University of Aberdeen.

Robert Smith   Department of Psychology, Gartnavel Royal Hospital, Glasgow.

Geoffrey Sparks   Department of Social Studies, The Polytechnic, Huddersfield.

Elizabeth Tarran   Department of Social Theory and Institutions, University College of Bangor.

Rex Taylor   MRC Medical Sociology Unit, Aberdeen.

Christina Victor   Welsh National School of Medicine, St. David's Hospital, Cardiff.

Glenda Watt   Royal Edinburgh Hospital.

David Wilkin   Withington Hospital, Research Section, University of Manchester.

The papers collected together in this volume were originally presented at the 1980 Annual Conference at the British Society of Gerontology, held in late September at the University of Aberdeen. It was generally agreed to have been a successful conference and many of the papers were deemed to be of a publishable standard. Accordingly, the Society invited the present editors to undertake the selection and editing necessary for the publication of a volume of conference proceedings. The present volume is the result of these endeavours.

Readers unfamiliar with the British Society of Gerontology might be interested to know that it was founded in 1973 to provide a multidisciplinary forum for researchers in the field of gerontology. Until 1979 it went under the longer title of the British Society of Social and Behavioural Gerontology. The original group of members included sociologists, psychologists, doctors and members of the caring professions. In more recent years, and particularly since the change to a less cumbersome name, this original membership has been broadened by the addition of numbers of historians, geographers, economists and architects. Membership is now open to all those who are interested in research into and understanding of human ageing processes and the contexts in which they occur. While the primary focus is on older people the society is also interested in ageing throughout the whole life span. There is growing awareness and activity within the membership relating to earlier life phases, and particularly to middle age. While the Annual Conference is the main event of the year, the society organises a variety of meetings on a wide range of age-related topics. It also publishes a newsletter – Ageing Times Bulletin – and its official journal – Ageing and Society – is published by Cambridge University Press.

The 1980 Conference was the tenth to be organised by the society and, unlike those of previous years, it had no single overarching theme. Instead of exploring one topic in depth, the conference ranged fairly widely over a number of the topics which currently animate social gerontology in Britain. The present volume reflects this diversity but the editors have selected and organised the papers into the following five topics, or areas: normal ageing, illness in old age, therapies and their evaluation, institutional and community care and methods and procedures of gerontological research. No claim is made for comprehensive treatment of these five areas, but the editors are confident that the papers devoted to each area will give the reader a good indication of current substantive and methodological issues. Considered collectively, the papers provide the best available sample of current thinking and research in British social gerontology, hence the title.

In preparing this volume the editors have been assisted in numerous ways by their uncomplaining spouses - Judy Taylor and Stan Gilmore. They would also like to thank Rose Parton, who did the typing, and Malcolm Johnson and Pauline Woodward, who helped in other ways.

Rex Taylor (Aberdeen)
Anne Gilmore (Glasgow)

May 1981

x

CLASS DIFFERENCES IN THE USE OF LEISURE
TIME BY THE ELDERLY

Mark Abrams

It is difficult to think of any areas of British life that have
not been explored in terms of class differences: incomes and expenditure patterns, education, accent, vocabulary, voting behaviour, food
and drink preferences, media consumption, household furnishings.
From time to time the findings of public opinion surveys endorse the
view that Britain is a class-obsessed society and that class
differences are of considerable importance in determining the personal
affairs of most people and the structure and manning of many
institutions that affect their lives. For example, a recent survey
carried out for the London 'Times' (published Sept.10, 1980) reported
that large majorities of the British public think that the class a
person belongs to is important in several ways: in social life ('who
you know and who wants to know you') - 61 per cent, in getting a good
job (66 per cent), getting promotion in one's job (59 per cent),
getting children into a good non-state school (70 per cent), in
getting elected to committees or being invited to become a magistrate
(62 per cent). And, with solid backing from the official mortality
statistics, they could have added that the class a person belongs to
has a considerable effect on peoples' years of life expectation.

One of the puzzling ommissions from our almost encyclopaedic
knowledge of British class differences is the almost complete lack of
information on class differences in the leisure activities of old
people. Thus, the report published on behalf of various government
departments ('Leisure and the Quality of Life', HMSO 1977) carried
out in the 530 pages of its second volume , 25 papers on different
research studies of leisure; the reported research findings are
usually related to age-bands, sometimes to terminal education age,
but only one of the papers analyses the material using the two
variables of age and class. This is the exciting and stimulating
paper by Alan Macheath ('Pre-experiment Leisure Survey in Clwyd
(Deeside)', but unhappily the total sample was small - 924
respondents and of these less than 200 were aged 65 or more, the
Deeside area of North Wales may not be representative of Britain as
a whole, and the interviews were carried out (in the first half of
1974) 'mainly by mature lady students ... on TOPS or secretarial
courses ... few of them had previous survey experience.'

In the hope of filling part of this gap in our knowledge of the
elderly I included some 'use of time' questions in my Age Concern
England survey of Spring 1977 and in this paper I shall present some
of the findings analysed by class of respondent. The total sample
consisted of 1640 men and women aged 65 or more (802 aged 65 to 74
and 844 aged 75 or more). The respondents were a probability sample
of elderly people living in four English urban areas - Hove,
Northampton, the Manchester parliamentary constituence of Moss Side,

1

and the London Borough of Merton. On the basis of respondent's (or
her husband's) occupation during the bulk of his/her working life
(many of the women had either never married or had been widowed in
early middle age), they were divided into four 'class' groups; their
designations and incidence in the sample are:

AB	=	professional or managerial	16 per cent
CI	=	other white collar workers	25 per cent
C2	=	skilled manual workers	36 per cent
DE	=	Other manual workers	20 per cent
			———
			97 per cent
			———

For 3 per cent of respondents mid-career social mobility was so
complex that allocation to one of the four classes was not possible.

    In order to obtain subsamples adequate for meaningful analysis
I have (very reluctantly) collapsed these four groups into two –
ABCI (called hereafter middle class), and C2DE (hereafter working
class). This collapsing was necessary since in analysing many other
data from the survey I had found it necessary and enlightening to
separate the younger elderly (65-74) from the other elderly (75 or
more) and then divide each of these into male and female groups and
then to go on and subdivide each of these age/sex groups into those
living alone and those living with others. This last subdivision
seemed to me to be one that would be of considerable significance
in examining the leisure behaviour of women where large numbers live
alone. The dimensions therefore of the sub-populations dealt with in
this paper (ignoring the 3 per cent of non-classified respondents
are:

			Middle class	Working class
			%	%
Men:	65-74		9	12
"	75		6	7
Women:	65-74	Living Alone	7	12
"	"	Not living alone	9	13
"	75+	Living alone	7	8
"	75+	Not living alone	4	6
			———	———
			42	58
			———	———

    Thus, our sample of middle class respondents constituted 42 per
cent of all those aged 65 or more; in the population aged less than
65 they would account for little more than 30 per cent of all adults;
this difference arises from the much fewer years of life expectation
of working class men and women in middle age. Again, in our sample
women outnumber men by 2 to 1; this is a much higher ratio than is
found in the population under 65 years of age and similarly is the
outcome of differences in mortality rates for elderly men and women.

    The shape of the analysis of the survey material emerged from
two broad assumptions: they are:

(a) That the point of retirement is also the point of consolida-
     tion of life-long social and economic inequality, i.e. that
     class differences in life-styles in old age are determined
     by class differences in youth and middle age.

(b) That since in all age groups the consumption of many leisure
     goods and services (e.g. taking holidays, belonging to clubs,
     owning a car, going to theatres, eating in restaurants)
     depends upon the ability to spend money. It would follow
     that substantial class differences in spending power among
     would generate substantial class differences in leisure
     activities.

     The existence of life-long social and economic class differences
(the starting point of the first assumption) is well documented in
several government publications. For example the most recent report
of the Family Expenditure Survey (for the year 1978 HMSO 1980) shows
that in the 65 per cent of all households where the head of the
household is an employee (i.e. excluding those where the head is
either retired, self-employed, an employer or unemployed) the gross
weekly income of the average middle class family (professional,
managerial, other white collar) was 30 per cent higher than that of
the average working class household (£149 compared with £115). In
both classes the age of the average head of household was 43, but
the number of children in the average middle class household was
fewer than in the average working class household (.86 compared with
1.06) and so in terms of gross income per equivalent adult head the
excess of average middle class household gross income over working
class income was nearer 33 per cent. The same survey shows that the
additional income of the middle class in the prime of life is largely
absorbed by greater spending on housing, durable goods, private
motoring, 'other goods' (e.g. travel and sports goods, newspapers,
books, gardening, materials, cameras etc.) and services (e.g.
telephone, theatre, education, holidays, club subscriptions, life
insurance, investment, and of course, income tax).

     Another source of relevant information on class differences in
the population at large is the 1977 General Household Survey. This
contained a question which asked about engagement in various leisure
activities during the four weeks before the interview. The latest
volume shows that many more middle class respondents, compared with
working class respondents, had engaged in outdoor sports – golf,
cricket, swimming, walking etc. – (34 per cent middle class, 22 per
cent working class); more indoor sports – squash, swimming, darts,
badminton etc. – (22 per cent middle class, 19 per cent working
class – in spite of the latter's much greater participation in
darts); the proportion of middle class respondents who had visited
historic buildings and museums, attended performances of opera,
ballet and theatre, and taken part in adult education classes, etc.
is almost double that recorded by working class respondents (51 per
cent against 26 per cent). As Hemingway pointed out to Scott
Fitzgerald many years ago, many differences between the life styles
of the well-to-do and those of the not-well-to-do are dependent on
the fact that the former have more money.

If my first assumption is correct - namely that class differences in life style before the onset of old age determine class differences among the elderly in the way they spend their leisure time - then from the above facts about pre-elderly inequalities one would expect to find very large class differences in the use of time among the elderly - if the inequalities of income found among the non-elderly persist in old age.

But do they? To begin with, the findings of the Family Expenditure Survey show that in 1978 the gross weekly income of the average household where the head of the household is aged 65 or more is very much less than that of households where the head is aged less than 65 - a mere £56 against the latter's £120; and even when allowance is made for household size and composition and these figures are turned into income per equivalent adult (by treating any child under 18 years of age as half an adult) the gap is not greatly reduced and in these terms the income of the average elderly person is little more than half that of the non-elderly person.

However, it is possible that inequalities of income are as great among the elderly as among the non-elderly, and that accordingly differences in life styles are not reduced by the mere process of ageing. Here again there is evidence from the Family Expenditure Survey. In 1978 of all households where the head was under 65 years of age the biggest single group was where the head was aged 30 to 49 (47 per cent of all such households) and the average weekly gross income was £134. In this group of non-elderly households the poorest 13 per cent had incomes which were less than half the average and the richest 13 per cent had incomes which were 50 per cent above the average.

Figures from the same source indicate that among households where the head is aged 65 or more the polarisation of incomes is even more marked. Here, as many as 30 per cent of households have incomes which are less than half the group's average and 18 per cent of households have gross incomes which are 50 per cent above the average. Thus, while the average elderly household has much less income than the average non-elderly household the former average emerges from a greater degree of inequality. And the 'affluent' elderly owe their good fortune not to the fact that the average head of the household is younger than the average head of the non-affluent elderly household (both are in their early 70's) but to the fact that the former is more likely to contain someone who is still working, or if not working, is receiving a private pension in addition to the State pension available to everyone aged 65 or more. Elderly people who are able to continue working beyond the statutory retirement age and/or enjoy a second pension of any financial consequence are almost invariably, as we shall see from the Age Concern survey, middle class people. It would seem therefore that we have to add a modifying sentence to our initial assumption that the point of retirement is also the point of consolidation of economic inequality - it is true that economic inequality is consolidated but it persists at a level where the incomes of even the most affluent minority of the elderly have incomes which are, on average, no more than those of the average skilled manual worker and are usually little more than

4

half of what they enjoyed (in real terms) before they reached the age of 65. In the light of this corollary to the initial assumption we would therefore expect that despite persisting class differences into old age, class differences in the use of leisure time would, for purely economic reasons be reduced.

The Age Concern England survey findings throw some light on this matter. Here, briefly, are some of the data.

1. Informant's sources of income

(a) Main source

The answers to the questions about respondent's sources of income are shown in Table 8; they relate not to all those in the sample but only to men and to women living alone - i.e. 68 per cent of the whole sample. For working class men and women almost without exception the State pension was the main source of income; only 2 per cent gave non-State pensions as their main source and 1 per cent gave savings. Less than two-thirds of all middle class men said that their main source of income was their State pension; 20 per cent said they lived mainly on a non-State pension, 7 per cent on earnings and 8 per cent gave dividends and interest as their main source of income. Middle class women living alone were more prone to describe their State pension as their main source of income (nearly 80 per cent of them), but 1 in 5 of them regarded income from their investments and from non-State pensions as more important.

(b) Secondary source

Most respondents, both middle class (94 per cent) and working class (88 per cent) had secondary sources of income but their origins differed considerably. For middle class men and women these were mainly from a non-State pension (31 per cent) and from the State pension (27 per cent), and from their investments (16 per cent). Working class secondary sources were either in the form of a Supplementary benefit from the State (39 per cent) or a non-State pension (20 per cent). (It should be remembered that four-fifths of the men in both classes were married and that most of these were married to a non-employed woman of pensionable age so that the household would be in receipt of a 'married couple' State pension).

2. Membership of clubs etc.

(a) Clubs specifically for old people

It is comparatively rare for elderly people in either class to belong to such clubs (7 per cent middle class, 13 per cent working class). Of all members in our sample three-quarters were working class and indeed 59 per cent were working class women. These groups are thus strongly over-represented in these clubs since among elderly people as a whole only 60 per cent are working class, and only 39 per cent are working class women.

(b) Church organised groups

    Here the class position is reversed. Of all members of such
groups in the sample nearly half are middle class. The predominance
of women however is even more marked - they constitute 80 per cent of
all members and this is largely because, compared with any other
organised bodies, they have a special attraction for middle class
women living alone.

    (A later question on attendances at religious meetings showed
that of all those who had been to a church, chapel or synagogue at
least once in the preceding month 79 per cent were women and 49 per
cent were middle class).

(c) Sports clubs

    In both social classes only very small minorities attend sports
clubs; the exceptions would seem to be middle class men in both age
groups and middle class women aged 69 to 74 living alone.

(d) Social clubs

    In both classes membership rates were low at 9 per cent; however,
the figures suggest that in both classes membership is lower among
respondents who live alone.

(e) Other organisations

    Respondents were asked separately about membership of lodges and
orders, political parties, trade unions, and 'other clubs'. In all
except the last of these membership was very low; with one exception
class and sex differences were negligible; the one exception was that
middle class women living with others were more prone to be members;
since these 'others' were nearly always a spouse it may well be that
membership by women of such clubs is dropped as middle class married
women become widows.

Use of time and social class

    Each respondent was questioned about the amount of time spent
'yesterday' on various pastimes and activities - watching TV,
listening to radio, reading, taking a walk, just resting, sewing and
knitting, and 'any other pastimes'. Table 5 presents the results in
six separate sub-tables.

    (a) Middle class and working class men aged 65 to 74
    (b)   "   "   "   "   "   "   " 75 or more
    (c)   "   "   "   "   " women living alone aged 65 to
                                                                            74
    (d)   "   "   "   "   "   " not "   "   " 65 to 74
    (e)   "   "   "   "   "   " living alone aged 75 or
                                                                           more
    (f)   "   "   "   "   "   " not "   "   " 75 or more

(a) <u>Men 65 to 74</u>

In both classes the total time spent on these pastimes was
approximately 10 hours, and in both the two largest slices of time
were those devoted to watching television and just resting. Working
class men spent more time on these two than did middle class men
(5.79 hours compared with 4.49 hours); the time thus gained by middle
class men was largely given over to listening to radio and going for
a walk.

(b) <u>Men 75 or more</u>

Here again the listed activities absorbed approximately 10 hours
for both classes; and again a great deal of this time was absorbed
by watching television and just resting (working class 5.92 hours,
middle class 4.80 hours); the middle class time gain was devoted to
more reading more walking and more 'other pastimes' - e.g. gardening,
stamp collecting, listening to the gramophone.

(c) <u>Women living alone, 65 to 74</u>

Again, for both classes the listed activities took up approximately 10 hours; for both groups the largest amount of time was spent
watching television, but 'just resting' fell behind listening to the
radio (apparently some of the time thus saved was taken up by sewing
and knitting) but these three basic time uses - T.V., radio, and
resting - between them filled slightly over 60 per cent of the
leisure time of both classes of younger elderly women living alone.

(d) <u>Women not living alone, 65 to 74</u>

Not surprisingly, in both social classes, younger elderly women
living with others - usually a spouse or offspring - devote less time
on the average day to the six listed pastimes. The middle class
group, compared with their class peers living alone, recorded a
reduction from 8.93 hours to 7.11 hours; and of this reduction of
almost 2 hours nearly 80 per cent was accounted for by spending less
time watching television, listening to the radio, and going for a walk;
some of the time thus gained was presumably spent attending social
clubs and miscellaneous clubs where the rate of membership among
these women was almost double that found among their class counterparts living alone. Domestic gregariousness apparently generates
among middle class women increased gregariousness outside the home.

The average working class younger elderly woman living with
others recorded a reduction of 1.38 hours spent on the average day
on the specifically named time-uses. Almost all of this saving was
made at the expense of less time spent on listening to radio, reading,
taking a walk, sewing and knitting; no less time was spent on watching
television and a little more was used for just resting.

(e) <u>Women living alone, 75 or more</u>

Women of both social classes spent approximately 10 hours of the average day on the listed pastimes, and both devoted approximately half this time on watching television and just resting. Middle class women gave nearly five hours to these two and working class women $5\frac{1}{2}$ hours.

(f) <u>Women not living alone, 75 or more</u>

As with the younger elderly women, both groups of older elderly women living in a family environment used less of their time on the activities dealt with in this question; both 'saved' at least one hour a day; this was effected largely by spending less time on listening to the radio, on reading, and on sewing and knitting. And within the group class differences were slight.

The general picture that emerges from all the above figures is that:

1. Among the younger elderly, middle class respondents spent less time on the listed pastimes than did working class respondents, and this was more marked among men than among women.

2. Among the older elderly there was a similar gap but of much smaller dimensions.

3. Respondents living alone, whether middle class or working class, spent more time on them than did those who lived with others.

4. The three main time-consuming pastimes for both social classes are watching television, listening to the radio, and just resting; between them they accounted for 65 per cent of the recorded time of middle class men, 70 per cent of the time of that of working class women's 'spare time'. In other words, the quantitative structure of time is very much the same for both classes. There may, of course, be quantitative differences. For example, the average working class man and his wife may spend their time watching 'Coronation Street', reading the Daily Mirror, and filling in football pool coupons, while their middle class counterparts give their leisure time to watching 'The Forsyte Saga', reading the Daily Mail, and playing bridge; which of the two patterns constitutes the more creative or intellectually stimulating life-style is a matter of taste. What the survey showed was that 65 per cent of middle class respondents expressed agreement with the statement: 'The things I do now are as interesting to me as they ever were'; and 67 per cent of working class respondents also agreed with the statement.

<u>Leisure and primary groups</u>

So far we have discussed the leisure of elderly people mainly in terms of their contact either with secondary groups (clubs, organisations etc.) or with mass media institutions. Most people, however, whether old or young, spend much of their leisure time with members of their primary groups - kin, neighbours and friends, and therefore this too was examined in the Age Concern survey. One of the more striking findings was that large minorities in every sub-section of the sample had never had any offspring and that of those who had the

majority, whether middle class or working class, had limited themselves to either one or two children. The following figures summarise
those in Table 2 and show that complete absence of offspring is
usually more common in the middle class than in the working class,
and is most common among middle class women living alone.

			Never any children		Average No. of children	
			Middle class	Working class	Middle class	Working class
			%	%	%	%
Men:	65-74		23	26	1.6	1.8
"	75+		27	16	1.7	2.3
Women:	65-74	LA	50	35	1.0	1.4
"	"	NLA	36	26	1.3	2.2
"	75+	LA	46	34	1.2	1.6
"	"	NLA	26	22	1.8	2.0

It is against this background that we must consider the findings
shown in Tables 3 and 4. Thus, compared with working class elderly
the middle class elderly were much less likely to be living in either
the same dwelling, the same street, or even the same neighbourhood as
any of their offspring (25 per cent middle class, 37 per cent working
class); they were much less likely to have seen any offspring at least
once in the fortnight before the interview (43 per cent middle class,
57 per cent working class). It might be argued that these differences
in parent/offspring geographical detachment merely reflect differences
in occupational and therefore residential, mobility with the children
of middle class parents going off to take professional and managerial
posts far from their parents' homes. But such an explanation over-
looks the fact that during the inter-war years the departure of
working class children from their parental homes took place on an
enormous scale - the daughters from the depressed areas in the North
went off in droves to obtain employment as domestic servants in the
South while the sons went to seek work in the factories of the
Midlands and the South.

The balance between the classes is, however, restored when the
definition of the primary group is widened to include friends and kin
other than offspring (e.g. siblings, in-laws). Of all middle class
respondents 70 per cent said they received visits from friends and
family at least once a week; and the corresponding working class
figure was 71 per cent.

When they were asked about the frequency with which they made
visits to friends and family the figures for 'at least once a week'
were lower for both social classes (not surprisingly, since people
in their 70s and 80s are more likely to be visited than to visit),
but the middle class figure (48 per cent) was even a little higher
than the working class ratio of 43 per cent.

More pointedly respondents were asked if they had any visitors
during the week-end before the interview. The replies from the two
class groups were almost identical: 45 per cent of middle class and

9

45 per cent of working class respondents said they had.

Some respondents had had more than one visit and so for all visits up to three they were asked to identify all their visitors as either family or friends. As far as the men respondents were concerned there was very little difference in the replies of the two social classes - in both a little over 70 per cent said the visitors were family and 25 per cent friends. Among women, however, there were very marked class differences. Of all those who had visited middle class women little more than half were family and the rest were friends; for working class women the corresponding figures were much higher for family (72 per cent) and much lower for friends (27 per cent). Thus, at least quantitatively it would seem that for middle class women in old age the companionship of friends, rather than family, is much more important than it is for either working class women or for middle class men.

THE DIFFERENTIAL TAKE-UP OF SUPPLEMENTARY BENEFITS

Scott A. Kerr

Alan Walker has recently argued that the 'elderly' are poor not
because of retirement per se, but because they have always been poor,
primarily because of their restricted access to resources in the past.
His work represents a major step toward a political economy of old
age, and makes it painfully clear that since this age cohort has
always been poor, it is very important that they maximise their
access to income support in the present, if solely to maintain an
already low standard of living.

But one of the first paradoxes that we encounter in broaching
this issue is that the elderly, who as a group are most likely to
need supplementary income, are also very likely to hold certain
attitudes and to suffer from certain conditions which restrict their
access to it. It is therefore critical to any full discussion of the
problem to account for both these attitudes and the 'multiple'
handicaps' of the cohort when looking at state provision for old age
and evaluating its success or failure from the consumers' perspectives. However, due to the limitations on time, I will be concentrating on the attitudinal aspects.

The plan of the paper is as follows. Firstly, I will summarise
the main benefits available to pensioners, in order to provide a
context for the later discussion of means-tested benefits. Secondly,
I will briefly look at their acceptability from the consumers'
perspectives, using 'take-up' rates as my yardstick. Thirdly, in
order to examine the consumers' perspectives in greater detail, I
will focus on one particular means-tested benefit, Supplementary
Pensions, and will summarise the results of past research which has
identified the reasons most frequently given by pensioners for not
claiming. However, policy should not be based upon the most
frequently given reasons, but upon the most important reasons.
Therefore, I will, fourthly, introduce some of my own research which
has attempted to identify the most important barriers to claiming.
This issue of frequency versus importance is of critical importance,
and underlies one of the major paradoxes of research in this area
which I will be discussing later.

1. Benefits for Pensioners

Table 1 summarises eleven benefits to which pensioners may be
entitled. In preparing this table, I have tried to use official
estimates wherever possible, and it must be noted that these
estimates are subject to sampling error. Where I have used local
study estimates (i.e. in the case of dental/optical concessions),
it must be noted that such estimates usually suffer from being

unrepresentative. Official estimates, in general, tend to be at least 15 per cent higher than are local estimates, and both suffer from a wide variety of deficiencies, which cannot be discussed here. Since many of you will be familiar with the majority of these benefits, I will confine my comments to pointing out their salient characteristics.

1. National Insurance Pensions (NIP) - the mainstay of pensioner income, entitlement based upon contribution record.

2. Non-Contributory Retirement Pension (NCRP) - for persons over 80 either not entitled to NIP or getting one which is below the NCRP rate (usually about one-half of the NIP rate). NCRP is so low that in all but exceptional circumstances, NCRP claimants would also be entitled to Supplementary Pensions.

3. Attendance Allowance - payable for people so physically or mentally handicapped that they require: By day - frequent attention in connection with bodily functions - or - supervision to prevent them from injuring themselves; By night - the same. Higher rate is payable if both day and night criteria are satisfied; Lower rate if only one is satisfied. There is a six month qualifying period during which no benefit can be paid.

4. Death Grant - £30 lump sum, paid on contributions of deceased, deceased's spouse, or sometimes on those of a near relative.

5. Dental/optical concessions - automatic entitlement to all on Supplementary Pensions, or to those who qualify on low income grounds (i.e. income being within about £2 of the SB line). Reduced costs for those marginally above this threshold. Low income grounds requires the SB means-test, which can lead to a claim for a Supplementary Pension.

6. Rent Rebates - for Council tenants, administered by the local authority, requires a means-test similar to the SB means-test, the notable exceptions being that it asks for investment income and not savings, and does not generally ask for information on personal health circumstances. More generous scheme than is SB.

7. Rent Allowances - same principles as Rent Rebates, but for privat tenants. Two distinct differences: (1) comes as a cheque to reimburse individual for rent payments and therefore requires substantial capital expenditure; (2) application usually requires contact with the landlord to verify rent or to set a 'fair' rent and this can (a) delay application, (endanger landlord-tenant relationship.

8. Rate Rebates - same means-test as rent benefits, but the responsi bility of the regional council rather than the district. Unlike the rent benefits, this benefit is payable to owner-occupiers as well as to renters.

Table 1.   Take-up Rates of Benefits by the Elderly

Benefit	No. in Receipt (thousands)	No. Eligible non-claimants	% take-up	Selection Principle
1. NIP	8,458	?	99+	group selectivity
2. NCRP	73	?	very high	"
3. Attendance (H)	97	?	?	"
Allowance (L)	81	?	?	"
4. Death Grant	455	5(?)	98	"
5. Dental/Optical	?	?	26/16	means-tested
6. Rent Rebates	600	150/200	75/80	"
7. Rent Allowances	170	130	55/60	"
8. Rate Rebates	2,000	800	70/75	"
9. Supplementary Pensions	1,670	610+	73	"
10. ECAs (heating)	1,186	524	69	"
11. ENPs	289	?	?	"

9. Supplementary Pensions - since I will be discussing this benefit
    in detail later, let it suffice to state here that Supplementary
    Pensions and rebates are mutually exclusive - one can be entitled
    to both, yet receive only one, since Supplementary Pension
    payments include an amount for the costs of rent and rates.

10. Exceptional Circumstances Additions (ECAs) - although they cover
    other areas of personal circumstances such as diet or laundry
    costs, I have given figures only for the discretionary additions
    for extra heating given on health or accommodation grounds.

11. Exceptional Needs Payments (ENPs) - lump sum one-off grants for
    clothing, bedding, etc. Means-tested. Prior to 24.11.80 anyone
    who met eligibility criteria could apply; after 24.11.80 receipt
    of Supplementary Benefit is a necessary pre-condition of
    eligibility.

2. Benefit Acceptability

Using percentage take-up (defined as the total number claiming
divided by the total number eligible, the latter being computed from
the known number of claimants plus estimates of non-claimants based
upon secondary analysis of Family Expenditure Survey findings as our
yardstick of acceptability, we can immediately see that benefits
working on the principle of group selectivity have significantly
higher take-up rates than do means-tested benefits. 'Group
selectivity' here means that the eligibility criteria are not
individual means-tests, and examples of these criteria would be
contribution status, degree of disability, etc. As we can see from
Table 1, of the means-tested benefit, rent rebates, rate rebates,
Supplementary Pensions, and Exceptional Circumstances Additions for
heating have take-up rates between 70 and 80 per cent, which may be
considered as reasonable, especially since 75 per cent efficiency in
industry would be highly desirable. But, considering the fact that
the 25 per cent failing to claim their entitlement are, by definition,
below the poverty line in most cases, the only acceptable take-up
rate is 100 per cent.

But hundreds of thousands of pensioners fail to claim the
benefits to which they are entitled. Why? And what can be done to
ameliorate this situation? In order to move toward a solution, we
must examine the situation in detail. Therefore, I will spend the
remainder of this talk focussing on what prevents pensioners from
claiming their entitlement to Supplementary Pensions.

3. Supplementary Pensions: Description and Research Findings

A. Who are the eligible non-claimants?

In 1977, they were 610,000 households who were due, on average,
£3. 10 per week. Two-thirds were married couples and most of
the rest were single and widowed women. About one-half were owner
occupiers without mortgages, one-third were council tenants, and
one-sixth were private tenants. They include many people already

receiving rebates but who would be 'better off' if they claimed
Supplementary Pensions; and finally, they include only a small
group of non-householders, about 12,000, but this group is due
the most i.e. about £6. 56 per week in 1976.

B.   How does one claim a Supplementary Pension?

In order to put non-claiming into perspective, we must understand
the requirements of the claiming process. Firstly, unlike with
rebates, an official interview is necessary. This can be arranged
via sending in the tear-off form on Leaflet SB1, or by phone, and
the interview can be conducted either in the pensioner's home, or
at the local social security office. Secondly, at the interview,
the pensioner must have available all relevant information on
pensions, savings, rent and rates, stocks and shares, etc., and
be prepared to answer questions about the state of his/her health
and the house (to assess entitlement to ECAs), as well as to
verify his or her finances. The social security officer completes
the claim form, and the pensioner is asked to sign it. It is
usually processed in 3-4 days, and comes as a cash addition to
the national insurance pension in 90 per cent of the cases where
it is paid. About one in every three pensioners who apply for a
Supplementary Pension turns out to be ineligible.

C.   Why have at least 610,000 failed to claim?

To begin to formulate an answer to this question, we will look at
the results of two general types of research into non-claiming:
(1) descriptive surveys, and (2) action research, which, through
the provision of information has attempted to increase claiming
amongst the eligible non-claimants.

By way of general introduction, a review of the literature on the
subject suggests that the main deterrents to claiming can be
sorted into a half-dozen categories:

1.   perceptions of 'no need' or that they are managing OK;

2.   basic lack of knowledge of the benefit and/or application
     procedure;

3.   perceptions that, for one reason or another, they are
     ineligible;

4.   expectations that the amount and/or form of the benefit is
     of low utility;

5.   expectations of difficulties with the application procedure;

6.   expectations that applying and/or receiving the benefit will
     lead to social outcomes (such as the family, friends or
     neighbour finding out) which are negatively valued.

All of these suggested explanations are highly interrelated, table 2 shows the frequency in which each was given for not claiming in four studies of the non-claiming conducted since 1966.

Table 2. Frequency of Reasons Given for not Claiming Supplementary Pensions (%s)

Reasons	MPNI (1966)	ACE(C)(1974)	ACE(N)(1974)	OPCS(1977)
1. Perception of 'no need' or managing OK	33	---	27	57
2. Ignorance	35	---	6	41
3. Perceived inegibility	---	---	---	21
4. Expectations of low utility	9	---	---	7
5. Expectations of difficulties with appli. procedure	3	25	11	7
6. Expectations of negative social outcomes	22	50	23	41
(Other)	---	25	33	15

Although nothing totally consistent crops up, it is clear that the major factors are expectations of negatively valued social outcomes (a category which includes perceptions of stigma and charity), perceptions of no need, and ignorance or low awareness. What is surprising is that the only aspects which can be directly changed by the DHSS - expectations about the application procedure - elicit little resistance in general.

A word of caution must be spoken about some of these percentages. Part of the variation in percentages across studies, especially in the 'ignorance' factor, is due to the fact that the threshold of knowledge implicitly set by researchers to be necessary to apply varies across studies.

The perception of 'no need' deserves special comment. Although it is frequently said that this answer given by pensioners is a rationalisation of their perception of the undesirability of the benefit, there is little evidence to support this. It seems more to be a logical response by pensioners who see themselves as being financially better off than their peers. The 1966 Ministry of Pensions and National Insurance study made this clear by demonstrating that eligible

16

non-claimants:

   - had smaller gaps between their income and expenses than
     did claimants before they claimed

   - were more likely to have disregarded income and substantially
     more savings

   - marginally more likely to have a state pension at the higher
     rate

   - had lower rents than did claimants

   - were more likely to state that they were in good health
     than were claimants.

From Table 2, we can see that 'ignorance' is indeed a substantial
problem. Although other deterrants have similar weight, 'ignorance'
was the only factor that government and researchers were able to
attack, considering the resources at their disposal and the unethical
nature of implementing programmes to change people's values. However,
the results of action research which provided these eligible non-
claimants with the information necessary to claim, have been
disappointing. These are shown in Table 3.

Table 3.   Results of Action Research

	DHSS(GHS) 1975	Inverclyde 1975	Bethnal Green 1974/1975	OPCS 1977	Kerr 1979
No. Informed	114	25	Take-up raised	46	25
No. Applied	17	9	from 86% to 98%	11	5
% 'Hits'	15%	36%	(Very small sample)	24%	20%

Although in many surveys 'ignorance' of many types comes out as
being one of the most frequently given reasons for non-claiming, the
results of action research indicate that even when informed of their
entitlement, relatively few apply. This finding comprises the second
paradox in this situation. Since beneath it lies the distinction
between frequency and importance, it deserves a special note. If
frequency and importance are isomorphic, then one would expect that
if 40 per cent express ignorance of their entitlement, then those
40 per cent should claim when informed of their entitlement. However,
this does not occur, and its failure to do so leaves us to conclude
that although ignorance is a frequently given reason, it is not all
that important as a deterrent. From this premise, it is relatively
easy to see that the estimates of the percentage who are 'ignorant'
are inflated, and this is due to an issue broached before - that the
threshold level of knowledge implicitly set by researchers as being

necessary to make a successful claim has been set too high. Most
studies have implied that anything less than a remarkably complete
understanding of how the scheme works and how entitlement is calculated
comprises a state of partial ignorance. However, referring to the
levels of knowledge possessed by actual claimants shows that, strictly
speaking, only the existence of the benefit and where to apply for it
are necessary to know in order to claim, if other factors (such as
'need') are conducive.

If 'ignorance' is not the most important factor, then even
greater emphasis must be put upon determining the relative importance
of the other factors. Previous research has yielded only general
findings in terms of perceptions of stigma, charity, feelings of
independence, and the like. But what is now necessary is to locate
specific sources of resistance in order to answer the question, 'what
is it, exactly, about the benefit that offends?'.

In a study I conducted last year, funded by the DHSS, I had the
opportunity to do exactly this.

4. Toward a Technique for Deriving the Importance of Specific

   Deterrants to Claiming

The aim of this study was to derive a technique which, when later
applied to a larger sample, would allow us to attach weights to
specific expectations and perceptions in order to determine empirically
how important the factors were. Although the large scale study is
only now underway, I can reflect on the feasibility study, and share
some tentative findings with you.

Our research design was a combination survey/action research
design, and it comprised six stages:

1. Locate a sample of eligible non-claimants

2. Determine their reasons for not claiming to date

3. Inform them of:
   (a) Their eligibility
   (b) The probable amount of their entitlement

4. Systematically inform them of the outcomes of applying
   and measure their feelings about these outcomes

5. Predict which will claim

6. Find out which claimed.

In Stages 3 and 4, we 'manipulated' the amount of knowledge
possessed by our respondents, and by informing them of their eligibility and how to claim we were able to hold constant their levels of
knowledge. This had the advantage of allowing us to study what

barriers would remain and what maximum take-up would be in the event
that every eligible pensioner was informed of his/her entitlement.
Unfortunately, it had the distinct disadvantage of failing to model
the real world, in which pensioners do not have such information.

Since previous research never attempted to validate the
relationship between espoused attitudes and actual behaviour, our
fifth and sixth stages involved making blind predictions and comparing
them against actual behaviour over the following two months.

The depth interviews were extremely thorough, each lasting about
two and a half hours. To give you an idea of the specificity of our
questioning, we discussed each of the following outcomes with our
eligible non-claimants:

Table 4. Outcomes Discussed in Depth Interviews and used to

Make Predictions
_____

Asking for Help

Family Finding out

Friends Finding out

Having an Interview

Involvement with DHSS

Interview Site

Interviewer Personality

Having to Answer Specific Questions
  (15 Types Included)

Having to Verify Income and Expenses

Getting the S P

Automatic Entitlement to Optical/Dental

Meeting Specific Needs (Elicited Individually)
  (up to 4)

Having to Give up Rent Rebate/Allowance
  and/or Rate Rebate

Figure 1 shows the main single and combined factors which
explain the application or non-application of twenty-four of the
twenty-five eligible non-claimants in the sample.

Some notes on interpreting this figure are necessary. Firstly,
the theoretical model which we developed to explain differential
application (and which is explicated in Kett (1980)) comprises a
series of thresholds above which a pensioner must fall in order to
be considered a potential applicant at any stage. Thus of the 24
correctly predicted, the main reason for the non-claiming of seven
was that they perceived no need. Of the 17 who perceived some need,

FIGURE 1. SUMMARY OF SUBSTANTIVE FINDINGS

25 OAPs BEHAVIOUR PREDICTED

1 INCORRECT PREDICTION

7 PERCEIVED NO NEED; DIDN'T CLAIM PEOPLE W/ EXTRA INCOME OVER-REP

5 NOT IN POSITION TO DECIDE; NO CLAIMS

10 EXPECT FAMILY ABLE TO HELP & TO DISCOURAGE THEM AND HAD REL. LESS PROBLEM MAKING ENDS MEET. SINGLES AND 70s OVER-REP.

24 CORRECT PREDICTIONS

17 PERCEIVED NEED; PEOPLE WITH EXTRA INCOME UNDER REPRESENTED

14 IN POSITION TO APPLY

4 EXPECT FAMILY UNABLE TO HELP TO ENCOURAGE THEM TO APPLY & HAD REL. GREATER DIFF. M.E.M. MARRIED COUPLES AND 70s+ OVER-REPRESENTED

three did not apply because their situations were ambiguous, even though they were attitudinally predisposed toward applying. (This represents a seventh factor which did not appear in previous literature.) Of the 14 remaining, 10 did not apply because of a combination of low perceived need and the expectation that their families could help them out if they asked. To the contrary, four applied because they perceived some need and expected that their families could not help them out if they asked. Although in our present large-scale study we will be deriving weights to attach to each of these factors, this could not be done in this study due to the small sample size.

Our other main findings were, firstly, that the majority of our respondents (24 out of 25) were already receiving rebates and allowances. Therefore, it is an issue of switching from one benefit to the other and not merely applying for Supplementary Pensions which is the crux of the matter. Secondly, none of the aspects of the Supplementary Pensions means-test either (a) raised much resistance, or (b) differentiated between claimants and non-claimants. And finally, even when told of (a) their entitlement, (b) the probable amount of their entitlement, (c) exactly how to apply, and (d) when left with all the necessary information, only five of the 25 applied. This bodes poorly for any publicity campaign, and makes it seem probable that take-up will never reach more than 80 per cent with the benefit as it stands.

But should this last finding surprise us? Not really, especially when we consider that nine in ten of the respondents were already receiving very large rebates and allowances. Despite the fact that they would have been financially better-off on Supplementary Pensions, they preferred rebates because:

- except for the private tenants, rebates are more convenient since they come as a reduction at source and not as a cash alternative

- they come from a local source and not from the 'state' or 'social security'

- the point of claiming is familiar (i.e. the rent office)

- many neighbours are already receiving rebates and allowances

- they didn't want to undergo yet another means-test

- they were confused as to how it was possible that they could be better-off, and preferred to stay on their rebates rather than to take a leap into the unknown.

The type of confusion that two systems of benefits, both with provisions for housing costs, can create for the elderly is exemplified in a quote taken from Syson and Young's 'Poverty in Bethnal Green' (1974):

I'm on the Assistance and the Assistance sent me like a
rebate - the Assistance stopped the rebate and the council
gave me a rebate. They stopped at one end and gave this
to me the other like.

- Mr. Ratchford, a pensioner.

The summary picture looks like this, then. The main theme is
that pensioners do not perceive applying for Supplementary Pensions
to be a matter of 'entitlement'. Direct evidence for this comes from
their statements that they <u>would</u> apply for the benefit because it is
their right - <u>if</u> they felt that they needed. The very necessity of
including an explanatory factor such as 'perceived need' substantiates
this view. Indirect evidence comes from several sources. First, the
vast majority of pensioners who had families and who were receiving
rebates would prefer to turn to their families rather than to the
State for help; second, virtually all the pensioners were substantially resistant to 'asking for help', yet over nine-tenths of those
who were entitled to rebates were receiving them; third, considering
that pensioners showed little resistance to the only real difference
between the substantive areas of questioning in both means-tests (e.g.
that SB assessment requires revealing savings rather than income
from investments), we tentatively conclude that the means-tests, in
substantive terms at least, are equally palatable.

It seems fairly certain that for this residual group of eligible
non-claimants, it is the connotations of the Supplementary Pensions
means-test and the social outcomes of applying that make this
benefit less desirable than rebates and allowances.

What is surprising is that there is nothing specifically to
which we can point and say 'this is a major cause of non-take-up
and must be changed'. The simple fact is that 'rebates' (leastwise
for this group of pensioners) along with state pensions are construed
as 'entitlement', whereas Supplementary Pensions are not, leastwise
not in any real sense.

To summarise, it seems very unlikely that take-up will ever
exceed 80 per cent, with the benefit as it presently stands, and the
progress from 73 to 80 per cent will be gained only by an inordinate
amount of effort and expenditure.

The forces militating against increased take-up are twofold.
First, and most important pensioners attitudes are against it. At
a very basic level, the benefit is not perceived as a 'right',
pensioners expectations of what they need are often very low, the
connotations of applying for Supplementary Pensions - that it is
asking for help - are unacceptable, and the expected outcomes of
applying - the potential insult to the family - are undesirable.
These attitudinal factors combine with what are generally called the
'multiple handicaps' of advanced years.

These multiple handicaps include restricted mobility, poor
health, low confidence and inarticulateness, poor hearing and vision,

potentially low reading age and possible psychological disorientation.

Considering the potency of these two sets of forces, it seems fair to conclude that so long as the onus is placed upon the individual to claim his entitlement, rather than upon the state to provide it, the situation will remain as it is, with the symptoms of age combining with long-held attitudes to militate against improving the financial welfare of the elderly.

FOOTNOTES

A substantially more detailed review of means-tested benefits and the elderly based upon this paper has been prepared, and is being submitted to the journal of <u>Ageing and Society</u>. This review paper is available from the author at the Department of Psychology, University of Edinburgh, Edinburgh EH8 9JZ.

REFERENCES

A complete list of papers and studies referred to in this talk can be obtained from the author. They are not attached due to their sheer number.

MIDLIFE INVOLVEMENT AND PHYSICAL ACTIVITY

R. Malcolm Reid

At present there is little comprehensive information relating to the involvement in physical activity of males in the middle period of life. Attention has tended to focus upon psysiological implications; personality traits or similar individual features. It is arguable, however, that a multi/inter-disciplinary approach is required for the area relates strongly to psycho/social/physiological factors.

Overt features of middle age, such as increased body weight, expanding girth, declining health and general withdrawal from active involvement, are accepted social and cultural norms. Thus a cultural stereotype of compliancy, predictable comfort seeking, stability, dependancy and conservation is inferred (Aronson, 1966). Mid-life in Western Society is therefore portrayed as a slowing down process co-existing with a settled way of life suggesting little in the way of change until old age.

Such predictability is now being challenged. This life-stage has recently been referred to as a 'festival of lipid migration', being considered second only to the teenage years in the degree of psychological, social and biological change (Stevens, 1979). Thus, notions of arresting the culturally implied decline are envisaged.

Conceptual Issues

It is clear that there are many features of mid-life about which little is known. It is equally clear that the term 'middle-age' is one which is both confusing and derogatory. Confusing because the process of ageing appears to progress at varying rates with different people, making it difficult to accurately assess chronological ages which begin and end the middle-age period. Derogatory, because it categorises and type-casts individuals. Relative to studies of this type, therefore, it is perhaps more apt to use the term middle-years. This signifies that youth in the generally accepted birth to maturity developmental sense, has passed, but old age relative to the physically degenerative and senescent state has yet to appear.

The term physical activity gives rise to conceptual difficulties and clouds issues. One clear definition is:

'A behaviour primarily characterised by observable and vigorous output. It can be differentiated from movement behaviour in that it implies a more vigorous and overt movement. Thus, physical activity is action denoted by movement of the large muscles, utilising large amounts of space*, with a moderate to maximum amount of effort involved'.

Cratty, 1967

In lay terms physical activity is linked with competitive sport and taking exercise. Such links create difficulties. Sport in Western Society is regarded as the perogative of youth, with some sports having social class overtones. In spite of numerous campaigns sponsored by Sports and Health Councils, these two factors make blanket participation unlikely. 'Taking exercise' has connotations of 'physical jerks' reminding contemporary middle-yeared males of their National Service, cold early morning showers and other such features regarded as eccentricities. It is, therefore, unacceptable to the majority, hinting at abnormality when those who are neither young nor high level performers are involved. The combination of the apparent social stigma attached to participation and the concept which implies that individuals are powerless to influence the physical and mental degenerative process of ageing, seems to exert a negative influence over the majority of middle-yeared males and their approach to regular participation.

Empirically, many social factors seem to influence involvement, although little is known of these. However, presentation of, and proximity to activity/activity areas, marital status, occupation and financial state are just some of the features of an individual's social environment which may be linked with the desire and opportunity to take part. In spite of the many negative social and cultural influences, however, physical activity is an acceptable part, although of varying degrees of importance, in the life-style of some middle-yeared males. Indeed, at the participatory end of the activity-inactivity continuum exercise addiction is thought to take place. It is defined as:

> 'A psychological and/or physiological dependance upon a regular regimen of physical activity. Additionally, exercise addiction is characterised by recognisable withdrawal symptoms when the need to exercise remains unfulfilled after 24-36 hours. These withdrawal symptoms may encompass both psychological and physiological factors, including feelings of irritability, tension, guilt, uneasiness and bloatedness'.
>
> (Sachs and Pargman,1979)

Although little is known of the complex motivational influences and activity patterns of those committed to participation, the probability is that psychological structures are significantly involved. Regular participants therefore, may not only show certain physiological benefits but also reveal trait combinations which differ from those less interested. Such combinations may be manifested in a drive towards involvement, which interact with physical activity interests, producing varied levels of participation.

* The author sees no need for this phrase to be included in the definition.

Methodological Difficulties

Recent attempts to investigate random samples of general population middle-yeared males (Reid, 1980) emphasised the difficulty of this exercise. Few problems are found in obtaining the assistance of males placed at the activity end of the activity - inactivity continuum. These men possibly similar to 'exercise addicts' (Sachs and Pargman, 1979), tend to be most co-operative beinf grateful for information regarding their own physical condition. In contrast, the majority who are less involved appear to lack motivation to participate, are dis-interested or are apprehensive about the outcome. This is a significant problem for the investigation of males who are moderately to minimally involved in physical activity may give rise to important findings.

Industry would appear to be an excellent source of subjects but this is fraught with difficulties, especially on the shop floor. Two major features arise. Firstly, the research interviewer is seen as a management 'snooper'. Secondly, interviewing may be considered to interfere with productivity. Shift work is also a problem. One possible source of subjects is via the factory canteen but this may lead to a biased sample being obtained.

Size of initial contact groups is a further problem. Response from larger groups of working men - especially relative to physical activity - is met with sexual and/or jocular comments. However, if contact groups are reduced to five or less, then response and rapport is usually good. An extension of this is to contact small businesses, especially those close to university/higher education establishments for they are often pleased to be involved. Once initial subjects have been obtained the sample can be increased, via the neighbours and friends of these individuals. Thus, the process tends to be a practical one of building up a sample rather than a comprehensive random number/telephone directory type of approach. However, this does lead to difficulties of extrapolition to the population at large for samples of males obtained in this way cannot be considered truly random.

Factors Associated with Participation

Taking cognisance of procedural difficulties contemporary evidence indicates that several factors individually categorisable in psycho/social, psycho/physiological domains, although quite clearly interrelated, have a significant bearing on physical activity participation, particularly among males in the North East of Scotland. These influences, four of which will be discussed here, range through the perception of exertion during physical performance, attitudes relating to the 'perceived instrumentality' of physical activity, personality traits and ageing.

(i)   Perceived Exertion

Recent work (Reid, 1980) shows that this psycho/physiological measure may be of significant importance. Regarded as a configuration

of total bodily inputs it is the subjective intensity of work being
performed which as a construct can be considered analagoud to pain.
Present information suggests that males who are regularly physically
active will perceive physical effort to be less demanding than those
who are not active. Those who participate regularly appear to be
able to adapt and accommodate to physical stress more easily. In
addition, it seems possible that there is some form of hierarchial
structure which regulates moderate sub-maximal effort to a position
of being considered less demanding physically, in comparison to
physiological responses, than is really the case.

In addition, the regularity of participation appears to be
reflected in attitudes towards physical activity, the body and
achievement behaviour which signify persistence. Thus, it is
possible that the continuity of participation by those who are
regularly active will tend to maintain a basic level of physiological
fitness and an approach to physical activity which will enable
moderate levels of physical stress to be both coped with and perceived
as being low, rather than high, in effort.

(ii) <u>Attitudes</u>

There are strong indications that attitudes held towards
physical activity also significantly influence involvement. Among
males categorised as general population, involvement is strongly
influenced by a combination of features provided by the attitudes
towards physical activity which have the 'perceived instrumentality'
(Kenyon, 1968) of health/fitness, catharsis and ascetism. The
implication is that the health benefits obtained from participation;
the release from tension, frustration and pent up emotions created
by the pressures of modern living; the rewards obtained by long
and strenuous periods of physical effort, (for many males in this
life-stage long and strenuous may possibly be interpreted as
continuity of participation) are in some way combined, to highlight
a long term positive health approach to health/fitness through
physical activity.

It is possible that a less demanding 'socially orientated'
approach is also a feature of this life-stage. Those sharing this
appreciation are aware of the health/fitness aspects etc., but
hierarchically their physical activity involvement is of a lower
order of importance than among those who have the 'positive health'
orientation. The social function of participation which tends to
be less physically involved, more friendly and outgoing is, therefore,
not required to meet the same needs as the 'positive health' approach.

At present one interpretation of the attitude results, may be
to imply that regularly physically active middle-yeared males,
having a 'positive health orientation' use participation as a
means to an end. Others who may be 'socially oriented', use it as
an end in itself.

(iii) Personality

There is strong support for the claim that males who participate regularly in physical activity will reveal personality traits relating to extraversion and stability (Ogilvie, 1967; Warburton and Kane, 1967; Brunner, 1969; Cooper, 1969; Ismail and Trachtman, 1972; Harris, 1973; Alderman, 1974). More recent evidence among middle-yeared males (Reid, 1976b; 1980) hints that such theories may not be totally correct. It seems that the influence of extraversion may be indirect rather than direct. It is clear that extraversion is evident in those who perceive their involvement in physical activity to be both an important influence on life-style and higher than normal.

However, the same data indicates that the traits of extraversion are not necessarily a feature of regular physical activity partipants per se. The traits of extraversion, therefore, appear to relate to the perceptual orientation to physical activity more readily than its practice. Earlier work by Brunner (1969) and Harris (1970) hints that this may be culturally biased.

(iv) Ageing

Except for a small percentage of the population regularly involved, the compatibility of ageing and participation in physical activity appears to be unacceptable among normal population. Anecdotally, ageing is thought to have an adverse effect on participation, with regular involvement being both unwise and undignified as well as narcisstic and self-masturbatory (Field, 1970). The author's work does not find total support for such notions. Support is found for the decline in physiological performance with age and that the lean are likely to become less lean via an increase in body weight/body fat.

Such features therefore, tend to underline the ease with which it is possible for the general population to subscribe to the view that as age increases, the ability to participate decreases. The indication is that such a notion is not correct, for although in absolute terms physically active males will show a decrease in physiological performance with age, they will, in relative terms, be sounder in physiological and body composition/positive health features, than their less active peers. They will also compare favourably with low active males some decade and a half their junior. In keeping with this it is clear that age will affect physiological performance but need not affect participation.

The major difficulty may therefore be conceptual. Present notions could arise as a result of confused thinking and a lack of information, for it is possible that participation is equated to performance. This implies some expected level of output from participants, which leads to a comparative approach, such as age versus youth etc. However, if comparisons have to be made, it may be more apt to do so against age related norms or within similar age groups. Once these features are appreciated, then it is possible that society may understand, support and relate to, regular participation along with the ageing process. The physiological evidence indicates that among similarly aged middle-yeared males regular physical activity participants are cardiovascularly more efficient and carry a lower percentage of their body weight as fat than those who participate infrequently or not at all. In addition regular participation in the later middle-years can lead to cardio-vascular and body composition features which compare favourably with those in the earlier years of this life-stage who participate irregularly. Furthermore, age group comparison implies that there is a less rapid decline in cardiovascular efficiency and body composition during the ageing process among regular participants.

Ageing and physical activity are readily discussed with regard to the rate of physical decline. However, not all factors related to this area should be viewed negatively, for the indications are that with age there is a more appropriate acceptance of the body, its functions and processes. Neuroticism also tends to decline. In addition, ageing brings with it a greater appreciation of the aesthetic aspects of physical activity. Thus it seems possible that age may gradually impose a form of physical tranquility, for with additional years, more emphasis may be placed on the sensuous rather than the vigorous nature of the activity involved.

Conclusion

The following broad conclusions may be drawn from this paper which dealt with issues arising from studies during the past decade. Firstly, cultural and conceptual anomalies appear to dominate society's thinking regarding ageing and physical activity involvement, for it is considered somewhat abnormal to regularly participate in physical activity as age increases. In addition most participation appears to be similarly categorised regardless of type or level of activity. It is probable that participants do not share these views. Thus, involvement in mid-life will be greatly facilitated if such factors are more clearly understood.

Secondly, there are practical difficulties in obtaining the necessary information to allow for a comprehensive understanding of physical activity in this life-stage. General population information, especially relative to irregular or non-participation, is important but difficult to acquire. Such problems may be overcome when investigatory techniques become more sophisticated, and the necessary finance made available to support team and longitudinal research.

Thirdly, it seems that difficulties normally attributed by society to physical activity participation and ageing may not be correct, for involvement is shown to be influenced by many variables. In particular perception of exertion is involved. This may be affected by regularity of participation and effort or it could be constitutional. Attitudes reflecting a health/fitness bias also significantly influence involvement. These and other factors hint that personality traits may be important but such features tend to relate more to perceptions of involvement rather than activity per se. It is clear, however, that many factors interact to bring about pa.ticipation. The probability is that particular combinations of relationships will both reflect and account for levels and styles of physical activity participation in this life-stage.

REFERENCES

Kenyon, G.S. (1968b). Six Scales for Assessing Attitudes Towards Physical Activity. Res. Quarterly, 39, 1.

Ogilvie, B.C. (1967). What is an Athlete? Paper presented to the American Association of Health, Physical Education and Recreation. Las Vagas.

Reid, R.M. (1976b). Participation in Non-Working Time Physical Activity - Psychological Correlates of Middle-Yeared Males, Social Classes III, IV and V. Scottish J. of Physical Education, 4,3.

Reid, R.M. (1980). Involvement in Physical Activity. Unpublished Ph.D. Thesis, Aberdeen University.

Sachs, M.L. and Pargman, D. (1979). Running Addiction: A Depth Interview Examination. J. of Sport Behaviour, 2,3.

Stevens, J. (1979). Adult Life: Developmental Processes. London: Mayfield Pub. Co.

Warburton, F.W. and Kane, J.E. (1967). Personality Related to Sport and Physical Ability, in Readings in Physical Education. Physical Education Association, London.

THE PROBLEM OF RETIREMENT: FARMERS IN
NORTH-EAST SCOTLAND

Mike Hepworth and Robert Anderson

Over the last two decades attitudes towards retirement from urban occupations have been gradually changing. The increase in the number of men and women over statutory retirement age who are mentally and physically active and who also have spending power has stimulated the emergence of a new 'retirement culture'. In America, the American Association of Retired Persons is pioneering 'the new world of retirement'. In Britain, the Pre-Retirement Association, now linked with the Over 50's Club, publishes a widely circulating magazine, 'Choice'. This is filled with recreational, cosmetic, do-it-yourself, financial, consumer, and medical advice designed to transform retirement into a specific 'lifestyle' for which active preparation during 'the middle years' is not only desirable but exciting. The transformation of the traditional 'pipe and slippers' image of retirement has, of course, been further stimulated by the even more recent creation of 'premature retirement' which has had the unintended consequence of rejuvenating the retired population.

These changes have made it easier for us to see retirement as a human process which takes place over a period of time.(1) Retirement can no longer, as Malcolm Johnson has argued, be reduced to a simple transition from work to leisure - the so-called 'final Phase of the occupational lifecycle' - to which individuals or specific groups of individuals adjust with varying degrees of success. Rather it can now be more clearly seen as a number of stages of which the act of leaving full time employment is only one. The sociological literature is less concerned as in the past with the personally and socially disruptive aspects of retirement and more with integrating retirement into the complete lifecycle of whoever is being studied. (2) In particular, this perspective must take into account the specific meanings of work and leisure for different sections of the population and the individual's perception of his past, present and future.

The time is therefore ripe for an outcrop of detailed studies of retirement grounded in the everyday experiences of selected occupational groups and set against the backcloth of the emerging 'new world of retirement'. Whilst massive socio-economic changes obviously cannot be ignored, retirement like ageing with which it is in Western culture allied, is not a single unitary event, but a complex of processes in their natural settings, (3) There is no point in describing retirement as a transition unless we know what a person is moving from: the subjective meaning in its cultural context of outwardly observable changes in his or her life.

31

As far as life in rural areas is concerned, there is an additional difficulty. Geriatrics and social gerontology, the two disciplines which have stimulated research into ageing, have slowly matured in a predominantly urban context. The concept of retirement is itself an urban/industrial construct which has thus far failed to produce any extensive sociological accounts of retirement from rural occupations. Studies have for the most part been carried out in urban areas where the structure and texture of daily life contrast sharply with life in the country, especially in the remoter parts of the UK. The result is that we tend to view retirement and ageing in rural areas through urban-tinted spectacles. To fill up the gap in our knowledge we fall back on an urban stereotype which, as Clare Wenger has shown in her analysis of social aspects of ageing in a largely uplands farming area in Wales, is far removed from the actual experiences of native inhabitants. (4)

The neglect of rural retirement can be attributed to a number of factors. Firstly, there is the problem of geographical isolation. In our research area - the Grampian and Highland Region - towns, villages and farms are widely scattered and in winter, the best time to interview farmers at any length, often difficult if not impossible to reach. Secondly, there is another kind of communication problem. The majority of farmers in the Region have spent the whole of their lives on the farm amongst members of a small community and it is therefore necessary for a researcher to have some familiarity with local farming and social customs in order to establish rapport and an easy atmosphere in which the kind of data other workers have shown to be relevant can be obtained. Experience shows that farmers are not infrequently suspicious of strangers asking what are seen to be personal questions, and a mutual interest in agriculture, or at least a mutual contact in the farming world, is invaluable to the researcher. There is also the problem of dialect. In the rural areas of North-East Scotland speech follows a number of variations with which an interviewer must be familiar if conversation is not to break down and fail to develop. Unfamiliarity with local speech patterns can quickly lead to misunderstandings and distorted data.

The pilot study reported here is, therefore, the result of collaboration between a sociologist with an interest in ageing but no knowledge or experience of rural life - having spent most of his days in the suburbs - and an agricultural economist with extensive knowledge of farming in North-East Scotland. Additional assistance was provided by agricultural advisors from the North of Scotland College who often accompanied us on our interviews, provided necessary introductions, and smoothed the conversational way. These men brought not only an intimate knowledge of the locality but also an apparently inexhaustible fund of information on kinship networks, family history, the agricultural competence of interviewees, and their economic circumstances. Because the work is time-consuming (large distances must be travelled) and is in its early stages, our conclusions are tentative but nevertheless useful pointers to the way ahead. By the time these words are published much more work will have been done.

The main problem of this kind of research in the North-East have already been outlined. To improve our chances of obtaining viable information we decided to place farm workers and other rural employees in one side (although we shall be approaching a sample of farm workers in the near future) and to concentrate on owners and tenants of family farms. The tentative conclusions with which this paper ends refer only to farmers and their families in this category. This is not, however, so great a limitation as may be imagined. In common with other parts of the UK, the typical farm is the family farm comprising 'that form of farm business organisation where management, capital and the bulk of labour to operate the farm are provided by the family living there. They may or may not own the land as well. A family farm need not be small but the requirement that the family provide a substantial proportion of the labour sets an upper limit on size'. (5)

There are in this part of the world, therefore, few large-scale farms. In the face of a steady decline in agricultural labouring, members of the immediate family normally supply the labour. The hereditary principle is strong: in the absence of alternative employment most of the farmers we have interviewed gravitated 'naturally' to farming when their brief school days were at an end. In other words, we are dealing with self-employed businessmen (and women) who may or may not own the land from which they make a profit and where they are likely to have worked for the greater part of their lives. In this situation retirement is very much a family matter.

The pilot study was carried out in the winter 1979-80. A sample of 25 farmers was taken from the lists of agricultural advisors in the Region. All were men aged 45 and over who had received assistance under the Farm and Horticultural Development Scheme (FHDS), which simply meant that advisors had collected detailed information concerning a farmer's economic circumstances, and interview time (often precious after a long journey) need not be wasted in fishing for details of income/expenditure etc. No part-time or 'hobby farmers' were included nor did we meet any of the 'white settlers' on the West Coast. Large-scale commercial farmers were also excluded as were the large estates. The typical farm was in the range 60-120 hectares based on cattle and barley production. The farming system was, in the main, simple and traditional but the farms were well equipped and the buildings solid and well maintained. No-one was seriously in debt and income levels were adequate to maintain what may be considered by urban standards to be a somewhat frugal lifestyle. No-one was making a fortune nor was anyone approaching the poverty line. Most interviewees had experienced difficult seasons in the past and were capable of tightening their belts if need be. Close family ties provided a firm basis for an independent attitude and pride in hard work and stockmanship. With the exception of a minor landowner who had been an army officer and an ex-professional man with a university education, all interviewees had spent their whole lives in the area and most of their working lives in agriculture.

The method was an unstructured interview with the farmer and if possible his wife and other members of the family; particularly those with more than a passing interest in the future of the farm. Because farmers' wives are usually involved in a working relationship with their husbands and therefore make more than a 'domestic' contribution, it was easier to include them in the interview than might otherwise have been the case. In most of the farms we visited their role was far less subordinate than in other comparable domestic groups. Indeed, in most instances they made clear their intention of participating fully in the discussion.

The aim was to obtain as full a picture as was possible during one preliminary visit of the farmer's attitude to retirement and his plans for the future. Since we already had detailed background information about the farmer's type and size of farm, main sources of income, capital, gross output, income level, debts, insurances, savings and investments, we were free to concentrate on his life history, health record, and on what we may call his 'world view'. In the time available we could not, of course, do justice to the biographical method but we were concerned to open the way for a biographical analysis. An integral feature of this project is a series of follow-up visits which the pilot study proved to be feasible and acceptable to all subjects. We therefore set out to establish rapport with the farmer and his family and in the context of friendly conversation about the problems of farming to introduce the issue of retirement and explore the reaction. Inevitably this approach can lead to variable results but during the winter months farmers living in relative isolation tend to have time to talk and reminisce; welcoming, once the initial contact has been made, the opportunity to talk over their lives.

The actual length of interviews varied from 1-3 hours, depending partly on the time of day. Because the farmer had received previous assistance through FHDS he did not feel his home was being invaded by strangers armed with alien questionnaires. At least one of the party had been proven to have a legitimate interest in his business and was known for his agricultural expertise. It was thus a relatively simple matter to raise the question of retirement not as a special and possibly traumatic future event but as part of the ongoing activity which, because a farmer is freer than other workers to retire when he chooses, might come sooner or later. Retirement was discussed in the context of personal and family commitment to agriculture, experience with relatives who had retired, alternative income and housing arrangements, holidays, leisure interests, lifestyle, and future hopes and fears. At the end of each interview the information was recorded (out of sight of the farm) on a pocket tape recorder and an interview schedule divided into three sections: economic and social circumstances; preparation for retirement; and lifestyle.

It is important to stress the value of this kind of informal approach using trusted intermediaries where necessary. It is our experience that farmers, in this Region at any rate, are not used to putting their lives into their mouths and will only begin to produce word pictures when they feel at ease. Once rapport has been established, however, the situation changes and a wealth of material emerges so that the interview is only beginning in earnest when one reluctantly has to leave. Our first interview began in the most unpromising manner. The subject was a retired tenant farmer: one of the unfortunates who had had retirement forced upon him by a heart attack which he had not expected to survive. During his illness he handed over control of the property to his son and was now confined reluctantly in an inactive fringe role which he clearly found frustrating. From this man we obtained a vivid picture of enforced retirement as it must have been experienced by some who survived in the old days. There's a tradition that farmers never leave the land until they go broke or die. In North-East Scotland their fate was semmingly, in the words of David Toulmin, an Aberdeenshire farm worker turned novelist, to be 'nailed to the cross of life with no escape but death and gathered at last to the cluster of gravestones that surrounded the kirk on the brae'.(6) According to our informant when you retire at 68 you might as well be dead. When asked what happened to people a generation ago he said they simply worked until they 'tummelled down' in the fields. This was his doorstep greeting: he couldn't really see there was anything to discuss; retirement was a closed book.

Once, however, we had gained access to his fireside he began to enlarge upon his life and to explain some of the reasons why retirement was for him such a dead end. It was not retirement it-self which was the problem but his approach to his life when he was active and closing his mind to the possibility of ill health. A man with tremendous and deserved pride in his skill as a farmer and place in the community, he had not considered what life might be like as an invalid. Retirement was for him a problem not simply because he had made inadequate financial provision, or because there are few services for the retired in the country (in any case he thought the urban experience of retirement irrelevant), but because he had failed to anticipate change and had so much of his dignity and status vested in the autonomy of his work. He was an object lesson in the need to understand retirement in the context of each individual life.

His attitude to retirement, like Toulmin's dismal picture, turned out to be representative of an older and fading tradition. Before starting our interviews we had listened to the story of a shepherd who, having worked well into his eighties, was finally forced to retire. He now sat, his cap on his head, his dog by his side, gazing steadfastly through his cottage window into the hills. At the present stage of our investigation it seems to us evident that this view of retirement is no longer accepted by the younger generation of farmers; those whose urban contemporaries are increasingly exposed to elements of the new 'retirement culture'. To be sure we encountered one or two retired farmers like the man whose hobbies were TV and cigarettes and who rose every morning at 6.30 to work on the farm he had handed over to his daughter. But this man refused to describe himself as 'retired': he was part of a world which equates retirement with the sociological concepts of disengagement, disqualification, and loss of status - a transition to the tomb. Anecdotes about older farmers for whom retirement was the kiss of death - the popular image in this part of the world is the last arthritic stroll round Huntley Square - abound. But these tend to be passed around in the form of cautionary tales: examples of the perils of over-identification with one's occupation. The majority of men we interviewed firmly voiced their intention of avoiding the pitfalls of unplanned retirement. Our preliminary findings suggest that retirement, at least for family farmers in North-East Scotland, is not a 'fearsome thing' (7) but in the context of rapid technological change, may be positively welcomed provided careful advance preparations can be made.

This, of course, is where the story really begins. For the questions remain: what do farmers mean by preparation for retirement? what do they mean by retirement?; and by implication, what are the meanings of work and leisure? In 1978 the Ministry of Agriculture, Fisheries and Food carried out a survey of 100 farmers in England with businesses of between 150-274 standard man days. Few, it was discovered, were facing up to the problems of succession, inheritance, and retirement. 'They possessed extremely limited knowledge of Social Security, capital taxation and the legal aspects involved. Neither were they making provision for ill health or old age by savings or insurance policies; especially was this so on small farms and tenanted holdings'. A second project, undertaken simultaneously with 102 elderly farmers revealed that only one third had made any kind of provision for retirement and even fewer had made plans to provide supplementary income on retirement.(8) With a very few exceptions the farmers we interviewed did not turn out to be financially unwary or unmindful of the future. But more importantly we confirmed that a purely economic approach to retirement, necessary though it is to have an adequate income, is too narrow a pathway to a complete understanding of the nature of retirement.

Our pilot study suggests that family farming in the Region can be sufficiently flexible to allow a gradual and self-sufficient approach to later life. In this connection it's worth citing the example of Tommy Dale of East Lothian, a retired farmer who is still very much alive. In May 1980 he drew attention to the advantages of farming compared with his conception of retirement from the civil service: a sudden casting off onto the scrapheap. By contrast, he wrote in 'The Scottish Farmer', retirement does not make the farmer useless 'it is at least pleasing to think how we who are farmers can, without loss of any face or place in the "pecking order" give up our duties (as seems appropriate) to those who follow us'.(9)

This agricultural version of the 'flexible future' has also been
aired in 'Choice', the magazine of the Pre Retirement Association
which seldom pays any attention to retirement in rural life.   In
1980 Ted Moult, Britain's most famous farmer, was featured on one
of the covers.   Like many of the celebrities who advertise the
wisdom of preparation for retirement, he has no intention of retir-
ing in the old sense of making a complete break with work.   At 53,
he no longer has all his eggs in one basket.   Starting his life with
a commitment to farming he has systematically diversified his
interests and created a flexible lifestyle which blurs the line
between work and leisure. (10)

     Far from being a sudden and traumatic break, retirement for
family farmers tends now to be a gradual process of personal adjustment and change involving a long-term process of interaction between
objective socio-economic factors, cultural context, and subjective
appraisals of the meaning of events.   The problems that arise are
not so much problems of retirement but of life in the particular
situation in which it has been lived and in which it may be lived in
the future.   As far as the future of our project is concerned, we
are now engaged in a more systematic study of the lives of a sample
of 112 family farmers selected from FHDS lists and representatives
of the whole Region.   We are following up the lines of enquiry
reported here and expect to have a much fuller picture of the processes of interaction underlying contemporary retirement in due course.

REFERENCES

(1)   Research into retirement, notes Malcolm Johnson, has tended
        to suffer from certain deficiencies: '...a large
        proportion of retirement studies are more concerned with
        the adjustment or readjustment of actually retired indivi-
        duals, rather than with explanations of social transitions'
        'That Was Your Life: a Biographical Approach to Later
        Life', in V. Carver and P. Liddiard (eds.), An Ageing
        Population, Hodder & Stoughton, 1978.

(2)   Phillipson, C. The Emergence of Retirement, University of
        Durham, Department of Sociology and Social Administration,
        Working Papers in Sociology, No.14.

(3)   For an important exploration of the specific social world of
        elderly tenants in a slum hotel in a large city in the
        USA see, J. Stephens, Loners, Losers, and Lovers,
        University of Washington Press, 1976.   In this she writes,
        '... let us have done with the tendency in gerontology to
        assign to some vaguely defined process called "ageing" the
        reasons for what elderly people do and do not.   Rather,
        let us look at specific populations of elderly men and
        women in their natural settings - whether it be the SRO

hotel, a suburban apartment, a retirement village in
Phoenix City – and get to the business of studying the
situated aspects of human behaviour'.

(4)   Wenger, O.C. 'The Social Aspects of Rural Ageing', paper
        presented to the British Society of Gerontology Annual
        Conference, University of Aberdeen, 1980.

(5)   The definition is Ruth Gasson's.
        See also her 'Use of Sociology in Agricultural Economics',
        Journal of Agricultural Economics', V, XXI, No.3, 1971.

(6)   Toulmin, D. Harvest Home, Pan, 1980.

(7)   Retirement has often been described as an object of dread.
        Thus, in his recent text Morton Puner observes, 'The act
        of retirement, its immediate prospects, continue to be a
        fearsome thing. Gerontologists consider that retirement –
        along with the death of a mate – are the two most shatter-
        ing, traumatic events of later life. The day his retire-
        ment starts, a man is apt suddenly to feel very old'.
        Such statements need to be qualified considerably. To The
        Good Long Life: What We Know About Growing Old,
        Macmillan, 1978.

(8)   Ministry of Agriculture, Fisheries and Food, Succession,
        Retirement, and Inheritance, Socio-Economic Papers No.10,
        627, 1978.

(9)   The Scottish Farmer, May, 1980.

(10)   Cole, N. 'Farmer Ted Moult Contemplates Retirement', Choice,
        August, 1980.

ADDITIONAL REFERENCES

Allright, D.W. 'Farmers and Pensions', Farm Management, V.3, No.12,
    1979.

Anderson, R. and Hepworth, M. 'Retirement from Farming: Some
    Economic and Social Considerations', Farm Management Review,
    13, January, 1980.

Henkes, R. 'Beating the Retirement Blues', The Furrow, January-
    February, 1981.

Featherstone, M. and Hepworth, M. 'Changing Images of Middle Age'
    in M. Johnson (ed), Transitions in Middle and Later Life, British
    Society of Gerontology, 1980.

Winter, D.M. Family Farming and The Development of Capitalism,
    unpub. paper, May 1979.

Winter, D.M. 'Job Satisfaction, Work Motivation and the Need for a
    New Direction in Agricultural Labour Science', <u>Journal of Agricul-
    tural Labour Science</u>, 7, 1978.

SOME SOCIAL IMPLICATIONS OF ACQUIRED DEAFNESS
IN OLD AGE

Katia Gilhome-Herbst

It is no exaggeration to say that deafness is a hated disorder and highly stigmatised. This proposition is made in the full confidence that most people have an elderly hearing impaired relative or elderly friend who will, in the face of obvious difficulties, hotly resist any notion that they may be a little deaf or hard of hearing. By their denial they acknowledge their awareness of prevailing attitudes. Why do people feel this antipathy to deafness and what are the wider implications of their denial?

Their attitude to their deafness and, possibly one's own, is tempered by a backlog of cultural dislike. Whereas most physical handicap, including blindness, cuts people off from things (usually doing things, which thus begs a helping hand), deafness cuts people away from other people and thus defies help. In this sense it may be seen as a form of dreadful isolation with only God as company, much as are many forms of mental disorder. There is also an apparent similarity between the symptoms of deafness and those of some types of mental disorder (particularly defects of reason) namely, indistinct speech, not answering when spoken to, or answering inappropriately or out of context, pitching the voice incorrectly and so on. These symptoms often encourage people to talk to and treat the hearing impaired as if their cognitive abilities were also impaired. From our work such public reaction is well perceived.

The dislike of deafness and the blurring in the popular mind between it and mental disorder are not peculiar to contemporary society. The ancient Greeks, particularly Aristotle (History of Animals, Bk. IV. No.9) also failed to differentiate between deafness and mental disorder or retardation. Aristotle's understanding of the matter remained established 'fact' right through until the Renaissance (Hodgson, 1953; Bender, 1970).

Aristotle's observations were focussed primarily on the pre-lingually deaf - that is those who are born deaf or who lose their hearing before the normal acquisition of language and not on the adventitiously deaf who constitute the bulk of elderly hearing impaired. Nevertheless, the stigma suffered by the one group seems to have rubbed off onto the other. The code of conduct expressed in Leviticus IX, v.14 'Thou shalt not curse the deaf', suggests that the early Hebrews recognised the indignities suffered by the hearing impaired. None-the-less, the deaf were subsequently penalised by the early Christians by the fact that they were deprived from hearing the word of God. Paul, in his letter to the Romans X, v.17, said 'So then faith cometh by hearing and hearing by the word of God'. By implication therefore hearing was Godgiven and deafness hindered faith itself. It is no wonder that for centuries, until, indeed, reading and writing became universal alternatives, deafness was regarded as the most horrendous of misfortune.

Deafness is regarded, proverbially, as a condition that can be turned on or off at will to break communication with another person in a pre-meditated sense. Hence the saying 'None so deaf as those who will not hear'. The implication being that deafness is a 'hoax' disorder which can be overcome if there is a will to do so. No parallel proverbs exists which accuses blind men of peeping when they want to see. Most similies related to deafness reinforce this rebuff by depicting it in relation to hard, solid, immovable objects: 'as deaf as a post', 'stone deaf', 'deaf as a door nail'. There is yet another cultural reason why deafness is so disliked and that is its close association with ageing. On the stage, in literature, if we want a quick sketch of an old person, we portray him as bent, grey haired and with his hand cupped behind his ear, misunderstanding what is said amidst peals of laughter and the gaiety of others. Deafness, when used in an allegorical sense as synonymous with old age usually represents a breakdown in meaningful communication with the world and is a component of .....'mere oblivion, sans teeth, sans eyes, sans taste, sans everything'. We openly mock deafness in the old as we would mock no other disorder.

But as with most situations that we laugh at, our laughter is accompanied by a definite feeling of unease. Lack of comprehension of speech in others is frightening - to many it still does verge on the 'inhuman'. Moreover, it is the one disorder which handicaps the unafflicted and we do not like it.

What then is the basis of the popular association of deafness with old age? The kind of 'deafness' that I am talking about is a significant handicapping bilateral hearing loss that would normally warrant the use of a hearing aid. Numerous studies have documented hearing loss alongside other conditions such as failing sight, poor teeth, bad feet (the well known art of screening for unmet needs). All of them have obtained their information either by asking the respondents whether they were deaf, hard of hearing, found it difficult to follow conversations and so on (Sheldon, 1948; Harris, 1962; Townsend and Wedderburn, 1965; Abrams, 1978) or by the observations of the clinician or interviewer (Williamson, 1964; Sheard, 1971; Cumbria, C.C. 1973). In this way, the prevalence of disorders of hearing amongst the elderly has consistently been assessed as affecting between 30 per cent and 40 per cent of the entire population of the so-called retired.

I would now like to turn to our own two year study whose main objective was to investigate whether the high prevalence of deafness thought to exist amongst the elderly is related to the high prevalence of mental disorder known to exist in that age group. A basic prerequisite for such a study was the systematic assessment of both the level of hearing (by means of pure tone audiometry) and the mental state of an elderly population living at home. The association that was found between deafness and mental state is reported elsewhere, (Gilhome Herbst and Humphrey 1980).

The sample consisted of all 365 persons aged seventy years and over, registered with the central surgery of a group general practice in an Inner London borough. Fortyeight people refused to participate and a further 46 were either untraceable, on holiday, or in hospital during the fieldwork period. Eighteen respondents were excluded after interview for a variety of reasons ranging from inadequate audiometry to poor English. Thus the final sample studied consisted of 253 persons, representing 69 per cent of the initial sample. This response rate is comparable to other medico-social studies of elderly populations living at home (Milne et al. 1971). There were no significant differences between the age and sex distributions of respondents and non-respondents.

Table 1:   Age and sex distribution of the sample

Sex	age in years				
	70-74	75-79	80-84	85+	total
	no.(%)	no.(%)	no.(%)	no.(%)	no.(%)
male	46(41)	34(46)	7(20)	5(16)	92(36)
female	66(59)	40(54)	28(80)	27(84)	161(64)
total	112(100)	74(100)	35(100)	32(100)	253(100)

The interview schedule, which took approximately $1\frac{1}{2}$ hours to complete, was administered during a single home visit to each respondent. Audiometric measurements were made and scales to screen for organic brain syndrone and depression, extracted from the Comprehensive Assessment and Referral Evaluation (CARE) Schedule (Gurland et al. 1977), were administered to each respondent. The interview also contained detailed questions about three other life domains: general health and use of primary and secondary health and welfare services; the experience of loneliness and contacts with friends and relations; the experience of deafness and use of aids where applicable.

Hearing loss was measured using pure-tone audiometry (air conduction) over the speech frequencies at 0.25kHz, 0.5kHz, 1kHz, 2kHz and 4kHz, for both ears. Masking was considered unnecessary. Audiocups were fitted to the Amplivox 2150 portable diagnostic audiometer used.

Validation of the audiometry was carried out by the Hearing Aid Centre at the Royal National Throat, Nose and Ear Hospital, London, to which a total of 44 referrals for hearing aids were made (19 requiring domiciliary visits). A very high level of agreement (an overall mean difference of 0.3B) was found between the average decibel levels of respondents re-tested under clinical conditions and their average decibel levels in the field.

42

All significance levels quoted in the text are derived using a simple chi-square test.

Using as a measure of deafness the level of impairment where it is normally considered necessary for patients to obtain the amplification of a hearing aid (an average loss of 35dB or more over the speech frequencies at 1kHz, 2kHz and 4kHz in the better ear), it was established that 60 per cent of the whole sample (70 years and over) were 'deaf'. Sixty nine per cent of those aged 75 years and over, 82 per cent of those aged 80 years and over and 84 per cent of those aged 85 years and over were 'deaf'. The proportion 'deaf' and severity of deafness increases significantly with age (p 0.001). In keeping with all other studies where no audiometry was performed, only 38 per cent of the sample responded positively to the conventional question on the interview schedule regarding hearing loss (Gilhome Herbst and Humphrey, 1981).

Thus by using audiometric techniques, we disclosed double the previous estimates of the prevalence of deafness arrived at by self report or clinician observation.

These figures compare favourably with unpublished results of the Edinburgh longitudinal health study on the elderly by Milne et al (personal communication) and with two studies carried out in local authority homes for the elderly (Burton, 1976; Martin and Peckford 1978).

Indeed from these results, deafness must now be seen as almost twice as prevalent as has hitherto been assumed. The popular image of the old as deaf is truer than one had thought. It must be seen as almost synonymous with ageing, and as such, a contributing factor to the social and psychological experience of nearly all old people.

The implications of deafness can be considered by reference to those factors which significantly differentiate the hearing impaired elderly from the normally hearing.

Nineteen persons assessed as probably suffering from marked dementia according to their scores on the organic brain syndrone scale are not included in the following analysis as their responses to the interview schedule were deemed to be unreliable. Thus the sample for the subsequent discussion comprises 136 deaf and 98 normally hearing.

The completed schedules of the sample were divided into deaf and normally hearing. ANOVA, a sub-programme of SPSS (Statistical Package for the Social Sciences, Nie et al. 1975) designed to produce a chi-square test for significance whilst allowing for multi-control of nuisance variables are age and socio-economic status. Both these variables are themselves significantly associated with deafness.

In this way the following eight factors on Table II were found to significantly differentiate the deaf from the hearing elderly.

		Level of Significance
1.	Self-assessment of health:	The deaf rate their health worse	$p\ 0.05$
2.	Extent of mobility:	The deaf are less likely to be able to get out without help	$p\ 0.01$
3.	Range of excursions in the past week:	The deaf have ventured out less far	$p\ 0.05$
4.	Satisfaction with amount of going out:	The deaf are more likely to say they do not get out enough	$p\ 0.0$
5.	Number of friends relative to the past:	The deaf are more likely to say they have fewer friends than in the past	$p\ 0.05$
6.	Having a relationship to which they make an active contribution:	The deaf are less likely to be assessed as having such a relationship	$p\ 0.05$
7.	Enjoyment of things relative to the past:	The deaf are more likely to say they enjoy less than previously	$p\ 0.01$
8.	Depression rating:	The deaf are more likely to be rated as depressed	$p\ 0.05$

None of these associations are exceptionally strong, but together seem to constitute a clearly interpretable picture of the aspects of life affected by deafness in old age. They show that deafness in old age may be said to contribute to a significantly impoverished quality of life. Using Harris's terms, (Harris 1971) deafness is both disabling in its influence on activity and handicapping in its effect on personal happiness. For deafness is significantly associated with depression, ill-health and isolation.

Firstly, as regards the first four variables on Table II deafness was found to be significantly associated with poor general health,* and, as such, could be seen to be linked with reduced mobility and a reduction in both range of activities and numbers of excursions outside the home. However, when general health status and limiting and non-limiting physical disabilities were controlled for, deafness was still found to be significantly associated with a restricted range of outdoor activities. Thus we have evidence to support the hypothesis that deafness may be a direct cause of reduced mobility outside the home due to fears of managing outside the home with poor hearing.

The second main area of influence of deafness (variables 5 and 6) was in its association with a significant reduction in personal contacts. No doubt in part this is due to reduced mobility, but a major cause of this diminution must also be because of problems with communication. This is indeed the most obvious and the most frequently noted effect of deafness in all age groups (von Leden,1977; Jackson, 1979; Thomas and Gilhome Herbst op cit. 1980).

Insofar as the reduction in mobility and reduction in personal contacts associated with deafness may be said (objectively) to constitute conditions of living which together create an isolated life-style, deafness in the elderly can be said to be working primarily as a determinant of isolation.

Deafness in old age appears by itself not to be a strong determinant of loneliness (which we may call the lack of companionship of the desired kind). In old age, loneliness is probably more a consequence of lack or loss of kindred spirits, or possibly follows a lifelong predisposition. The very normality of deafness in old age probably renders it less influential in disrupting such relationship as remain.

Thirdly, the cumulative handicapping effect of the restrictions I have just discussed can be seen in the association of deafness with reduced enjoyment of life as a whole (variable 7) and with depression (variable 8). Indeed, the first seven variables are each themselves

* Thomas and Gilhome Herbst (Thomas and Gilhome Herbst,1980) also noted this association of deafness with poor general health in their study of the hearing impaired of employment age.

significantly associated with depression. This association of deafness with depression confirms how, in the extreme case, the handicapping effect of deafness may engender disturbance. It also underlines
the notion that deafness must be seen as a disorder requiring
treatment and care.

One point which should be considered is how all eight factors on
the Table present a picture which one might easily associate with the
conventional notion of ageing per se. One can now see more readily
why deafness is popularly synonymous with ageing and may thus be
overlooked. Variables 1,2,3, 5 and 6 in particular may be viewed
from a disengagement perspective as 'normal' ageing.

It would be useful at this point to discuss how society's pre-
conceptions about ageing and attitudes to the age-related disorder in
particular, have inhibited the proper use of rehabilitative services.
At time of interview, in a sample of elderly people of whom 60 per
cent were significantly deaf, 8 per cent said they made use of a
hearing aid.* (Yet 97 per cent possessed spectacles and wore them
when necessary). Nearly 40 per cent of the whole population did not
know of the free hearing aid service under NHS - a service that has
been available since the NHS began over 30 years ago and only one
individual had ever been to a lip reading class. Why should this be?

Let us first consider the attitudes of the elderly to deafness.
You will remember that audiometric techniques produced double the
previous estimates of prevalence based on self-report. The
discrepancy in these figures suggests that approximately one third of
the hearing impaired elderly do not readily admit to their hearing
loss. When we compare this to other health-care studies using
screening techniques, we may say this is <u>not</u> an unusual finding. Yet
even after producing 'scientific' evidence of a hearing loss, 27 per
cent (36) of the sample of hearing impaired still refused to admit it.
This 'denial' group were nonetheless substantially deaf with a mean
loss in the better ear of 44dB (Sd 10-1).

Some part of apparent denial of hearing loss must be attributable
to the kind of life-styles of some elderly people whereby they are in
a position of not <u>needing</u> better hearing. Our experience showed such
people to be those living neither particularly isolated nor particularly gregarious lives where being able to hear well matters far more.

----

* Community studies such as Townsend and Wedderburn's estimated in
   1965 that only 6.3 per cent of their sample of elderly people
   possessed aids. By 1978, Abrams estimated that 9.2 per cent of
   those aged 65+ had aids. Of those who do admit to a hearing loss,
   there is some indication that about one third will possess an aid
   (Harris, op. cit.1962; Sheikh and Verney,1972; Gilhome Herbst and
   Humphrey op. cit. 1981).

However, overt denial of trouble with hearing, in the face of
difficulties, seems to be far more common and had already been noted
in previous studies which relied on self report (Wilkins, 1948;
Sheldon, op. cit; Townsend and Wedderburn op. cit.).

Seventy five per cent of our sample who admitted they were
having difficulties in hearing, confided that they did not tell
anyone about their hearing loss. The mean dB loss of this group was
55.8dB (sd 14.5). By witholding information about their deafness,
all these people are fuelling commonly held stereo-types about the
parallel of mental disorder with deafness. Deafness is a hidden
disorder. Any 'unitiated' person interacting with people with such
degrees of hearing impairment may be forgiven if they begin to doubt
their cognitive abilities.

Consequently 24 per cent of those who admitted they were deaf
said they often felt that their deafness was mistaken for 'absent
mindedness'. Consequently, 54 per cent also said that other people
got irritable with them - because of their deafness. This reticence
to tell other people of their hearing impairment results in an
incredible 40 per cent who did not know anyone else who had difficulties with their hearing - a situation which is totally improbable
but mirrors the findings in our previous work on the hearing impaired
of employment age (Thomas and Gilhome Herbst, op. cit.) and causes
people to feel 'odd', 'ashamed' and alone with a problem.

Our analysis showed that overt denial was due not only to the
desire to 'pass as normal' in response to having a disorder which
they recognised as being stigmatized, but also to the expectation of
being hearing impaired at their age, and the belief that any
difficulties had to be borne with fortitude and not mourned over
(for a broader analysis see Gilhome Herbst op.cit.1981).

In that the hearing aid service is offered on demand, we now
arrive at some understanding as to why a 'deafness labelling' device
such as a hearing aid may be resisted - if it is known of.

Attention is now drawn to the attitudes of professionals who,
as members of our society, probably hold prevailing attitudes to the
disorder. Amongst our sample who admitted to their hearing loss
about 65 per cent said they had been to see their general practitioner
particularly about their hearing loss. In that they are dependent
for a hearing aid upon their general practitioner's recommendation to
the local hearing aid clinic, it is some indication of general
practitioner attitudes that over half these people were sent home
and told not to worry 'it was normal' (which of course it is) and
that they did not therefore need an aid. The near dB loss of people
who had seen their doctors and had not been recommended for an aid
was 56.3dB in the better ear! (Discussed in full in Humphrey,
Herbst and Faruqi, 1981 in press).

The present system is hampered by the fact that doctors may not
notice hearing loss in their elderly patients. If clinicians (such

as Kay et al 1964; Hoskinson, 1973) specifically interested in hearing loss, failed to detect deafness, without audiometry, in a substantial number of their patients during stylized clinical and research investigations, busy general practitioners with other matters on their minds may be forgiven for failing to detect hearing loss amongst their patients - particularly when conventional clinical techniques or conventional 'bed-side talk' is used and expected by the elderly patient.

Johnson (Johnson,1972) makes the very valid point that in many medico-social studies using screening techniques, vast areas of apparently unmet need are recognised by doctors but not by the elderly. To some considerable extent, of course, we have found the same. But we also have here the reverse situation: here we have a significant number who report their disorder to their doctor and are told that their problem does not constitute a need.

As we have seen, deafness is essentially a social malady derived from a physical impairment. Evidently many doctors do not recognise social disorders which are as prevalent and 'normal' as deafness as requiring medical attention. Indeed, there is ample research evidence to show that because they receive little encouragement to do otherwise, the elderly either defer demand for hearing aids indefinitely, or are encouraged to postpone it for as long as possible - usually until they are very old, very frail and almost 'stone-deaf' (Alberti, 1977; Brooks, 1979; Ward, Gowers and Morgan, 1979).

There is a danger, that attempting to initiate aural rehabilita-tion with the very old is a wasteful use of staff time. The mean dB loss of those with aids was 69.5dB (sd 16.6) in the better ear. We must compare this to waiting to wear spectacles until almost total blindness.

Rumour of the considerable failure of rehabilitative measures when undertaken at this very late stage may well reinforce the belief of the unrehabilitated elderly, their doctors, and their supporters that there is little point in getting an aid. So the original causes of withholding recognition of deafness and therefore demand for an aid, namely the stigma of deafness, the expectation of poor hearing and life-styles which apparently demand little communication, come full circle to disrupt attempts to overcome the disability by making early, appropriate or sensible use of existing services. Whilst deafness very clearly thwarts personal autonomy and contributes significantly to isolation and depression, we need to attack the notion, still upheld by many, that because it represents a stereo-type and is 'normal' it may be left as it is.

REFERENCES

Abrams, M. (1978) Beyond Three-Score and Ten. A First Report on a Survey of the Elderly. Age Concern Research Publication: Mitcham.

Alberti, P.W. (1977) Hearing aids and aural rehabilitation. Journal of Otolaryngology; 6: Supplement No. 4.

Bender, K. (1970) The Conquest of Deafness, The Press of Case Western Reserve University, Revised edition.

Brooks, D.B. (1979) Hearing aid candidates - some relevant features, British Journal of Audiology: 13: pp.81-84.

Burton, D.K. (1976) Hearing Impaired Residents in Local Authority Homes for the Elderly, Unpublished M.Sc. dissertation, Salford University.

Cumbria County Council (1973) Survey of the Handicapped and Impaired and Elderly Over Seventy five in Cumberland, Cumbria County Council.

Gilhome Herbst K.R.(1981) Psycho-social Consequences of Disorders of Hearing in the Elderly. Chapter VIII in Medicine in Old Age - Hearing and Balance ed. Hinchcliffe, R. Churchill Livingstone, (In press).

Gilhome Herbst K.R., Humphrey, C. (1980) Hearing impairment and mental state in the elderly living at home, British Medical Journal: 281: pp.903-905.

Gilhome Herbst. K.R. Humphrey, C. (1981) The prevalence of hearing impairment in the elderly living at home, Journal of the Royal College of General Practitioners, in press (accepted 1.9.80).

Gurland, B.H., Kuriansky, J.B., Sharpe, L., Simon, R., Stiller, P., Birkett, P. The Comprehensive Assessment and Referral Evaluation (CARE) - rationale, development and reliability, International Journal of Aging and Human Development: 8 (1): pp.9-42.

Harris, A.I. (1962) The Social Survey, Health and Welfare of Older People in Lewisham, London: Central Office of Information.

Harris, A.I., Cox, E., Smith, C.R.W. (1971) Handicapped and Impaired in Great Britain. Pt. I. London: HMSO.

Hodgson, K. (1953) The Deaf and Their Problems: A Study in Special Education. London: Watts & Co.

Hodgkinson, H.M. (1973) Mental impairment in the elderly, Journal of the Royal College of Physicians, London: 7 (4) pp.305-317.

Humphrey, C.M., Gilhome Herbst, K.R., Faruqi, S. (1981) Some characteristics of the hearing impaired elderly who do not present themselves for rehabilitation. British Journal of Audiology, (In press).

Jackson, P.H. (1979) Special problems of the hard of hearing, Journal of Rehabilitation of the Deaf; 12 (4): pp.13-26.

Johnson, M.L. (1972) Self perception of need amongst the elderly: an analysis of illness behaviour, Sociological Review; 20: (4).

Kay, D.W.K., Beamish, P., Roth, M. (1964) Old age mental disorders in Newcastle upon Tyne, Pt. I: A study of prevalence, British Journal of Psychiatry; 110: pp.146-158.

Martin, D.N., Peckford, R.W. (1978) Hearing impairment in homes for the elderly, Social Work Service; 17: pp.52-62.

Milne, J.S., Maule, M.H., Williamson, J. (1971) Method of sampling in a study of older people with a comparison of respondents and non-respondents. British Journal of Preventive and Social Medicine; 25: pp.37-41.

Nie, N.H., Hadlai Hull, C., Jenkins, J.G., Steinbrenner, K., Bent,D.H. (1975) The Statistical Package for the Social Sciences, Second Edition, McGraw-Hill, Inc.

Sheard, A.V. (1971) Survey of the elderly in Scunthorpe, Public Health London; 85: pp.208-218.

Sheikh, J., Verney, A.R. (1972) Report on the Survey of Hearing Impaired Persons in Blaby Rd. Leicestershire County Council, Social Services Dept.

Sheldon, J.H. (1948) The Social Medicine of Old Age, Report of an Enquiry in Wolverhampton. London: Oxford University Press.

Thomas, A.J., Gilhome Herbst, K.R. (1980) Social and psychological implications of acquired hearing loss for adults of employment age. British Journal of Audiology; 14: pp.76-85.

Ward, P.R., Gowers, J.I., Morgan, D.C. (1979) Problems with handling the BE10 series hearing aids among elderly people. British Journal of Audiology; 13:(1): pp.31-36.

Wilkins, L.T. (1948) The Social Survey, Survey of the Prevalence of Deafness in the Population of England Scotland and Wales. London:

Williamson, J., Stokoe, I.H., Gray, S., Fisher, M., Smith, A., McGhee, A., Stephenson, E. Old people at home: Their unreported needs. Lancet; i: pp.1117-1120.

THE EFFECTS OF AGEING ON CONSULTATION
AND PRESCRIBING PATTERNS

Deirdre Jones

Introduction

The elderly, that is the over 65s, form just over 12 per cent of
the population but consume 30 per cent of the National Health Service
drug bill (Caird, 1977). Drug prescribing in the elderly can be
considered to be important from two points of view; the cost to the
Health Service and the well-being of the elderly themselves. It is
the second with which I am primarily concerned; the cost can only
reasonably be discussed when we know the quality and appropriateness
of the prescribing and the effectiveness of the drug therapy.

The most important single cause of iatrogenic disorders in old
age is the improper prescription and ingestion of drugs. The
frequency of major side effects from drugs increases steadily with age
(Hurwitz, 1969). Hurwitz claimed that adverse drug reactions occur
in 21 per cent of the 70-79 age group.

Many studies have produced consistent results concerning drug
elimination. 'Clearance rates have almost always been shown to be
reduced and this is undoubtedly the most important pharmocokinetic
principle in the elderly'. (Caird, 1977)

Polypharmacy is particularly hazardous to the elderly as the
frequency of inter-reactions rises with age. Also it is well documented that they have difficulty coping with complicated regimens
because of visual and manual impairment, for example, reading the
labels, differentiating between tablets, opening complicated packages.
Errors in drug-taking are directly related to the degree of mental
impairment. (Davidson, 1974)

My own interest in elderly prescribing was aroused when analysing
a study I carried out on a general population (Jones et.al.1980).
From there it seemed that this area needed researching in more depth
and that such a study would need to be prospective in design and
based on lengthy interviews. The results which I shall present today
can only serve as a basis for future studies, they provide an overall
picture without answering the hows and whys of the situation.

The Study

In 1978 we carried out a study to investigate the different
patterns of consultation and prescribing in Wales and England. Both
consultation and prescribing rates are significantly higher (30 per
cent) in Wales than England. Today I shall present the data from

this study in order to demonstrate the effect of ageing on consultations and prescribing.

Random samples of electors were chosen in Bristol and Cardiff - two cities that are similarly classified for socio-economic factors. The prescribing rate for Bristol is the same as the average for England, and Cardiff is slightly lower than the average for Wales. A postal questionnaire was sent to the subjects requesting details of the prescriptions that they had received during the last four weeks, the total number of prescriptions over the last three months and consultations and self-medication in the last four weeks. The response rate was 89 per cent.

Table 1 shows the details of the sample. There 793 and 798 in each area, 172 being over 65 in Cardiff and 160 in Bristol.

Consultations

Firstly we looked at the consultation pattern, that is how many subjects had actually seen a G.P. during the previous four weeks. Table 2 summarises those results: in both of the cities there is a noticeable increase in the rate of consultation with age, apart from the over 75 males in Bristol and the 65-74 in Bristol females. There is a more consistent and noticeable increase in Cardiff with a very high rate in the over 75s. The difference between the elderly and others is very significant. As one would expect, there is a noticeable difference between the sexes in both samples. In almost every age group females consulted more than males. It is interesting to note that the oldest group see their G.P. far more often in Cardiff than in Bristol. Is this an alternative to home consultations?

Table 3 shows the percentage of subjects who had a visit from their G.P. at home. Males and females have been combined for this table because the numbers were inevitably so much smaller. There is a significant difference between the elderly and the rest of the population, and a very consistent increase with age in both cities. The frequency is very much higher for the over 70s. Cardiff over 75s receive markedly more home visits than those in Bristol. Home and general practice consultations do not appear to be alternatives. G.Ps see their elderly more often in Cardiff. This could have several possible explanations.

The G.Ps in Cardiff may have a policy of seeing their elderly more often; the subjects may demand to see their G.Ps more often; it may be easier to travel to a G.P. in Cardiff or there may be greater morbidity in Wales.

The consequences of the consultations are summarised in Table 4: this table shows the percentage of people consulting a doctor who received a prescription. All age groups have a very high chance of their consultation resulting in a prescription. The elderly in both cities have a significantly higher rate than the rest. The numbers

in the 75+ age group are rather small. Again a higher percentage of
females receives prescriptions than do males. This is interesting in
the light of previous research which shows that G.Ps consider 60 per
cent of visits to be trivial and that less than 50 per cent of
patients require a prescription from consultation.

Prescribing

We then started to look at prescribing rates generally.

In Table 5 we see the percentage of all subjects who had a
prescription during the previous four weeks. A significantly higher
percentage of the elderly receive prescriptions over a four week
period than do the rest of the samples. This increases consistently
with age in both cities with the exception of the over 75 males in
Bristol being particularly noticeable. Again more females than males
receive prescriptions in a four week period - more than 50 per cent
of Cardiff elderly women.

As a higher proportion of the elderly are unwell at any one time,
it is perhaps not surprising that more of them are taking medicines.

Table 6 demonstrates the proportion of subjects that are having
several prescriptions over a longer time period; of three months.
This information gives us some idea of how many people are on regular
medication. Significantly more elderly are receiving more than three
prescriptions in three months. Apart from the age group 65-74 in
Bristol females, there is a consistent increase with age in both
cities and in both sexes. In Cardiff the sex difference reduces in
the older age groups, but in Bristol the very elderly males appear
to have less than one might expect.

It seems then that not only are more elderly on medication at
any one time, but more of them receive it regularly.

Table 7 summarises another measure of regular medication: the
average number of prescriptions received during the previous three
months. Once more there is a consistent increase with age in both
citied. Again this demonstrates that not only do more of the
elderly receive prescriptions, but that they have more of them.

Items

As well as the frequency of prescriptions we were also
interested in the number of different medications being received at
any time. The average number of items per script is shown in Table 8,
from which it appears that the elderly have on average more items on
each script. Not only then do they receive more scripts than younger
people, but each of these contains more items. What we cannot tell
from this, of course, are the quantities prescribed not the dosages.
This increasing average is remarkably consistent in each town in both
sexes. Females at every age apart from the Cardiff over 75s have
more items than the males.

This is interesting and important bearing in mind the dangers of polypharmacy in the elderly. It is also known that the elderly have more problems coping with the management of several different drugs with different instructions for each.

Classes of Drugs

So far we have looked at the frequency of consultations and prescriptions in the elderly, but not at their medication.

In Table 9 we see the major classes of drugs that the elderly are prescribed. Cardiff and Bristol have been combined together for this table but the sexes are separate in order to demonstrate the differences. The first two columns show the percentage of all prescriptions that are in each of the major classes and the second two columns show what percentage of subjects receive drugs in these major classes.

We can see that over a third of all the prescriptions are in the cardiovascular class and that subjects must receive more than one of this type of drug, a higher percentage of females than males being given drugs of this type. The second most frequent drugs are the psychotropics: 16 per cent of females were prescribed psychotropics, but 20 per cent of the prescriptions for females were for psychotropics, so that some are receiving more than one. Many more females than males were prescribed them.

The third most important group of drugs are the analgesics, including anti-inflammatory: 10 per cent of the female subjects had been prescribed analgesics, but for this group the percentage of prescriptions for males was higher than for females. Respiratory and alimentary drugs are the next most frequently prescribed drugs. With anti-microbials being prescribed much less than would have been expected. The major therapeutic classes are therefore cardiovascular, psychotropic and analgesic. So far we have confined ourselves to medication that has been prescribed, but what about medication that the elderly have bought?

Self-Medication

The percentage of subjects who had used self-medication during the previous four weeks is shown in Table 10. Here we see a complete reversal of the trend in all the other tables: self-medication being significantly lower in the over 65s. There is a marked decline throughout the age groups in both cities, but there is no consistent pattern between the sexes. This pattern held for all types of self-medication, but the fall off was most dramatic for the treatment of headaches.

Conclusions

The results of this survey show that the frequency of contact that the elderly had with their general practitioner increased with age. As one might expect, home consultations were much higher in the older age groups with a noticeable difference between the cities.

Over three-quarters of the subjects who had consulted a general practitioner had received a prescription - again the percentage rising consistently with age. With the exception of Bristol males over 75, more of the elderly received prescriptions and those who had them had more of them. Also, the number of items on each script is higher among the elderly.

Cardiovascular, psychotropic and analgesic medications accounted for two-thirds of those drugs prescribed to the subjects.

The frequency of self-medication, in contrast to consultations and prescribing, declined markedly with increasing age.

This study presents an essentially 'macro' approach that indicates certain problems and areas that need further investigation in depth. Prospective work is now required to study the expectations, relationships and interactions that underlie these results.

Prescribing and consultation among the elderly are issues that affect a large proportion of the elderly population living in the community, inevitably leading to morbidity and lower quality of life.

REFERENCES

1.   Caird, F.I. (1977), British Journal of Hospital Medicine,
         June: pp. 610-613.

2.   Hurwitz, N. (1969) British Medical Journal: p.536.

3.   Davidson, J.R. (1973), Journal of Hospital Pharmacy, 31: 180.

4.   Jones, D. et al (1980) Journal of Epidemiology and Community
         Health, 34: 2.

TABLE 1
Age and Sex of Sample

	Bristol	Cardiff
Males		
$<$ 45	191	167
45 –	135	132
65 –	59	49
75 +	26	19
Females		
45	168	183
45 –	129	144
65 –	46	70
75 +	39	34
Total	793	798

TABLE 2.
Percentage of Subjects who Consulted a General Practitioner
During Previous Four Weeks

	Bristol	Cardiff
Males		
$<$ 45	18	20
45 –	25	24
65 –	31	33
75 +	19	47
Females		
45	26	28
45 –	32	38
65 –	20	40
75 +	36	59

x_c^2 under 65 vs. over 65 = 9.5

p   0.005

56

TABLE 3

Percentage of Subjects who Received a Home Consultation
During Previous Four Weeks

	Bristol	Cardiff
Males and Females		
$<$ 45	0.6	0.9
45 –	3	2
65 –	5	9
75 +	11	26

x_c^2 under 65 vs. over 65 = 37.4

p $<$ 0.0005

TABLE 4

Percentage of Consulters who Received a Prescription
During Previous Four Weeks

	Bristol	Cardiff
Males		
$<$ 45	74	73
45 –	91	81
65 –	94	88
75 +	80	100
Females		
$<$ 45	68	81
45 –	90	87
65 –	100	96
75 +	93	95

x_c^2 under 65 vs. over 65 = 10.3

p$<$0.0005

TABLE 5

Percentage of Subjects who Received a Prescription
During Previous Four Weeks

	Bristol	Cardiff
Males		
< 45	14	16
45 -	29	24
65 -	37	37
75 +	31	58
Females		
< 45	21	29
45 -	34	40
65 -	37	50
75 +	51	59

x_c^2 under 65 vs. over 65 = 46.2

$p < 0.0005$

TABLE 6

Percentage of Subjects who Received 3+ Prescriptions
During Previous Three Months

	Bristol	Cardiff
Males		
< 45	3	6
45 -	12	11
65 -	17	22
75 +	31	32
Females		
< 45	7	12
45 -	20	21
65 -	13	29
75 +	41	32

x_c^2 under 65 vs. over 65 = 49.9

$p^c < 0.0005$

58

TABLE 7
Average Number of Prescriptions Received During Previous
Three Months

	Bristol	Cardiff
Males		
< 45	0.4	0.5
45 -	0.7	0.7
65 -	1.1	1.1
75 +	1.4	1.7
Females		
< 45	0.8	0.9
45 -	1.1	1.3
65 -	1.2	1.5
75 +	1.8	1.5

TABLE 8
Average Number of Items Per Script

	Bristol	Cardiff
Males		
< 45	0.2	0.2
45 -	0.5	0.5
65 -	0.7	0.9
75 +	0.7	1.6
Females		
< 45	0.3	0.4
45 -	0.6	0.8
65 -	0.8	1.1
75 +	1.6	1.4

TABLE   9

Major Classes of Drugs Prescribed for the Over 65s

Therapeutic Class	% of all prescriptions		% of subjects	
	Males	Females	Males	Females
Cardiovascular	35	36	15	22
Psychotropics	11	20	8	16
Analgesic	18	11	12	10
Respiratory	10	7	8	5
Alimentary	7	5	6	5
Anti-microbial	2	2	2	2
Dermatological	1	1	0.7	1
Genito-urinary	1	1	0.7	1
All others	15	17	10	11

SOCIAL ASPECTS OF SENILE DEMENTIA

Mary Gilhooly

The main objective of this preliminary study is to investigate the needs and problems of those caring for confused elderly persons in the community. This is an important area for investigation as the burden of care for the mentally impaired elderly still falls primarily on relatives. In 1964 it was found that less than 20 per cent of those with severe senile dementia are being cared for in a hospital or institution, (Kay, Beamish and Roth) and there is not much reason to expect that things will be any different in the 1980s.

Study Population and Method

The sample for this study was drawn from two Aberdeenshire day hospitals. All the patients selected for study were diagnosed as suffering from senile dementia. The patients' main care agents, or supporters are, however, the focus of the study.

It was noted that there were two main groups of supporters. Group I supporters lived in the same household as the dementing elderly person; Group II supporters did not live in the same home. Group I is a larger group than Group II. To date 25 supporters in Group I have been contacted although five of these interviews are incomplete. Ten supporters have been contacted in Group II, and one of these interviews is incomplete.

In Group I, 12 supporters were spouses, 7 were daughters, one a son, there were two daughter-in-laws, and three sisters. Including the incomplete interviews, there were five daughters, two sons, two daughter-in-laws and one sister in Group II. Thus, excluding 'spouses', the burden of care in these groups falls primarily on females, mostly daughters. It is important to note that where a son was interviewed as the main care agent, the son's wife was found to be contributing heavily to care.

The study involved intensive interviews with supporters, plus assessments of the day hospital patients. The interviews with supporters took from 3 to 12 hours. In most cases the schedule was completed in three sessions of about two hours each. Although most of the data for the study was gathered through open-ended or structured questions, several standardised measures were incorporated, at least in a modified form. The following are the measures used:

The Elderly Mentally Infirm Subject/Patient

(a)   Instrumental Activities of Daily Living Scale (IADL) (Lawton and Brody, from Lawton, 1971)

(b)   Physical Self-Maintenance Scales (PSMS) (Lawton and Brody, from Lawton, 1971)

(c)   Modified Crichton Royal Behavioural Rating Scale (D. Wilkin, personal communication)

(d)   Performance Test of Activities of Daily Living (PADL)(Kuriansky et.al., 1976)

The Supporter

(a)   Questions on physical health from the General Household Survey, 1979.

(b)   Present State Examination Schedule (PSE) (Wing et. al., 1974)

(c)   Kutner Morale Scale (Kutner et. al., 1956)

Only results from the use of the Physical Self-Maintenance Scales, a measure of impairment in the patient, and Kutner Morale Scale, a measure of the supporter's well-being are reported here.

Areas covered in the interview schedule included the patient's mental state and behaviour patterns, the supporter's physical and psychological limitations and resources, and environmental and social conditions. Time was also spent examining the history or care and the supporter's perceptions of the dementing illness, as well as help from the statutory services.

Perceptions and Knowledge of Senile Dementia

One of the things which came out very clearly at the start of the study was how uninformed supporters were about senile dementia. Only three out of 34 supporters contacted produced the response 'senile dementia' when asked 'what is wrong?' With reference to Table 1 six supporters said their relative was 'going senile', although this was rarely the first response to the question. The figures in Table 1, which show the 'causes' of the disorder as given by the supporters, represent multiple codings. 'Old age' was most frequently given as causal, followed by 'hardening of the arteries'. The response 'I don't know' was also given by eight supporters, i.e. a quarter of the sample.

Although most of the supporters gave more than one cause, what these figures do not reveal is the quite considerable confusion that supporters exhibited over causation. For example, several of

the supporters talked about the disorder in terms of 'morality'.
In other words, they could not understand how or why this had
happened as the patient had always been a 'good' person.

TABLE 1

Frequency of 'causes' given by supporters for the
dementing disorder. The codings represent answers
to a general question 'what is wrong?' and represent
multiple codings.

F	'Cause'	(N = 34)
3	Senile or Arteriosclerotic Dementia	
6	'Going Senile'	
8	Hardening of the Arteries	
3	Brain has gone/Brain deterioration	
5	'Shock', Stroke, C.V.A.	
6	Physical Illness	
1	An Operation	
9	Old Age	
6	An emotional Event	
2	A hard life	
2	Personality of dependant	
2	Loneliness/Neglect by relatives or friends	
7	OTHER	
8	Do not Know (response of respondent)	

One supporter considered that everything started when her
mother fell and broke her hip and had to go to hospital for an
operation. However, later questions on memory and orientation
revealed that her mother had been extremely forgetful and disoriented for 6 years prior to the hip operation. Two supporters implica-
ted the start of the disorder to a housebreaking incident which was
thought to be particularly upsetting for the patient. In these
cases the housebreaking, or emotional event, occurred several years
before there were signs of loss of memory or disorientation. In
one case I was told that the illness was related to an event which
took place about 20 years prior to signs of impairment for example
that the disorder was the result of a head injury in which someone
had thrown a brush out of a tenement window, hitting the patient
on the head.

There are two possible explanations for such accounts. (1) The supporter is describing what has been called the 'threshold effect' by psychogeriatricians, and/or (2) the accounts are a 'search after meaning' on the part of the supporter. A 'threshold effect' refers to a process in which up to a certain limit the destruction wrought by degenerative brain changes can be accommodated within the reserve capacity of the brain. Thus, the illness or event described by the supporter could, in fact, have caused just enough damage to push the elderly subject beyond the threshold. Of course, this does not explain accounts in which the causal event some time prior to the development of dementia. Such accounts can really only be explained as a 'search after meaning'.

Retrospective Attitudes to Clinical Management

Why do the supporters have to 'search after meaning'? Surely the nature of the disorder has been explained to the relatives by their family's medical practitioner.

Table 2 gives the frequencies of 'No', 'Yes' and 'Unsure' responses by supporters, plus responses that were not codable and where the question was not asked. The questions were (1) Do you feel you have been given enough information about ( )'s problems? (2) Has a doctor discussed the problem with you? and (3) Were you given enough information on how to manage the problem? Only 5 out of 28 supporters said that they were given enough information about the problem, only 8 said that a doctor had discussed the problem with them, and none of the supporters said they had been given enough information on how to manage the problem.

Some of the conversations that went with responses to these questions were most revealing. For example, one of the female respondents said, when asked if she had been given enough information about her husband's problem, 'Well..eh...yes. They'd given me as much information as to say that there's nae betterness. They've given me that information'. Quite a few of the supporters who said that they had talked to a doctor about the disorder said that they didn't really regard the talk as a proper 'discussion'. I was also frequently told that the GP was not 'interested', and a great deal of resentment was expressed by many of the supporters about the lack of concern and visits from the old person's doctor.

In interpretation of these findings it may be that general practitioners may not consider it to be their role to counsel the supporters of the mentally infirm elderly, or they make take the view that if supporters want to know they will ask about the disorder. However, most of the supporters in this sample did not, and would not, ask, but did expect the GP to volunteer information.

As the majority of the supporters in the sample were working class, this data is supportive of numerous studies showing that doctors experience more difficulties in communicating with lower

class patients, and give significantly fewer voluntary explanations
to lower class patients (Pendleton and Tate, 1980). These are,
unfortunately. the people most often in need of such information.

TABLE 2

Frequencies of responses to three questions about
information given to supporters by doctors. (N = 28)

QUESTION	No	Yes	Unsure	Unsure of Response	Not asked
Do you feel you have been given enough information about ( )'s problems?	13	5	2	8	0
Has a doctor discussed the problem with you?	14	8	0	5	1
Were you given enough information on how to 'manage' the problem?	19	0	0	4	5

However, it must be remembered that the GP is the person
through whom the dementing elderly pass in their progression through
the services and that the role of communicator of information should
not be neglected.

Burden and Psychological Well Being

It was assumed, when this study was started, that the greater
the burden or dependency of the patient on the supporter, the
greater would be the adverse effects on the supporter's psychological well-being. Thus, it was predicted that Group II supporters,
those not living with the dementing old person would have higher
morale than Group I supporters. Furthermore, the greater the level
of impairment in the patient, the lower the morale of the supporter.

Interestingly, comparing Group I and Group II for averaged
morale and averaged disability scores gives some support for these
predictions. As can be seen in Table 3 Group II patients are less
disabled than Group I patients, and Group II supporters have higher
morale scores. However, level of impairment and dependency taken
as cohabitation are confounded variables.

65

TABLE 3

Averaged impairment ratings on the Physical Self
Maintenance scales by day hospital staff for Group I
and Group II patients, and mean scores on the Kutner
Morale Scale for supporters. The higher the impairment score, the greater the impairment; scaled 0-3.
The higher the morale score, the higher the group's
morale; scaled 1-7.

	Impairment	Morale
Group I	1.37	2.53
Group II	0.98	3.16

If impairment as rated by day hospital staff on the Physical
Self-Maintenance Scales is plotted against supporter's morale, the
expected negative association of impairment and morale is not
found.

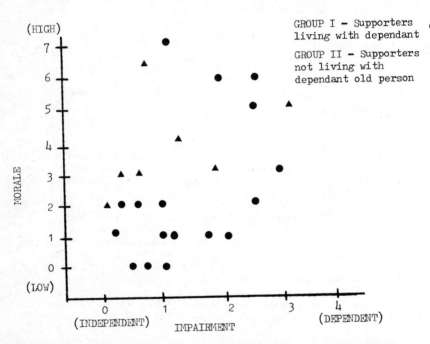

Figure 1 - Mean ratings by day hospital staff on the Physical Self-
Maintenance Scales (PSMS) and supporters' morale score. N = 26,
p = .392, p < .10 (Note - Group I, p = .546, p < .10; Group II, p = .463,
NS)

Instead, and as can be seen on Figure 1, the greater the impairment, the higher the supporter's morale. Although not highly significant, a rank-difference correlation of .392 between impairment and morale could not have occurred entirely by chance (p. .10). Furthermore, removing the Group II supporters, that is, those not living with their dependent relative, increases the correlation to .546 (p .10). The rank-difference correlation between impairment and morale for Group II supporters is .463, which is not significant.

How does one explain a positive association between impairment and morale? It may be that when dementia is newly started, that is, when the impairment is less, the supporters are unsure as to whether or not certain behaviour, especially behaviour like verbal abuse, garrulousness, or some of the more deviant behaviours, are self-motivated. Furthermore, when the patient still has considerable contact with reality it is harder for the supporter to ignore the patient. Further, when the disorder is newly started the supporters have had less time to adjust to the constraints on their time and freedom. However, plotting how long the supporter has had to cope with the burden against the supporters' morale does not indicate that the time factor is significantly correlated with

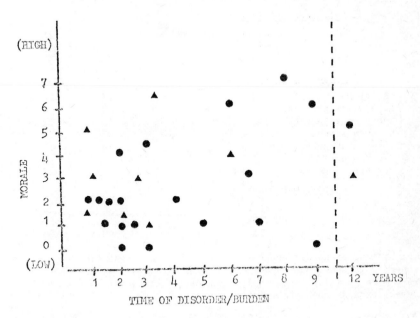

Figure 2. Reported length of disorder or burden to supporter and supporter's morale (p = .260, NS)

67

morale (p = .260), although the correlation is positive. (See Figure 2).

Social Contacts, Help from Relatives and Friends, Loneliness

A fairly large proportion of interview time was spent examining the kinship and friendship networks of supporters, as well as the feelings of social isolation, frustration and loneliness. Table 4 shows the amount of contact with relatives and friends and the help given, for Groups I and II. There are no major differences between the two groups.

TABLE 4

Contact and help from relatives and friends for Group I (supporters living with dependant) and Group II (supporters not living with dependant). The figures represent percentages.

	Group I	Group II
Contact with Relatives		
Every Day	15	33
2-3 times per week	45	11
About once a week	30	11
once a week, once a month	10	0
Less than once a month	5	22
No contact	0	0
Unsure of Respondent's response	0	11
Help from Relatives		
A Lot	20	11
Some	30	55
None	50	33
Contact with Friends		
Every Day	10	22
2-3 times per week	20	0
About once a week	15	22
once a week, once a month	25	22
Less than once a month	15	11
No contact	10	0
Unsure of Respondent's response	5	22
Help from Friends		
A Lot	0	0
Some	10	22
None	90	88

The lack of group differences is surprising as these tables were expected to show that supporters living with a dementing relative were more socially isolated than those not living with their dementing and dependent relative.

The results also indicated that supporters living with a

dependent relative do not report feeling more forgotten, lonely, etc. than those not living in the same home. However, questions concerned with social isolation - e.g., Have you had to stop visiting friends? Have you had to give up social gatherings? Did you used to go out more often? - did reveal group differences. As can be seen in Table 5, supporters in Group I more often reported giving up social gatherings, having gone our more often before care began, and no longer visiting friends.

TABLE 5

Percentage response rates on three questions concerned with social isolation. Group I (n = 20) supporters are living with the dependant. Group II (n = 9) supporters did not live in the same home as the dependant.

Question	GROUP	No	Yes	Unsure of Response	Not Asked
Have you had to give up club meetings or social gatherings because of caring for ( )?	I	35	50	10	5
	II	67	11	22	0
Did you used to go out more often?	I	5	60	10	25
	II	22	44	22	11
Have you had to stop visiting friends or going out because of caring for ( )?	I	15	50	15	10
	II	78	0	11	11

It was certainly the case that those living with a confused elderly person more often spoke, spontaneously, about feelings of social isolation. The problem, of course, with tables like this is that contact with relatives and friends may be relatively high, but the quality of contact may not be what the supporter wants or expects. For instance, one could feel quite differently about being able to go out of the home to see a relative or friend - something which many of the supporters in Group I said they could not do - as opposed to having friends or relatives come to one's own home. Also, having friends or relatives visit often provoked a great deal of anxiety in the supporters in Group I. Some of the supporters were so embarrassed about the patients, and worried so

69

much about the unpredictability of deviant behaviours that they had
ceased to invite friends and relatives to the home.

The questions about contact with relatives provided interesting
information on family conflict. There were supporters who said they
got very little help from relatives, or rarely saw a relative, but
it transpired that a daughter, son, or sibling visited nearly every
day. In a couple of cases it was said that relatives helped a lot,
but indeed it was found that the relatives visited only. In certain
cases little help was received by the supporters even though the
kin network was large. It seemed that once one person had formally
taken on the responsibility of care, the rest stopped helping at
all. Sometimes the supporter felt considerable resentment about
the lack of help, and in other cases the supporter felt that there
were quite genuine reasons for the lack of help. As might almost
be expected, when there were both sons and daughters who could
potentially give assistance, sons were rarely expected to give as
much help as daughters.

It was anticipated that the more contact supporters had with
relatives, and the more help given by relatives, the higher would
be the supporter's morale. However, as can be seen in Figures 3
and 4, frequency of contact was not positively associated with
morale, nor was the amount of help given.

Again, frequency of contact may not be as important to the
supporter's morale as the quality of contact. One of the supporters, for example, saw his children quite often, but family arguments seemed to always develop during visits about how often the
children ought to visit and how much help they ought to be giving.
This man had not spoken to one of his daughters for two years
because of a disagreement about the frequency of her visits.
Another supporter had fallen out with all but two of her six siblings over the care of their father. The most interesting case,
however, was a family which had arranged to pay a daughter-in-law
to do the 'nursing'. None of the other members of the family
helped in any way and she, of course, felt she could not ask for
help. There was even conflict in families where relatives gave a
lot of practical help. Few relatives seemed to be willing helpers
and supporters described methods which might be termed 'emotional
blackmail' to get relatives to help.

Why Supporters Continue with Care

Why are some people willing to take an old and confused
relative into their home? Why do some people resist institution-
alisation for their elderly relative? Or, for that matter, how
many of these supporters want to continue with home or community
care? Several investigators (Isaacs, 1971; Townsend and Wedderburn, 1965) have suggested that willingness to care is the result
of a good relationship prior to the development of dependency.
One might, therefore, expect that supporters in Group II

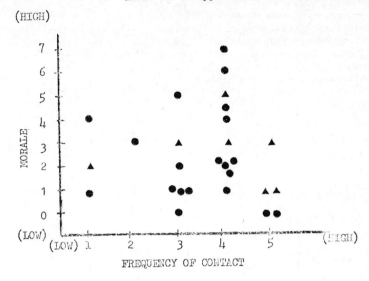

Figure 3.   Frequency of contact with relatives not living
in the same household and the supporter's morale.

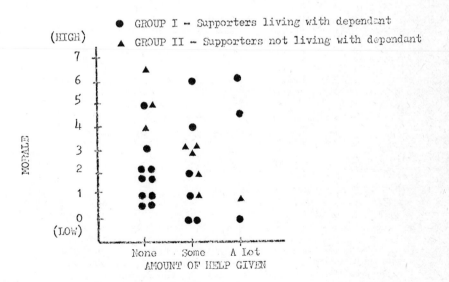

Figure 4.   Amount of help from relatives not living in the
same household and supporter's morale.

71

(supporters not living in the same household) were more likely to
have had a poor relationship with their dependent relative before
the development of senile dementia.

Plotting ratings (Figure 5) of the quality of the past relationships and the respondent's desire to have or keep the old person at home gives only marginal support for the hypothesis that
willingness to care is associated with a good past relationship
between dependant and care giver.

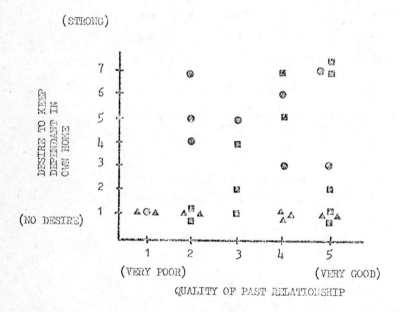

⊙   GROUP I - Spouses

⊡   GROUP I - Daughters, siblings, etc.

▲   GROUP II - Daughters, siblings, etc.

Figure 5. Quality of past prior relationship between supporter
and dependant and supporter's desire to keep the dependant in
his or her own home.

Although the points in Figure 5 appear to be distributed
somewhat randomly, the reader will note that most are below the
diagonal. This is especially true if the 'spouses' of Group I
are excluded from consideration. Thus, if the relationship was

72

very bad prior to the development of dependency, the daughter, sibling, etc., is unlikely to want to have the dementing relative in his or her own home. However, the past prior relationship may have been very good, and the supporting relative still have no desire to keep the dementing relative at home.

I have not yet looked very closely at the data to be able to say how is it that the daughters, sons, etc., come to take in a confused relative? In most cases the supporter and patient were living together before the development of dementia. In only 3 out of 13 cases in Group I was an arrangement or change made in which the dementing old person was moved into the supporter's home. One respondent said that she and her husband married so that the mother-in-law would have care. In another case two sisters set up house together to provide care for a dementing sister.

Thus, it appears to be rare for supporters to take confused relatives into their own homes, and even when they did it was often somewhat unwillingly, or because they thought it would only be for a short time. One lady, for example, told me that she thought her mother would die fairly soon after the development of the disorder and would never have taken her mother into her home had she known in advance that she would have to be a full-time psychogeriatric nurse for so long - <u>only</u> one year at the time of the interview.

How Supporters Cope with Care

Most of the spouses, and many of the daughters in Group I said it was their duty to care for their confused relative. There are, of course, numerous reasons for why people take on the role of care giver, not least of which is the desire to avoid the stigma attached to having a spouse or parent in a mental hospital, or 'asylum', a term used by many of the supporters in this study to refer to the hospital most likely to take these patients in the near future. But, no matter <u>why</u> these people take on care, they still have to make quite considerable personal sacrifice (although few said so), and have to find some way of coping with a situation which many of us would find intolerable.

Coping responses can be divided into two types, (behavioural, and (2) psychological. Behavioural coping responses include finding out about and making use of health and welfare services, plus actively organising help from friends and relatives. Psychological coping refers to attempts to modify or control the meaning of the stressful experience. There are, of course, numerous ways in which an individual can alter the meaning of a stressful experience.

Pearlin and Schooler (1978) describe the following psychological strategies which are used to cognitively neutralise threats

(1) <u>Making positive comparisons</u> - The hardship is evaluated as being an improvement over the past or as the forerunner of an easier future.

73

(2) <u>Selective ignoring</u> – Casting about for some positive attribute or circumstance within the stressful experience. When a positive attribute is located, the unpleasant aspects of the experience are ignored.

(3) <u>Re-ordering of life priorities</u> – Moving or keeping stressful experiences in the least valued areas of life. The aim is to shrink the significance of the problem.

(4) <u>Converting hardship into a moral virtue</u> – This method of coping is expressed in sentiments such as 'take the bad with the good' and 'try not to worry because time itself solves problems'.

Table 6 below indicates those supporters who used behavioural coping responses, supporters using the four methods of cognitively neutralising threats discussed by Pearlin and Schooler and those who could not be classified with this system. The supporter's morale score is also shown in Table 6.

The most obvious finding is that those utilising behavioural responses, that is, making use of services, getting relatives to help, etc., have relatively high morale and are male. Those who could not be said to be using either behavioural responses, or the four methods of psychological coping, have very low morale and are female.

Although most supporters could be placed into each of the four categories of psychological coping on the basis of the definition for the response there was a need for an additional and different category. For example, the case of R13 might have been more correctly described as using 'denial' as a coping strategy. This woman thought the future would get better (a positive comparison) because she believed that her husband would improve in the summer when it was warmer.

Had I developed by own categories of coping after the data had been collated an additional category might have been 'Ignoring the Dementing Relative'. Several of the supporters spoke of leaving the room when, for example, the strain of hearing the patient repeat something for the tenth time got to be too much. One lady said that she just put on her coat and went for a walk when the frustration of having her husband follow her from room to room got to be too much. Many supporters coped by ignoring their dementing relative.

<u>Conclusions</u>

Although still at an early stage of the project, the results of this study seem to have implications for service provision and therapy. First of all, the data suggests that a better understanding of senile dementia would relieve some of the distress

experienced by supporters. It seems unlikely that GPs will ever
have the time to thoroughly discuss the problem with the supporter,
nor would many GPs consider it to be their role. Counselling the
supporters of the dementing elderly could perhaps be a role for
psychologists.

TABLE 6

Supporters (by number) making use of behavioural
coping responses and the four methods of cognitively
neutralising threats described by Pearlin and Schooler
(1978). The supporter's morale score on the Kutner
Morale Scale is also shown.

	Morale Score
Behavioural Coping Responses	
R2 – male	6
R3 – female	6
R6 – male	7
R8 – male	3
R16 – male	4.5
Psychological Coping Responses	
1. Making positive comparisons	
R1 – female	2
R13 – female	2
2. Selective ignoring	
R16 – male	4.5
3. Re-ordering of life priorities	
R3 – female	6
R4 – female	5
R6 – male	7
4. Converting hardship into a morale virtue	
R8 – male	3
R7 – female	0
R9 – female	2
Unclassified	
R5 – female	1
R10 – female	1
R14 – female	0
R12 – female	1
R11 – female	0

The second conclusion which might be offered is related to therapy with the dementing elderly, in particular Reality Orientation and its extension to the home environment. The fact that so many of the supporters interviewed appeared to cope by ignoring their dementing relative indicates, to me anyway, that attempting to teach supporters to use Reality Orientation is doomed to failure from the outset. A technique which would require supporters to constantly focus on behaviours which they can only cope with by ignoring is unlikely to succeed, and could cause supporters considerable distress.

REFERENCES

Isaacs, B. Geriatric patients: Do their families care? British Medical Journal, 1971, 4, pp.282-286.

Kay, D.W.K., Beamish, P., and Roth, M. Old age mental disorders in Newcastle upon Tyne. British Journal of Psychiatry, 1964, 110, pp.146-158.

Kuriansky, J., Gurland, B., Fleiss, J., and Cowan, D. The assessment of self-care capacity in geriatric psychiatric patients by objective and subjective methods. Journal of Clinical Psychology, 1976, 32, pp.95-102.

Kutner, B., Fanshel, D., Togo, A.M., and Langer, T.S. Five Hundred Over Sixty, New York: Russell Sage Foundation, 1956.

Lawton, M.P. The functional assessment of elderly people. Journal of the American Geriatric Society, 1971, XIX, pp.465-481.

Pearlin, L.I. and Schooler, C. The structure of coping. Journal of Health and Social Behaviour, 1978, 19, pp.2-21.

Pendleton, D. and Tate, P. Research and training in the skills of communication between general practitioner and patient. Paper presented at the annual conference of the British Psychological Society, Aberdeen, 1980.

Townsend, P. and Wedderburn, D. The Aged in the Welfare State. London: G. Bell & Sons Ltd., 1965.

Wing, J.K., Cooper, J.E., and Sartorius, N. The Measurement and Classification of Psychiatric Symptoms. Cambridge University Press, 1974.

MORTALITY AMONG THE ELDERLY: EXAMINATION
OF THE O.P.C.S. LONGITUDINAL STUDY

Christina Victor

INTRODUCTION

Ecological community studies have consistently identified marked
variations in mortality between socially defined groups. Of the
criteria investigated, socio-economic status has emerged as the
parameter most consistently linked with differential mortality,
(Office of Populations, Censuses and Surveys, 1978). Geographical
studies have indicated that mortality differentials possess a clear
spatial component (Pyle, 1971). Such studies have, however, tended
to emphasise the socially based mortality differentials of the younger members of the community. Little specific attention has been
given to the mortality experience of the elderly.

Employing data derived from the OPCS Longitudinal Study, this
paper describes the mortality of a 1 per cent sample of the elderly
(i.e. those aged 65+ years) population of England and Wales both in
terms of a variety of social parameters defined by the 1971 census
and spatially. In particular, two inter-related questions pertaining
to mortality amongst the elderly are discussed. Firstly the existence of socially based mortality differentials amongst the elderly
is investigated. Secondly, mortality variations, where identified,
are compared with those illustrated by the younger members of the
L.S. sample. When comparing these two groups it was hypothesised
that the mortality differentials could display one of three alternative trends. Firstly as the population ages the differences between
social groups could decrease (i.e. illustrate a convergent trend).
Alternatively, the ageing process could exacerbate existing variations
(i.e. demonstrate a divergent trend). The final option is for the
variations not to alter as the population ages.

The mortality information described in the text relates to the
period 1971-1975 and deaths from all causes. No cause specific
information is presented. An indirect mode of standardisation is
employed to compare thepopulation sub-groups. Standardised mortality
ratios (S.M.Rs) were calculated for 10 year age bands with males and
females described separately.

The L.S. consists of a 1 per cent sample of the population of
England and Wales initially selected from completed census schedules.
Some longitudinal studies such as those based upon birth cohorts
follow a single sample over time (Douglas, 1964). However, the OPCS
study provides a dynamic population by continually updating the
sample using information routinely gathered by the Office. Therefore
as individuals leave the study through death or emigration they are

replaced. At any one point in time, therefore, approximately half a
million individuals are included within the sample.

Population estimates for 1977 suggested that 11.6 per cent of
males and 17.2 per cent of females were aged over 65 years. The
proportions derived from the L.S. were 11.1 per cent and 16.8 per
cent respectively. This close correspondence between the two data
sources is encouraging as each employs a unique population denominator. The population estimates are based upon an up-dating of information derived from the decennial census and so relate to total persons enumerated. In the L.S., however, each individual 'ages' with
the study and his/her exact contribution to each five year age group
for each year of the study is calculated. Obviously each person's
contribution ceases when they leave the study. Thus it is the
number of person years at risk, rather than individuals, which
constitutes the population demoninator for the L.S.

Death rates for the L.S. sample, based upon the above popula -
tion denominator, compare favourably with those derived from the
more traditional data source. Only in the younger age groups do
there appear to be any marked variations in death rates between
data sources. It is also clear that, for the elderly in particular,
death rates derived from traditional mortality statistics and the
L.S. are comparable. As would be expected, death rates increase
with age. However, females in all age groups record consistently
lower death rates when compared with males.

1) Household Status

At the 1971 enumeration, a distinction was drawn between
persons living in the community (i.e. in private households) and
those living in institutions (i.e. in non-private households). For
all ages, irrespective of sex, mortality rates are consistently
higher for persons enumerated in institutions (Figure 1). With
increasing age, mortality rates in both household status categories
decrease. Explanation for this apparent contradiction of S.M.Rs
reducing for both groups with age (whilst remaining constant for
the two combined) is to be found in the fact that the proportion
of individuals enumerated in institutions increases with age.
Approximately 4.3 per cent of the population aged 65-74 years was
enumerated in institutions - for the 85+ group the proportion had
risen to 20 per cent.

In addition, the distribution of persons between the various
types of non-private household changes. Below the age of 65 the
number of individuals enumerated in institutions such as prisons,
hotels and educational establishments matches the number in homes
and hospitals. For those aged 65-84, irrespective of sex, the
majority of persons were in either homes or hospitals, whilst the
majority of the very elderly (i.e. those aged 85+) were in residential homes (Table 1).

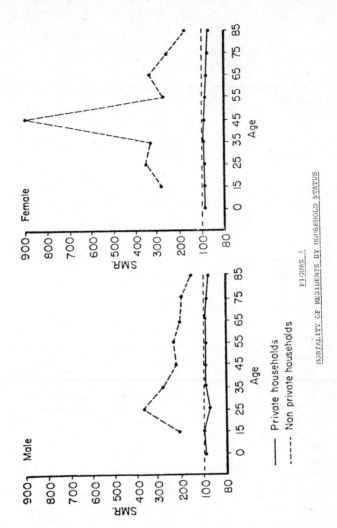

FIGURE 1

MORTALITY OF RESIDENTS BY HOUSEHOLD STATUS

79

TABLE 1

ELDERLY PERSONS ENUMERATED IN INSTITUTIONS
(L.S. 1971-1975)

1) Elderly persons enumerated in institutions(%)

AGE	65-69	70-74	75-79	80-84	85+
Male	2.10	2.39	3.14	5.13	8.62
Female	1.96	2.37	3.42	6.38	12.79

2) Elderly persons enumerated in residential homes (%)

AGE	65-69	70-74	75-79	80-84	85+
Male	0.25	0.54	1.09	2.50	5.06
Female	0.30	0.61	1.31	3.42	7.41

In both absolute and proportional terms, the institutionalised sector represents only a small proportion of the population. Data from the L.S. indicates that 2.0 per cent of elderly males and 3.78 per cent of elderly females were classified as either resident or visitors to institutions. However, mortality was generally high in this group. Approximately 10 per cent of total deaths were recorded in non-private households. (Table 2).

TABLE 2

DEATHS BY AGE IN INSTITUTIONS
(L.S. 1971-1975)

	0-64	65-74	75-84	85+	All 65+	All Ages
MALE Deaths	700	304	206	117	627	1327
% Total	17.3	6.6	5.6	8.0	6.5	9.7
FEMALE Deaths	683	536	228	140	904	1587
% Total	26.6	16.9	4.9	4.4	8.3	11.8

For elderly males and females the proportions of deaths recorded in institutions were 6.5 per cent and 8.3 per cent respectively. The dichotomy between the proportion of persons in institutions and deaths is less marked for the elderly than for the younger population. This suggests that with increasing age the type of person admitted to an institution changes. Younger people are more likely to be sick, whilst the elderly are more likely to be disabled, frail and no longer able to care for themselves in the community, than seriously ill.

2) Marital Status

In addition to providing information about the mortality of the elderly, the L.S. provides a useful insight into the social characteristics of the elderly population of England and Wales. Few elderly included in the sample were divorced/separated. This proportion varied little with age. With increased age the proportion of married individuals decreases – this is matched by a rapid increase in the number categorised as widowed. Although general to both sexes, it is a trend exemplified by females. The proportion of single males shows little variation with age in contrast with the considerable increase of single women with age. (Table 3).

TABLE 3

MARITAL STATUS OF THE ELDERLY
(L.S. 1971-1975)

	MARITAL STATUS (%)			
	Single	Married	Widowed	Divorced
65-69				
Male	7.7	83.9	7.4	0.8
Female	12.3	58.9	27.3	1.3
70-74				
Male	7.1	79.5	12.7	0.6
Female	13.3	46.1	39.5	0.9
75-79				
Male	6.4	71.9	21.3	0.3
Female	14.3	32.8	52.0	0.7
80-84				
Male	6.0	61.3	32.2	0.3
Female	15.2	20.1	64.1	0.3
85+				
Male	7.0	43.6	45.9	0.1
Female	15.4	10.3	73.9	0.3

Within each particular type of household group distinct variations in mortality by marital status are observable. In non-private
households the relative mortality for each marital status category
decreases with age (Figure 2). This trend, which is common to both
sexes, is most evident for the single, suggesting that those without
a spouse or offspring are more readily admitted to an institution.

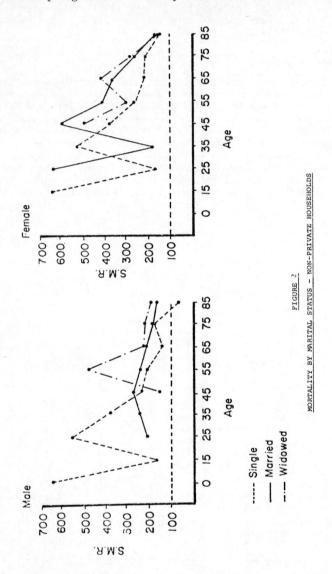

FIGURE 2

MORTALITY BY MARITAL STATUS — NON-PRIVATE HOUSEHOLDS

82

Whilst the males continue to manifest a difference in relative
mortality between marital status categories in old age, very
elderly females illustrate a total eradication of relative mortality
differences.

In private households married males exhibit a consistently lower
relative mortality than either the single or widowed (Figure 3).
This difference is most extreme before the age of 55. With ageing
these extreme mortality differentials are eroded. The situation
for females varies slightly from this pattern, with the convergence
of mortality differentials being more marked in the elderly age
groups.

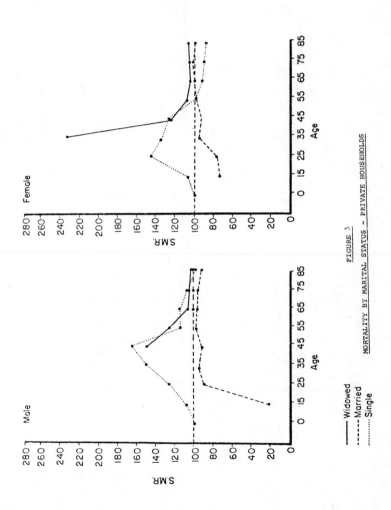

FIGURE 3

MORTALITY BY MARITAL STATUS - PRIVATE HOUSEHOLDS

3) Housing Status

Two aspects of the housing status of persons enumerated in private households are measured by the deccenial census – namely tenure and housing quality. The relationship between mortality and both these aspects of housing status is discussed.

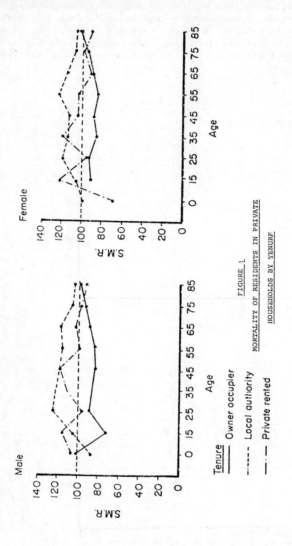

FIGURE 1

MORTALITY OF RESIDENTS IN PRIVATE

HOUSEHOLDS BY TENURE

84

a) Tenure

Three basic types of housing tenure are discernible from the census
schedule. These are home ownership, Local Authority rented accommodation and private rented property. Included within this latter
category are individuals renting furnished and unfurnished accommodation and those whose tenure was unstated on the census return.
Compared with the younger age groups a higher proportion of elderly
persons were enumerated in the private rented sector of the housing
market, whilst fewer were enumerated in the public sector. The
proportion of elderly persons resident in owner occupied dwellings
matches that recorded for the younger age groups. Figure 4
illustrates that of the three tenure categories the home owners
have the lowest relative S.M.R. and the Local Authority tenants the
highest. This generalisation applies equally to both males and
females. However, with age some convergence in mortality differentials is apparent. For both sexes, relative mortality rates for
home owners increase for the 65+ age group. In contrast those
recorded for the two forms of rented housing decrease.

b) Housing Quality

Dwelling standards, as defined by the 1971 census, were measured
in terms of two specific aspects - occupation densities and amenity
provision levels.

Occupation Densities . The occupation density of dwellings is, in
census terms, measured by the number of persons per room. The
standard definition of over-crowding used is 1.5 persons per room
(p.p.r) and over. Obviously this standard is based upon dwelling
rooms - kitchens and bathrooms etc. are excluded from such calcula-
tions. Table 4 illustrates the mortality experience of males
included in the L.S. categorised by dwelling density. There is an
obvious trend for relative mortality, at all ages, to increase with
dwelling density. However, within each density classification,
relative mortality decreases with age. Hence a convergent trend
is evident with ageing. A similar trend is characteristic of the
female L.S. population.

Amenity Provision. In terms of amenity provision the census
schedule recorded whether a household had sole (i.e. exclusive)
use, shared use or no use of a variety of facilities. Compared
with those aged under 65, the elderly were equally well provided
with such basic amenities as a sink, a cooker and hot water. Few
elderly persons had non-exclusive use (i.e. no or shared used) of
these amenities. However, the elderly were less well provided
with a bath, fewer had an inside W.C. and a greater proportion had
use of an outside W.C. Defined in these terms, the elderly were
less well housed than the rest of the community. A marked decrease
in housing standards with increasing age is evident. Largely this
reflects the older age of the property inhabited by elderly persons
and hence its lower level of facility provision.

TABLE 1

OCCUPATION DENSITY IN PRIVATE HOUSEHOLDS - MALES (L.S. 1971-1975)

		AGE								
		0-14	15-24	25-34	35-44	45-54	55-64	65-74	75-84	85+
PERSONS PER ROOM										
0.5										
	Deaths	2	4	24	44	184	759	1852	1601	638
	S.M.R.	95	59	129	293	113	91	93	97	99
0.5 - 0.75										
	Deaths	34	47	38	92	401	1139	1965	1362	462
	S.M.R.	101	115	76	100	94	100	237	102	104
0.75 - 1										
	Deaths	19	26	18	35	102	154	156	84	45
	S.M.R.	79	122	105	72	78	105	129	100	83
1 - 1.25										
	Deaths	34	25	25	39	173	245	334	241	81
	S.M.R.	97	81	110	66	109	124	122	103	97
1.25 - 1.5										
	Deaths	9	6	6	10	37	28	24	10	3
	S.M.R.	120	82	171	100	143	133	151	136	48
1.5+										
	Deaths	7	4	4	12	23	16	20	14	5
	S.M.R.	114	67	142	150	133	98	116	189	80

(Brennan and Lancashire, 1976) found that non-exclusive use of a fixed bath/shower was most highly correlated with childhood mortality. For this reason, access to a fixed bath was used to analyse mortality in the elderly. Figure 5 illustrates that for males relative mortality rates are highest in the group which lacks the use of a fixed bath/shower. These differences are at their most extreme in the younger age groups. The relative mortality for those sharing a bath decreases markedly with ageing. Whilst the relative mortality for those without exclusive use of amenities also decreases with age, it remains substantially higher than the mortality of elderly people with exclusive use of this amenity. Females illustrate a similar trend for mortality to decrease in each amenity access group. Wilst there is obviously some convergence of the mortality differential with age, it is more weakly defined than in previous examples.

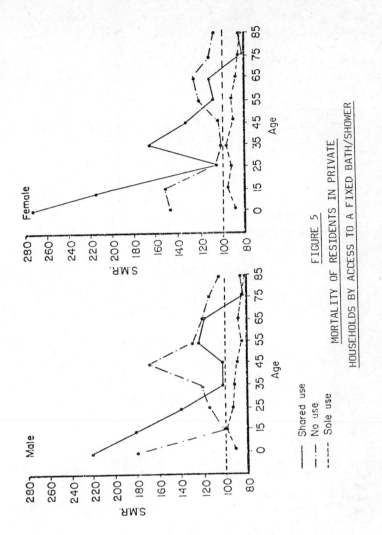

FIGURE 5

MORTALITY OF RESIDENTS IN PRIVATE
HOUSEHOLDS BY ACCESS TO A FIXED BATH/SHOWER

4) Social Class

Social class variations in mortality have been identified by
several workers and Figure 6 illustrates that for males the L.S.
confirms this general finding. Inter-class mortality differentials
are most extreme before the age of 45 years. After this age the
differential between the extremes of class hierarchy (i.e. classes
I and II and IV and V) remains constant.

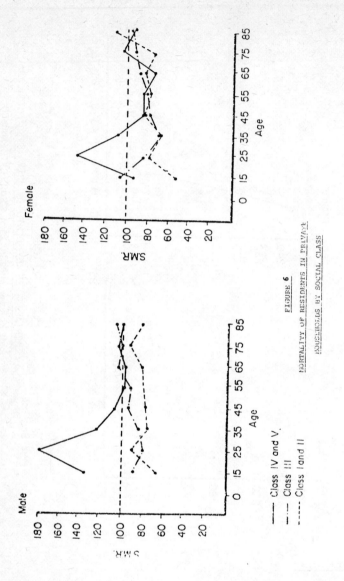

FIGURE 6

MORTALITY OF RESIDENTS IN PRIVATE
HOUSEHOLDS BY SOCIAL CLASS

The differential does not appear to converge with age. The employment based origin of the social class information means that the data is of little interpretative value for the female population.

Spatial Variations in Mortality

The previous section has indicated that amongst the elderly population of England and Wales social parameters do exert an influence upon mortality. The following section now investigates the spatial component.

Employing the nine standard regions defined for the 1971 census, Table 5 compares the standardised mortality of the young and elderly populations in the L.S. sample. For both males and females there was little variation between the two age groups. Regions with a high mortality for the 0-64 years age group maintained a high mortality for the elderly. Overall there is an obvious trend for the elderly in the north and west to experience markedly higher mortality than their southern counterparts.

TABLE 5

Standardised Mortality by Region

(L.S. 1971-1975)

REGION	Female		Male	
	0-64	65+	0-64	65+
North	104	107	107	110
Yorks. & Humberside	104	109	102	103
North West	118	107	115	113
East Midlands	106	100	113	97
West Midlands	97	104	103	104
East Anglia	70	83	96	93
South East	90	93	86	92
South West	99	95	91	93
Wales	113	112	121	112

By examining the elderly population in more detail, it is possible to identify the effect of ageing upon this general spatial distribution. Table 6 presents the mortality for each region of the elderly male population subdivided into three age groups - 65-74, 75-84 and 85+ years. The four regions of England and Wales which had initially high mortality - North, North West, West Midlands and Wales - all illustrate a decrease in mortality with age. This is accompanied by increase in mortality in the regions which initially had mortality rates below the national norm. Hence

89

with ageing, there is a decrease in the mortality differential between regions, although it is not completely eroded. A similar pattern emerges for females.

TABLE 6

S.M.R. (All Causes 1971-75)

- By Standard Region

	65-74	75-84	85+
MALES			
North	113.1	111.7	96.3
Yorks. & Humberside	98.4	108.1	107.3
North West	116.3	111.0	112.7
East Midlands	98.1	91.4	109.1
West Midlands	109.9	101.7	90.8
East Anglia	87.3	95.9	100.5
South East	90.7	93.2	96.2
South West	88.1	96.6	99.1
Wales	120.0	108.3	97.7
FEMALES			
North	111.7	111.5	95.6
Yorks. & Humberside	117.9	109.3	101.7
North West	107.1	107.4	109.1
East Midlands	93.4	100.7	106.2
West Midlands	104.2	112.6	94.0
East Anglia	84.5	82.3	83.5
South East	90.9	91.0	98.8
South West	88.9	95.2	98.6
Wales	119.8	108.9	109.4

Discussion

The above descriptions demonstrate that both social and geographical variations in mortality are observable for elderly persons. However, the intensity of the differential varies.

Visual examination of the evidence described above suggests that most of the parameters in terms of which mortality was discussed illustrated a convergent trend with ageing. An erosion of mortality differentials with ageing was characteristic of the household status, marital status, housing and regional factors. Whilst no variable seemed to increase its differentiating power with ageing, the social class measure, for males at least, illustrated a status quo situation.

This convergence in mortality differentials for the elderly may be explained by reference to two separate processes. Firstly there is the very obvious tendency for elderly people to move out of the community into institutions as their health deteriorates. In conjunction with this is the tendency for older persons, no longer able to cope for themselves, to move in with their offspring. These two 'selecting out' procedures leave a residue of fairly healthy individuals remaining in the community and hence help to dilute mortality differentials.

In conclusion this paper has described socially based variations in mortality for the elderly population of England and Wales. Whilst such differentials were discernible they appeared to be less marked than for younger people and appeared to converge with age.

REFERENCES

Brennan, M.E. and Lancashire, R. (1976) Association of childhood mortality with housing status and unemployment, Journal of Epidemiology and Community Health, 32. pp.28-33.

Douglas, J.W.B. (1964), The Home and the School, London: Macgibbon and Kee.

Office of Population, Censuses and Surveys 1978, Occupational Mortality 1970-1972, Registrar General's Deccenial Supplement, Series D.S. No.1, London: HMSO.

Pyle, G. (1971), Heart disease, cancer and stroke in Chicago, Research Monograph No.134, University of Chicago.

SOME ASPECTS OF PSYCHOTHERAPY WITH OLDER PATIENTS

Peter Hildebrand

Psychoanalytic theory has its paradoxes. Sigmund Freud said in his paper of 1905 on psychotherapy that 'near or above the fifties, the elasticity of mental processes, on which the treatment depends, is as a rule lacking - old people are no longer educable'. This is an interesting remark coming from a man aged 49, who was shortly to recast his whole metapsychology and give the world a completely new theory of mind. Freud also said in 1913 'it is a well known fact and one that has given much ground for complaint, that after women have lost their genital function their character often undergoes a peculiar alteration, they become quarrelsome, vexatious and over-bearing, petty and stingy, that is to say that they exhibit typically sadistic and anal erotic traits which they did not possess earlier during their period of womanliness. Writers of comedy and satirists have in all ages directed their invectives against the old dragon into which the charming girl, the loving wife and the tender mother have been transformed. We can see that this alteration of character corresponds to a <u>regression</u> of sexual life to the pre-genital sadis- tic and anal-erotic stage in which has been discovered the disposi- tion to obsessional neurosis. It seems then to be not only the precursor of the genital phase but often enough its successor as well, its termination after the genitals have fulfilled their function'. Sadly this citation demonstrates rather better Freud's well known male chauvinism than to his insight into the ageing process.

It is good to know that Freud's attitude was not completely shared by Karl Abraham (1948), who reported in 1919 a series of successful analyses of patients in their fifties and who made the seminal observation that 'the prognosis in cases even at an advanced age is favourable, where the neurosis has set in in its full severity only after a long period has elapsed since puberty, and if the patient has enjoyed for several years a sexual attitude approaching the normal and a period of social usefulness. The unfavourable cases are those which already have a pronounced obsessional neurosis etc. in childhood and who have never attained a state approaching the normal in the respects just mentioned. These, however, are also the kind of cases in which psychoanalytic therapy can fail even if the patient is young'. This observation of Abraham is very helpful in that he points the way towards a life-span developmental psycho- logy with as its major collorary, the existence of a phase-specific critical periods as individuals age. Psychoanalytic theorists generally have far too uncritically accepted a hypothesis of continuous psychic and psychosomatic development with a rising curve of growth from birth to adulthood, a long refractory period and then a terminal stage of psychic deficit and social withdrawal preliminary to dying and death itself.

While this may be a familiar model, it is suggested that it is an over simplified one. Kagan (1979) has recently shown that cognitive development even in infancy and childhood - including such major phenomena as object constancy - is discontinuous, while there is a new and increasing psychological literature which suggests that psychic and somatic function in the second half of life is far more complex and less regular than hitherto supposed.

If a developmental view is taken then a psychotherapeutic approach to patients in the second half of life becomes not only practicable but logical. The approach which is suggested and which is congruent with the work of David Gutmann, George Pollock and Jerome Grunes moreover differs in emphasis from that of English psychoanalysts, such as Eliot Jacques, Pearl King and Anne-Marie Sandler, who tend to be far more reductionistic in their thinking about the later periods of human development. Jacques (1965), for example, speaks of a mid-life crisis; 'The crisis is universal and there are few people in whom a decisive change cannot be seen in the quality of their work and in whose work the effects of their having gone through a mid-life crisis cannot be discerned'. This mid-life crisis is described as depressive and the consequence of defence against depressive anxiety. It is essentially a period of purgatory, of anguish and depression. Such a crisis is equated with critical phases, change points, severe and dramatic efforts so that it is difficult to know whether Jacques is describing something which is an event, a process, a period of life or a cause or an effect. Moreover it is considered that Jacques in his exposition concentrates far too exclusively on the question of creativity and ignores the many other developmental lines which are most certainly involved as Anna Freud (1966) has shown. Jacques reduces the mid-life phase to a reworking of the depressive position of the hypothetical Kleinian infant, and links this at age 37 to the acceptance by the individual of his inevitable death.

While this has been a very fruitful hypothesis in terms of directing attention to the mid period of an individual's life, emphasis has been placed less on this type of reductionistic reliance on very early infantile processes as primary explanations for later life phenomena and more on the elucidation and resolution of phase-specific problems. It is suggested by this author that there are at least five major factors which need to be met and worked through in long term psychotherapy and psychoanalysis with older patients, and that these may occur either in terms of critical periods or as long drawn transitions in the age range 45 years to 70 years (which is defined as the older adult period of life) during which in modern times people can live in good health before the beginnings of physical and psychological defect. It may well turn out that there are other factors which are equally important.

The first major factor which is often met in these patients aged 45-70 is the individual's narcissistic involvement in the identity which he or she has elaborated for themselves in the course of their adult lives. Pearl King (1974) gives a list of six areas which characterise this problem of identity. In particular feelings of futility, the lack of satisfaction in their achievements and the alienations from themselves and others are difficult for patients who suffer from narcissistic problems. King describes such people as developing a false self which has acted as an intermediary between the narcissistic requirements of the individual and the demands of external reality. Such a character organisation is threatened by possible illness or redundancy, owing to the fact that the sense of identity has become parasitical on the role at the price of appropriate ontological security. A second factor also suggested by King is that the actuality of the ageing process highlights difficulties in object relations which have been obscured by marriage and child rearing with their strict differentiation of roles and the fact that the passage through the late forties and fifties demands a re-valuation of relationships between spouses as well as between individuals and their ageing parents. A considerable change in object relations therefore becomes inevitable.

Further in the course of his cross cultural studies, David Gurmann (1977) has suggested that younger males in the age range 35 to 54 are characterised by a stance of active mastery. They are invested in production and competition, they strive to acquire control over the resources upon which their security and the security of their dependents is based. In the pursuit of these goals they rule out much of their capacity for tender feelings, for sensuality and for dependence, while giving priority to agency over community. By contrast older men in the age group 55 and over are more diffusely sensual and they can become particularly interested in not what they can produce but in that what is produced for them, good, pleasant sights and sounds and uncomplicated supportive social contacts. In effect the older men reverse the priorities of the younger males and orient themselves towards community rather than agency.

Women age psychologically in the reverse direction, even in normally patriarchal societies like the one in which we live. Women become more aggressive in later life, less affiliative and more managerial or political. One does not have to look beyond No. 10 Downing Street in our present society for an excellent example. Unlike the easy going older men, the older women become less interested in community and more turned towards agency. Thus over time and across gender lines Gutmann suggests that a massive transcultural gender shift seems to take place. During the post parental years, he says, the husband who used to support his wife both physically and emotionally now becomes more dependent on her as a kind of maternal authority. In short sex becomes something of what the other used to be.

Gutmann assumes that late onset disturbances reflect older people's inability to assimilate - that is to transform into newer executive capacities - the potentials that are released in the post parental period of the life cycle. Many men, like adolescents, are frightened by the emergence of a new feminine side to their sexual nature so that they produce severe reaction formations against

threats from an emerging feminine side of self. In the same way
many older women are profoundly troubled by the emergence of a
hitherto closeted competitive masculine and aggressive component of
the self.

Finally one must be concerned with the question of sexuality.
Stanford Finkel in Chicago has recently presented a fascinating
(but as yet unpublished) study of sexual behaviour in later life to
the Society of Life Cycle, which demonstrates that for the great
majority of the aged, sexual function continues normally until
extreme age and in some individuals can continue into the 90's.
Sexuality as one ages becomes less a matter of discharge of hormonal
tensions, and far more the expression of what Butler (1976) in a
recent book entitled 'Sex Past 60' has described as 'the opportunity
for the expression of passion, affection and loyalty; affirmation of
the value of one's body and its functions, a means of self assertion
and affirmation of life, the pleasure of being touched and caressed,
the defiance of the stereo type of ageing and a continuing search
for sensual growth and experience'. This is true for women equally
as for men and there seems to be positive evidence suggesting that
not only that women over 40 want more in the way of sexual relationships but that the relationships should not be only with their
partners or peers, but in social terms often optimally with younger
men. Moreover, masturbation in older women, which does not fall
away to the extent which it does with men, is both healthy and life
enhancing. On existing evidence there is a sexually deprived out-
group in our culture in which the divorced, separated, single and
widowed women may be found whose sexual needs and problems are now
viewed as sympathetically as those of the older man. With the rapid
change in morality it seems likely that older women, whether through
feminist groups or the Grey Panthers will assert themselves more
sexually in the near future. It is known that there are a great
many social, cultural and stereo-typic resistances to recognition
of changes in sexual behaviour amongst older people, but it is
becoming clear that there also needs to be more open recognition of
the existence of sexual needs and experience in the elderly. This
argument is directed away from the rigidly mechanistic Freudian view
tied to a mythical attitude towards hormonal secretion (Freud gave
up intercourse at 41 for good contraceptive reasons) - after all
things have changed in the last 100 years. Where there is time,
fitness and expectation, later life is a period when people can
allow themselves the pleasures of sexual and sensual exploration.
It follows that classical psychoanalysis - as Stoller has unceas-
ingly pointed out - has got it all wrong. While Balint (1957) might
say 40 years ago 'in the face of flagging genitality, infantile
sexuality resumes the importance it had in early life in the form of
renewed interest in pornography, voyeurism and exhibitionism,
masturbation, homosexuality and eroticisation of vegetative (autono-
mous) functions' and Bibring (1960) 20 years ago that 'any change in
life if readjustment fails can cause psychological distress, so that
the individual is confronted with new and specific problems in
ageing such as the end of reproductive function with its loss of
self respect, the end of professional activity for men and child

rearing for women, which brings about an aggressiveness which may direct itself towards the individual itself and cause depression. Illness, reduction in physical strength, loneliness due to the death of friends and lastly the awareness of approaching death itself may be experienced as punishment, the hostility as the actualisation of masochistic aspirations or as the reactivation of <u>castration anxiety</u>'. In today's world Balint and Bibring are overstating their case precisely because they are so infant centred in their approach to genitality and particularly the genitality of later life. Perhaps a more cogent approach is defined by George Abraham and his collea- gues (1980) when they say 'in the elderly, genitality and pre- genitality merge together to produce not an amorphous mass but rather a dialetic exchange far richer than in the young person.'

So therapeutically psycho-therapists are faced with a popula- tion who differ markedly from the young people in the first half of life on whom so much theorising is based. One may well be in disagreement with both Freud and received psychoanalytic wisdom that older people are not amenable to either analysis or analytical psy- chotherapy. Several reasons for this belief are cited together with some brief clincial examples. Keeping in mind the five previously mentioned factors i.e. narcissism, object loss, reversal of cultur- ally determined role patterns in both men and women and the change in sexual drive from the physiological to psychological outlets, ways may be formulated of helping older people which need not be governed by an unduly reductionistic and infantomorphic theoretical system.

There is first of all the question of rigidity. Freud suggests that older patients are too rigid for psychotherapy. Recent evi- dence suggests that unless irreversible brain damage has taken place, older people have learnt considerable flexibility in the use of their resources and while in some senses their defences may be more rigid, they also possess demonstrable capacity to use exper- ience, varying frames of reference in a creative and plastic way. What the links of such creativity may be to the depressive position or capacity to work through mourning in each stage of the life cycle are beyond the scope of this paper, but may possibly be worked out in the coming decades.

Together with this learned flexibility older people should be credited with greater ego strengths. After all they have been there in the way a 25 or 30 year old has not. They have been hardened and tempered by life and where their defences have not cracked they seem to have a good deal of capacity to delay gratification, allow problems to resolve and to take the long view. Moreover they often have much greater self reliance than do younger people and can be left to get on with things by themselves. Older people are capable of using briefer experience of therapy than younger people, partly because as Dr. Johnson said 'the prospects of execution concentra- tes a man's mind wonderfully.' Older patients don't have the time to hang about contemplating their navels, they want to get on with things - but different things. David Gutmann has re-analysed David

Malan's Tavistock sample of brief therapies and shown that while the
younger males in the sample were pre-occupied with oedipal themes,
the older males, with whom on the whole better results were obtained,
were involved more in questions of dependency and independence.
Younger men presented with problems of unresolved struggles with
dominant fathers, while older men had to face the problem of the
newly aggressive wife, while they were beginning to explore their
own dependent wishes. These problems of dependence of the older
male and aggression for the older female are equally immediate and
equally crucial in their resolution. Depressed older women are less
depressed about the loss of their procreative function, the empti-
ness, the husband's disinterest or the pain of widowhood; their real
losses are more apt to be internal. They are based on losses of
self esteem, provoked by developmental advances which relocate the
inner life around unacceptable needs and identifications. These
are focal internal issues which are reversible and treatable but
unfortunately as with the older male they are too easily ignored in
favour of concentration on trying to support people through the loss
of external figures, or psychological functions such as menopause.

On the question of the transferance with the older patient
there are on the whole few difficulties if one is a contemporary.
No more certainly than when a young psychotherapist works with an
attractive young patients of the opposite sex. However, the young
therapists often are somewhat hesitant about working with older
patients. In fact one often finds an inverted transference which
if understood, can be very productive. The young therapist becomes
in the transference the son or daughter of the patient and is
invested in the usual way with idealised or denigrated feelings or
attitudes by the patient. He or she is treated as the repository
of hopes and fears, shames or delights, aspirations or guilt, but
in terms not only of the past but also of the future. It is a
future, moreover, which may or may not include the older patient
for whom personal death is a far more concrete reality than for
the younger patient. The possibility of linking such attitudes to
the patient's life review are increased and as Guntrip (1975) has
shown in his most moving account of his own therapy in his 60s with
Winnicott, the patient can indeed win through to tranquility and
acceptance of their life and its burdens. The most difficult areas
for the young therapist to accept are the voyueristic elements
implicit in the work. Certainly things become rather tense when
you take a sexual history for the first time from a 69 year old lady
who tells one cheerfully of her ongoing sexual activity, perhaps
with several men, or indeed of her continued masturbation with her
masturbation fantasies. In our culture those past the conventional
age of reproduction are somehow supposed to become asexual. Our
homes for the aged separate them and treat them as if they were pre-
pubescent children, perhaps to defend the staff against confronta-
tion with the fact of their ongoing sexuality of the elders and all
that it implies. Therapists too have now to come to terms with our
built-in fantasies and cope with the facts of (later) life.

Here it may be helpful to illustrate these arguments by clinical examples. <u>Clinical Case 1</u> Mrs B was a lady aged 49 who presented for therapy complaining of depression and anxiety in social situations. Following the break up of her marriage of 24 years duration to an eminent public figure she had gone to pieces. Her life had been centred around first her father, then her husband, a classical English schizoid intellectual. A passionate woman she had acquiessed in his various perversions, including voyeurism and sparring with boxing gloves as a preliminary to sexual intercourse (perhaps a legacy of a traditional English public school), but she had eventually refused his request that they set up a menage a trois with his much younger mistress. She had great difficulty in coping with their subsequent divorce, his financial ill-treatment of her and his leaving their four adolescent children in her sole care. She had managed to find a job and maintain herself but lived celibately and was constantly threatened by doubt, fear, depression and feelings of inadequacy. She had difficulty in accepting her older children's independence, particularly their sexual independence and although they were living openly with partners at university she refused either to allow them to bring their partners home or let them share a room in her house. She could not discuss her feelings about herself at her divorce with her children and expected them to use her more as a doormat and provider of clean linen and food, rather than parent, which they naturally being invited to do so, did.

We offered Mrs B. a course of 15 sessions of brief psychotherapy. The workshop agreed that the focus of the treatment should be her unexpressed anger with men related to her father, her husband and the psychotherapist in the transference. It was a stormy and not apparently a successful period concentrated mostly on the here and now relationship, her rage over her impotence in her present position rather than on her infancy and childhood and she plainly needed to reject and destroy interpretations and their implications for her. However, nine months later at follow up it was clear that something major had happened in her life since she was now symptom free, had initiated both on a major and a minor sexual affair simultaneously and was saying that she had never experienced proper sexual and sensual satisfaction before, though she had always been orgasmic. She had changed her job to a more appropriate and rewarding one in which her social poise and background could contribute to her success. She has faced her husband down over money and obtained an appropriate settlement so that he supported the children and paid for their school fees. She had told each of her lovers about the other, which they had accepted so that she could carry on her active sexual life without undue guilt. Most importantly she had told her children, who had accepted her new sexual maturity without demur. Furthermore, she now allowed their sexual partners to stay with them in the house. Finally, she acknowledged that the therapy with its focus on her own activity and right to be aggressive towards men just might have something to do with the satisfactory state of affairs.

<u>Clinical Case 2</u> Mr. C. a police constable of 49 was referred

because of anxiety attacks and panic fears. His older son had been killed in a motor cycle accident some years before. It seemed that he needed to work through an unresolved mourning situation. It rapidly became clear that he was an extremely controlling man with enormous difficulty in relinquishing his objects. On several occasions he was nearly able to cry in the therapy with me but always stopped himself from doing so. He was and is clearly terrified of the shift from aggressive macho masculinity which was referred to earlier to a more accepting and feminine dependency in himself. He was quite unable to accept this even though he had become far more sensitive in his relationships with his many women and actually able to allow them to look after him to some extent. Unfortunately his second and surviving son had a schizophrenic breakdown during his therapy and this had made him more resistant to change in the direction of allowing himself to depend on others. He continued to work on the problem weekly but so far without marked success and he would be considered as a clinical failure. It is less the external realities which have caused this to be such a refractory problem, but rather the need to hang on to an internal psychic structure, which he finds enormous difficulty in giving up.

Clinical Case 3 Miss Y, is a 69 year old unmarried woman, suffering from anxiety symptoms, masking a quite severe depression. She was attached deeply to her father until his death when she was aged 40, whereupon she began her sexual life with simultaneous affairs with three married men, although one of them has since died. She continues to have sexual relations with the other two men with the knowledge, although the consent, of their wives, is in doubt. She feels that such relationships are of the utmost value to her as they make her feel close and valued. She is entering the eighth decade of her life terrified of being left alone and dementing as her mother did before she died. In her life review she now finds much to value and she is struggling to integrate both the disappointment of no marriage and no children and the successes as an artist and physiotherapist of her life into her view of herself as a woman on the threshold of old age. It should be underlined that she in no way sees herself as a sexual castrate and feels that the sexual aspects of her life are extremely important and productive for her at this time in helping her to try and resolve her very difficult problem of facing her last years on her own.

Clinical Case 4 Mrs P. This lady who is 70 years old exemplifies the potential of this group of patients for the psychotherapist. She presented complaining of mood swings from despair to maniac activity, of loneliness, panic attacks, vertigo, loss of energy and drinking bouts. The symptoms are acutely manifested when her relationship with one of her two adult daughters becomes troublesome. Mrs P. is divorced. She has made two unsuccessful suicidal gestures, one 10 years ago and one six years ago. When the problem was discussed it was decided to focus on Mrs P's relationship with her daughters, who said 'We both are sick and tired of the depression we have had to put up with for the last ten years. We don't think we can handle it if you came to live with us'. It should be noted that Mrs P. has an advancing arthritic condition, vertigo and 70 per cent blindness in one eye and these conditions have impinged on her life style. For her ageing is equated with senility and the physical reminders of ageing induce a panic when they flare up. She is convinced that her intellectual abilities will rapidly deteriorate as well.

Mrs. P was diagnosed as having a personality disorder with strong narcissistic features. In the past her emptional problems were dealt with through maniac activity and it is only in the last ten years that she has found it difficult to negotiate relationships, in particular those with her daughters. As a child Mrs.P was extremely restricted by her mother and educated at home until she was 8. Her mother felt that she had to be protected from either negative or destructive features of the external world in order to raise a fine young woman. Her father was reserved, the classic picture of a courteous English gentleman. Her mother died of sclerotic dementia at 48, her father died in his 50s very unexpectedly with great feelings of loss. A younger brother was homosexual and commited suicide at the age of 45. Mrs. P describes her background as typical English middleclass, which promoted an immature perfectionistic personality type. In reaction to this she adopted a manic thirst for life and became involved in many political cultura and educational activities. She married a man 11 years her senior, described as similar in character to her father and they had two daughters. After 16 years of marriage they were divorced on the grounds of her desertion, after living in another country during most of their marriage. She took her daughters back to this country with her but the husband did not follow her. After a stormy time following the divorce, Mrs P. has maintained a very active social life. Seven years ago at the age of 62 she returned to university as a mature student and gained a degree. She secured part-time employment, took up squash for the first time and became a foster grandparent. These activities were in addition to her enthusiasm for classical music concerts and theatre. When interviewed she posed many problems of vulnerability and rejection and it was decided that her very complex and difficult relationship with her own controlling mother appeared to have been the prototype with which she identified and defended against in her own adult relationships. As a result of her advancing age and its associated physical and social complications she has a very tentative notion of self at this period of her life.

The history suggests the following hypothesis - In the past, Mrs P. has employed narcissistic and manic defences to cope with life stresses. Genuine accepting relationships were not developed, in part as a result of her defensive style. She primarily related in terms of altruistic beliefs and ideologies as opposed to commitment to people. She now finds herself at a transitional juncture where her defences are inadequate. The biological and social onslaughts of ageing have diminished their value. Having not allowed herself to be involved in a healthy relationship, Mrs P feeds herself by her need for others. As her daughters grew up, they functioned more like narcissistic extension of their mother's ideals. Currently, she expects her daughters to provide the love of which they have been deprived for many years.

Mrs P's panic feelings, mood swings, alcohol consumption etc. seem to be in response to an intense need for the kind of relationships against which she has been defending. Her early relationship with mother may have satisfied her infantile dependence needs at the expense of any sense of her own ability to master conflicts. 'My problems revolve around my genuine lack of knowledge and understanding of relationships'. So much of Mrs P's energies were directed into activities of survival (immigrants, job opportunities, raising two daughters), that little time remained for what she now sees as the 'important things in life'.

If psychotherapy was to help Mrs P. there should be some evidence of resolution of least some of these problems:

1. Acceptance of the accompaniments of the ageing process; diminishing physical capabilities, restrictions on activities.

2. Within the therapeutic relationship, a shift should occur from a pre-occupation with self to an acknowledgement of others and feelings.

3. Less reliance on activities and alcohol as means of filling the void. She should utilise therapeutic actual relationships with others to satisfy dependency needs.

4. Re-investment in interests.

5. More flexibility of general attitudes towards people. Evidence of a capacity to behave with compassion and concern towards those with whom she has contact.

6. An appreciation and respect for the separate lives of others, particularly her daughters. Recognition of the fact that others co-exist in the same world.

As other issues were elucidated, then it became possible to work with mother, daughter therapist transference. The patient became much less manic, drank less and became more contemplative. Her relationshp with her daughters improved and she lived more contentedly. Ageing is no longer equated with senility and the pleasures of life can be accepted more passively. With her daughters, her demands became less overwhelming and she began to realise that she might meet some of her needs from her own internal resources. Mrs P. had some difficulty in acknowledging what she had got from the relationship, but despite that changed considerably.

The acceptance of aggressive drives in the case of Mrs B, the difficulties of giving up narcissistic investments in the case of Mr. D, the continuing importance of sexual activity with Miss Y. and the workings of the transference with a much younger therapist with Mrs P, illustrate the workings of factors previously outlined.

If one is only used to seeing states such as hysterical personality, phobic anxiety states, anorexia, in statu nascendi or follow them through their early development, as we do with younger patients, then the opportunity to look at such life long experiences retrospectively with an elderly patient is absolutely fascinating and gives an altogether different perspective on such experiences and their meaning for the patient. When Felix Deutsch (1957) anathematised Dora, he provided a misleading precedent for those who wished to understand the course of psychological illness.

Older patients show us aspects of the life cycle which are only available to novelists. When one thinks of the later Oedipus, blind Oedipus at Colonus, and his gift of good fortune to Thesus who offered him shelter, it seems not too inappropriate a task for a therapist to undertake.

BIBLIOGRAPHY

Abraham, George, Kocher, P. and Goda, G. (1980) 'Psychoanalysis and ageing', International Review Psycho-Analysis, Vol.7, pp.147-156.

Abraham, Karl. (1948) 'The applicability of psychoanalytic treatment to patients at an advanced age' in Sel. Papers on Psycho-Analysis, London, Hogarth.

Balint, M. (1957) 'The psychological problems of growing old' in Problems of Human Pleasure and Behaviour, London, Hogarth, 1957.

Bibring, G. (1966) 'Old age: its liabilities and its assets in Loewenstein et.al. 'Psychoanalysis - A General Psychology', N.Y. Int. A. Press cited in Abraham, G. above.

Butler, R.M. and Lewis, M.L. (1978) 'Sex after Sixty', N.Y. Harper and Row.

Deutsch, F. (1957), A Footnote to Freud's 'Fragments of an Analysis of a Cure of Hysteria', Psych. 26, pp.159-167.

Finkel, S. (1978) 'Late life sexuality - clinical, psychological, social and aesthetic perspections'. Paper read to Society for the Life-Cycle, Chicago, 1978.

Freud, A. (1966), 'Normality and Pathology in Childhood', London, Hogarth.

Freud, S. (1905) 'On Psychotherapy', S.E.7.

Freud, S. (1913) 'The Disposition to Obsessional Neurosis', S.E.12.

Guntrip, H. (1975), 'My experience of analysis with Fairburn and Winnicot', 2, pp.145-154.

Gutmann, D. (1977) 'The Cross-Cultural perspective: notes towards a comparative psychology of Ageing' in Bimen, J.E. and Schair,E. eds. 'Handbook of the Psychology of Ageing', N.Y. Van Norstrand.

Jacques, E. (1965) 'Death and the Mid-Life Crisis', Int. Journal Psychoanalysis, 44, pp.507-14.

Kagan, J. (1979) 'Form of Early Development: Continuity and Discontinuity in emergent competences Arch. G. Psychiat, 36. pp. 1647-1654.

King, P.H.M. (1974) 'Notes on the Osychoanalysis of Older patients, J. Analytical Psychol. 19, pp. 22-37.

EVALUATING REALITY ORIENTATION WITH PSYCHOGERIATRIC PATIENTS

John Greene, Robert Smith and Marie Gardiner

Previous Evaluative Studies

Of the four major approaches to the behavioural management of the elderly confused patient – stimulation and activity programmes, behaviour modification, reality orientation, milieu therapy (Woods and Britton, 1977) – reality orientation is the one that to date has been the most empirically evaluated. Since 1974 at least one controlled study has appeared each year. These are the studies by Barnes (1974), Brook et. al., (1975), Harris and Ivory (1976), Citrin and Dixon (1977), Holden and Sinebruchow (1978) and Woods (1979). All of these studies have been concerned with evaluating the efficacy of R.O. in various institutional settings, in a controlled fashion.

The reason why reality orientation has been the object of such experimental work may lie in the fact that of the four approaches it is the one most amenable to experimentation. This is partly because of the simplicity of the technique itself and partly because of the relevant and clear cut objectives of the procedure, namely an improvement in orientation. And indeed there is now very good evidence that R.O. is effective in doing precisely this. In four of the above studies (Brook et. al., 1975; Harris and Ivory, 1976; Citrin and Dixon, 1977; Woods, 1978) significant improvement in orientation, as assessed by objective tests, have been demonstrated in patients receiving R.O. as compared with a control group receiving no R.O. Furthermore Woods (1979) found a parallel improvement in other cognitive functions such as short term memory using standard psychometric tests. Barnes (1974), in his study, although finding no significant improvement in his patients during R.O., did find a significant fall in orientation after R.O., thus suggesting that for his group, R.O. was arresting deterioration. In only one study, that of Holden and Sinebruchow (1978), has no improvement in orientation been found as a result of R.O.

All of the foregoing studies however have been carried out on institutionalised patients, either in psychiatric or geriatric hospitals, or in residential homes for the elderly. Yet, if R.O. is effective, it could be argued that it should be of more value to elderly people still living in the community, who are perhaps showing early signs of dementia. There would also be greater scope for orienting people still living in the community as opposed to those living in an unchanging institutional setting.

R.O. with Day Hospital Patients

An ideal group for such an approach would be elderly patients

attending a psychogeriatric day hospital. These patients spend most
of their time in the community but spend some time at a place where
they could obtain R.O. from professional staff in a consistent and
systematic way, this being an essential part of any behavioural
approach. There is now evidence (Greene and Timbury, 1979) that a
major function of day hospitals is to maintain elderly dementing
patients in the community, and at the same time to provide some
relief to relatives, until such time as long term in-patient care can
be provided. Attendance at day hospitals is thus, in part at least,
determined by the degree of behavioural disturbance shown by the
patient at home.

The main area of interest for elderly day hospital patients
would therefore be the extent to which any behavioural change occurs,
concomitant on improvement in orientation. This is the problem of
generalisation. That is, whether or not a purely cognitive change
can give rise to change in behaviour, in this case a decrease in the
level of disturbed behaviour. This would seem a not unreasonable
expectancy, as it could be argued that in the case of the elderly
confused person, the loss of orientation for time, place and person
is a critical deficit. In which case such loss might be seen as
giving rise to at least some of the disturbed mood and behaviour of
these patients. Yet there is still little good evidence of a
generalisation effect from R.O. Although almost all researchers
have commented that the impression of ward staff was that patients
had shown some degree of behavioural change consequent on R.O., in
only three of the above studies has there been any indications of
behavioural change using systematic and controlled ratings. Brook
et. al., (1975) found an improvement on a global rating of intellectual and social functioning in the experimental group (those receiving
R.O.) in contrast to no change in the control group. In the Harris
and Ivory (1976) study, on only one of several ratings of behaviour,
that of disturbed speech, was there a change, while in the study by
Citrin and Dixon (1977) although there was a significant difference
between the experimental and control group on a behaviour rating
scale post-treatment, this was primarily due to the control group
becoming worse. The evidence for a generalisation effect from R.O.
to behaviour is therefore limited. And indeed in another, recently
completed study, Hanley et. al., (1981), while again finding R.O.
effective in producing some measure of improvement in the verbal
orientation of dementing patients, found no change in any other
aspects of behaviour, as assessed by a standard rating scale.

Single Case Studies

Our studies began with day hospital patients by using R.O. with
patients individually. The reason for doing this was that we wished
to personalise the information as much as possible, by including items
relating to the patients family and neighbourhood, in addition to the
more general time and current affairs items. Our primary interest at
this stage was to find out the extent to which these patients could
be re-orientated to information of this sort and also to see if we
could obtain generalisation effects. Single subject experimental
designs (Hersen and Barlow, 1970) were used for this purpose. All

patients were diagnosed by a consultant psychiatrist as suffering from senile dementia.

Results showed (Greene et. al., 1979) that it was possible to markedly improve the orientation of day hospital patients to a degree greater than that reported with institutionalised patients. Furthermore this was accompanied by parallel changes in some other aspects of cognition and behaviour within the day unit, as rated by observers. This generalisation effect however was limited, following a 'gradient of generalisation', depending on the degree to which the particular piece of behaviour was dependent on current orientation. Thus there was a high degree of generalisation to other items of related information, followed by generalisation to behaviour which had a major cognitive component such as performance in Occupational Therapy tasks, and lastly little generalisation to social behaviour in a group setting. These effects tended to level or fall off, depending on the severity of the patient's dementia when R.O. was stopped.

A Group Study

These results were encouraging, but individual R.O. is not cost effective for everyday purposes and no attempt had been made in these single cases to assess behavioural change at home in any controlled or systematic way. It was decided to extend this work by carrying out a group study of R.P. in which generalisation effects to behaviour at home would be investigated by obtaining a relative's assessment of the patient's behaviour at home, and in addition, the relatives own response to any change obtained. For this purpose it was necessary to construct two rating scales. One to obtain from the relative, an assessment of the patient's behaviour at home, the other to assess the degree of upset experienced by the relative.

Preliminary results from this study, the data from which is still being analysed, indicate that as before orientation can be markedly improved using R.O. and that there is some generalisation to other cognitive functions as measured, this time, by psychometric tests. As orientation improved there was also a parallel tendency for disturbed behaviour, as rated by relatives, to decrease. This was accompanied by an alleviation of self-reported stress on the part of the relative during the R.O. period. Initial conclusions are that exposure to R.O. while attending the day hospital can be accompanied by observable and measurable changes within the home situation. The actual mechanism through which these changes occur however is not yet clear and requires further investigation and analysis.

Conclusions

It is concluded that R.O. is a useful adjunct to the management of the psychogeriatric day hospital patient and that further investigation into its use with these patients is justified. At the moment a third study is underway in this day hospital for the purpose of developing and evaluating a unit based R.O. programme of a more informal sort, similar to '24 hour' R.O., and involving all patients

and staff. The long term objective of this exercise is to establish
R.O. as a permanent feature of unit management policy.

REFERENCES

Barnes, J., (1974) The effects of reality orientation classroom
in memory loss, confusion, and disorientation in geriatric patients.
The Gerontologist, 14, pp.138-142.

Brook, P., Degun, G. and Mather, M. (1975) Reality orientation, a
therapy for psychogeriatric patients: A controlled study. British
Journal of Psychiatry, 127, pp.42-45.

Citrin, R.S. and Dixon, D.N. (1977) Reality orientation: A milieu
therapy used in an institution for the aged. The Gerontologist,
17, pp.39-43.

Greene, J.G., Nicol, R. and Jamieson, H. (1979) Reality orientation
with psychogeriatric patients. Behaviour Research and Therapy, 17,
pp.615-618.

Greene, J.G. and Timbury, G.C. (1979) A geriatric psychiatry day
hospital service: A five year review. Age and Ageing, 8,pp.49-53.

Hanley, I.G., McGuire, R.J. and Boyd, W.D. (1981) Reality orientation
and dementia: A controlled trial of two approaches. British Journal
of Psychiatry, 138 (in press).

Harris, C.S. and Ivory, P.B. (1976) An outcome evaluation of reality
orientation therapy with geriatric patients in a state mental
hospital. The Gerontologist, 16, pp.496-503.

Hersen, M. and Barlow, D.H. (1976) Single Case Experimental Designs:
Strategies for Studying Behaviour Change. Pergamon Press, Oxford.

Holden, U.P. and Sinebruchow, A. (1978) Reality orientation therapy:
A study investigating the value of this therapy in the rehabilitation of elderly people. Age and Ageing, 7, pp. 83-90.

Woods, R.T. and Britton, P.G. (1977) Psychological approaches to the
treatment of the elderly. Age and Ageing, 6, pp.104-112.

Woods, R.T. (1979) Reality orientation and staff attention: A
controlled study. British Journal of Psychiatry, 134, pp.502-507.

REALITY ORIENTATION OF THE RESIDENTIAL
CARE OF THE ELDERLY

Ian Hanley

Reality Orientation, or RO for short, first described by Folson (1968) and more recently by Drummond et al, (1978), is well established in North America as a practical approach to the care of the confused elderly person. It is an approach which, although specifically designed to prevent, halt or reverse signs of disorientation and memory loss, also implicitly recognises the importance of maintaining an elderly person's sense of identity and his need for an awareness of and involvement with the world about him. It is an approach based on strong positive attitudes towards old age which is intended to benefit the elderly person's psychological and social well-being as well as the morale and attitude of the care staff. In these days of staff shortages and cut backs the cost-effective slant of RO towards optimally utilising existing staff resources has considerable appeal.

Twenty-four Hour Reality Orientation

There are two forms of RO: a main form called Twenty-four Hour Reality Orientation (24RO) which runs all the time and involves all staff members and a more formal supplementary procedure called Class Reality Orientation which is a small group activity for selected residents run by a therapist for about 30 minutes each day.

The emphasis of 24RO is on the attitudes, expectations and behaviour of all those who come in contact with the confused person. The way staff interact, in particular the way they communicate, influences the resident's level of awareness and involvement. This is what the Americans term an 'aide-centred' approach intended to be cost-effective in utilising all existing contacts between all staff and confused resident as therapeutic interactions. The basic idea is that in order to compensate for poor memory for recent events, information, explanations and expectations need to be presented clearly and routinely to a confused resident in a tone that ranges from friendly to matter-of-fact but is never condescending or negative. Many regard such communication as totally natural and commonsense and do it already. Others, for one reason or another, do not. Busy with procedures and daily routine, many care staff need to be encouraged, indeed taught, how to communicate effectively with the confused old person.

The principle is simple - in the day to day sameness of an institution efforts have to be consciously made to provide residents with relevant information about time place and person. This is done through personal communication and reorganisation of the living environment to provide orientation aids. How else, over an extended time period, can anyone - even someone not confused - stay in touch with the day to day world?

Specifically 24RO encourages:

(1) the reorganisation of the physical environment to provide greater stimulation and simple orientation aids such as large clocks, calendars, notice-boards and signposts;

(2) the use of all existing staff contacts with a confused resident to remind him of details of time, place and person;

(3) the development of positive expectations of a confused resident by reminding him or explaining to him an activity or procedure, allowing time for a response and then praising or otherwise reinforcing that response when it occurs;

(4) the correction of confused behaviour when it occurs.

1. Orientation Aids

At the Old People's Home it has been found that orientation aids are very effective, especially when care staff direct the resident's attention to them. Bedroom doors are decorated with personalised emblems made by the residents themselves in handicraft. For the ladies, these take the form of arrangements of favourite flowers cut out of felt. For one elderly man, a lifelong supporter of a famous Scottish football club, the team crest in the appropriate colours makes it easy for him to find his bedroom along the main corridor which has no less than 15 doors off it! Other areas, of interest to all residents, are marked with three dimensional signs large enough to compensate for most visual impairments. These identify, through clear black and white motifs, the functional significance of the different areas. As well as obvious examples such as cut-out figures to represent bathroom areas, novel signs were designed to represent rooms where different activities are available, e.g. a cut-out old fashioned gramophone to indicate a sitting room with a record player, a cut-out television to indicate a television room etc.

Data derived in the experimental work indicates that these signs improve the accuracy with which confused residents identify different ward locations. Hanley (1980) has demonstrated that before improvements are evident staff often need to explain the signs and train residents to use them. By being able to move more easily and accurately from one place to another, dignity and independence are restored and aimless wandering, so tiring for the elderly, is reduced.

Many of the orientation aids such as the signposts described above are used by the non-confused residents. A large noticeboard opposite the dining room door announces forthcoming events in clear bold print, seeks resident volunteers for different activities and gives the next day's menu. This is referred to by many residents on a daily basis. Staff also wear name tags with the Christian name only spelt in large black letters on a white background. As a result residents call the staff by name more often and their person orientation has improved. Some residents have been provided with diaries and active encouragement to use them to record important events such as visits from relatives, trips out etc. Where possible, orientation aids are provided with a view to encouraging resident activity and self-reliance. The signs allow residents to negotiate their living environment more freely themselves. A bright red postbox in the corridor for example, encourages them to both write and post their own letters. One resident has volunteered to collect the post at a set time each day. Thus time orientation is encouraged.

The aids to orientation help the staff as well as the residents by reminding them of the existence and the purpose of the RO programme. The presence of tangible orientation aids also helps staff to communicate effectively with residents.

2. Verbal Orientation

Staff were encouraged to use all existing contacts with confused residents to remind them of details of time, place and person. They were encouraged to speak slowly, clearly and simply. The need for repetition of basic information was stressed. In particular staff were asked to address the resident by name, introduce themselves by name and converse in a fashion that related activities in the home to details of time and place. This communication, although generally focussed on orientation to the present, takes cognizance of the resident's past life. In order to understand residents better and facilitate conversational contacts, detailed personal histories of residents were obtained from relatives and visitors. Staff found this information changed their perception of resident's capabilities and made conversation easier. Information related to the past was then linked with orientation to the present.

As RO is essentially a team approach relying heavily on consistency to be effective, good communication between staff members is vital. This can be greatly helped by the attitude and approach of the supervisor and by making adequate provision for record-keeping and evaluation meetings. In the programme at the Old People's Home, each care staff was assigned responsibility for keeping in close touch with a particular resident or residents and making a daily note of relevant progress for others to read. Thus changes in mood, behaviour and orientation could be flexibly monitored and shared.

3. Facilitation of Purposive Behaviour and Activity

The main emphasis in 24RO is the maintenance, through active practice, of as yet unimpaired behavioural functions. To achieve this staff adopt an attitude of positive expectancy; they prompt and encourage all residents to carry out daily activities for themselves, allow time for these activities to be completed and reinforce through positive attention the efforts that are made.

A Kardex system also allows specific goals to be recorded. For one resident this involved the encouragement of greater social interaction. For another, it was something as practical as locating their own clothes in their wardrobe or remembering to wash in the morning. Thus behavioural deficits can be tackled.

This illustrates how 24RO relates to the behaviour of residents. Orientation nearly always has a purpose other than the simple acquisition of verbal information. Staff, busy as they are, must not only provide information to residents, but encourage the residents to use that information. This must involve allowing the resident more time to respond and carry out an activity for themselves. Many studies have demonstrated the reinforcement value of appropriately managed staff attention and Brody et al (1971) have demonstrated that specific behavioural improvements e.g. in self-care activities, can be achieved with the confused elderly.

In line with the staff's increased awareness of the resident's past functioning and interests, several new recreational and social activities were introduced with the goal of increasing resident's general activity level and 'engagement'. For example an indoor garden was acquired for residents with a gardening interest and card games were introduced for residents who had once been regular bridge players. The need for a staff approach based on prompting and reinforcement, in order to encourage optimal participation by residents has been highlighted in several recent behavioural studies (McClannaghan and Risley, 1975, Blackman et al 1976).

Of course activities per se do not constitute RO. It is important however to have confidence in the sort of 'reality' towards which we wish to orientate the confused elderly. If we speculate that someone is happier confused, are we not in most cases acknowledging deficits in the care environment rather than deficits of the person?

4. Correction of Confusion

Twenty-four hours RO also stresses the need to correct confused behaviour when it occurs. Confusion is seen as reversible provided all staff consistently correct it in a similar prescribed manner. While not disputing that this may well be the case, our experience has been that one must be selective in deciding what to correct. Many care staff are not happy to remind residents of unpleasant aspects of reality e.g. that a close relative is dead. Some residents clutch false beliefs in a way that suggests more than simple confusion. On the other hand, many of those who have gone through a period of acute confusion describe it as extremely distressing. Simple confused behaviour such as wandering in the corridor poses little problem for correction. Other evidence of confusion is difficult to interpret never mind correct.

Success can be achieved however. One elderly gentleman, suffering from an organic dementia, who had been in the Home for two years, regularly became agitated and asked staff if he had stayed there the night before and was his sister still alive. With regular RO and visits to see his sister his confusion and agitation were reduced and he became easier to manage.

The attractive thing about RO is that every interaction with an old person suddenly has potential. For many staff their job becomes more interesting as they are presented with a rationale for dealing constructively and personally with the residents they care for. The procedural aspects of care no longer assume absolute priority and an improvement in atmosphere and morale, unfortunately a difficult thing for a researcher to measure, seems to develop.

Class Reality Orientation

Class RO is the other, often optional, form of RO. This is a small group activity for the more disorientated residents which provides more intensive reorientation for a short period daily in a specially equipped area under the auspices of a trained therapist. At the Home an informal atmosphere was created for these meetings by holding them round a wall-fire in a room which had large windows and the air of an old fashioned drawing room. Residents were selected for class RO if they showed signs of cognitive (mental) impairment on a psychological test battery. The room was equipped with an RO or information board, large calendars, posters and occasional displays of seasonal flowers, fruit, etc.

Meetings generally commenced with residents introducing them - selves and learning each others names. Then the blank spots on the RO board were filled in with residents encouraged to provide the information on such things as the day, the month, the year, the place, the weather and the nature of the next meal. Where a resident could not provide the answer, other residents were encouraged to assist. The therapist provided information the group could not provide and involved the residents in placing the information on the board. Units of information placed on the RO board were made of large white letters on black plastic strips. These were magnetised and could easily be put on and pulled off the board by the residents. Perhaps surprisingly, these very simple activities were obviously enjoyed by the residents - even those only mildly disorientated.

Formal as these group procedures sound, a considerable amount of social activity was engendered during the sessions, a sense of humour was often evident and the communications were surprisingly matter of fact and adult. Of ten residents participating in two groups of five, only one dropped out saying she would rather not attend. Many of the group members were often waiting outside the room before the groups were due to start and some complained when the groups were stopped for a period!

Drummond et al (1968), the developers of RO in the Veterans Hospital Service in America, advocate two levels of class RO; a basic level as described above and a more advanced level for those who are either less disorientated to start with or who benefit sufficiently from the basic class. At Greenlea, we rolled both into one and after going over the basic information, finished each class with discussions and activities based round advanced orientation themes. On the morning of Burns Night, for example, group members discussed who Burns was, where he lived, recited some of his poetry and discussed the

112

preparation and content of the traditional haggis supper. Another
popular orientation theme involved examining postcards of famous
Edinburgh buildings, naming them and locating them on a map of the
city. Many such themes were developed which related closely to
people, places and the ongoing passage of time. The common denomina-
tors in each were that residents were encouraged to make active
contributions and relate information acquired in the past to the
present day.

The effects of class RO were evaluated experimentally. Although
gains were modest and not always statistically significant, residents
attending class RO displayed improvements in verbal orientation
(Hanley et al 1981). Such improvements have been reported in other
studies, notably that of Woods (1979) and Greene et al (1979).
Increased social interaction both in the groups and on the section was
readily apparent to many staff members, though empirical data which
might support this has not yet been analysed. Group members were
noticed to seek out each others company when back on the section.

The RO classes which were introduced six months prior to 24RO
proved a valuable staff training resource. Many care staff expressed
interest in the groups and appeared to benefit from attending them.
The administration at the Home has recently decided, with a view to
possibly expanding RO into other sections of the home, to introduce
as many staff as possible from these other sections to the RO groups
and thereby the RO approach to care.

Overall then, positive results have been obtained from the
application of both Twenty-four Hour Care Reality Orientation. It
is unfortunate that as yet no comprehensive RO manual, suitable for
use in this country, has yet been produced. Plans are underway to
produce such a manual and possibly a video training film.

<u>REFERENCES</u>

Blackman, D.K., Howe, M. and Pinkston, E.M. (1976). Increasing
Participation in Social Interaction of the Institutionalised
Elderly. <u>The Gerontologist</u>, 16, 1, pp.69-76.

Brody, E.M., Kloban, M.G., Lawton, M.P., and Silverman, H.A. (1971).
Excess Disabilities of Mentally Impaired Age. Impact of Individualised Treatment. <u>The Gerontologist</u>, 11.

Drummond, L., Kirchoff, L., and Scarbrough, D.R. (1978). A Practical
Guide to Reality Orientation. <u>The Gerontologist</u>, 18, 6, pp 568-
573.

Polson, J.C. (1968). Reality Orientation for the Elderly Mental
Patient. <u>Journal of Geriatric Psychiatry</u>, 1,2.

Greene, J.G., Nicol, R. and Jamieson, H. (1979). Reality Orientation
with Psychogeriatric Patients. <u>Behaviour Research and Therapy</u>, 17,
pp.615-618.

Hanley, I.G. (1980). The Use of Signposts and an Active Training
Procedure to Modify the Ward Orientation of Female Senile Dements.
Proceedings of the World Congress on Behaviour Therapy, Jerusalem.

Hanley, I.G., McGuire, R.J., and Boyd, W.D. (1981). Reality
Orientation and Dementia: A Controlled Trial of Two Approaches.
<u>British Journal of Psychiatry</u>, 138 (in press).

McClannahan, L.E. and Risley, T.R. (1975). Design of Living
Environments for Nursing-home Residents: Increasing Participation
in Recreational Activities. <u>Journal of Applied Behaviour Analysis</u>,
8, pp.261-268.

Woods, R.T. (1979). Reality Orientation and Staff Attention: A
Controlled Study. <u>British Journal of Psychiatry</u>, 134.

SOME CONFLICTS AND ANOMALIES IN TERMINAL
CARE MOVEMENTS

Nicky Smith*

To provide an environment for a 'good death' is a common aim
between antagonistic groups – the hospice movement and the euthanasia
lobby. This paper explores these two movements as different means to
the same end and outlines some anomalies in both.

Two incidents have occurred which brought my attention to the
fact that groups I had thought to be rigidly opposed to each other,
do have some fundamental links. The first was the sudden realisation
that both the hospice movement and the Voluntary Euthanasia Society
(since renamed 'Exit, the Society for the right to die with dignity')
claimed that they wanted to provide the environment for a 'good death',
or for the greater illumination of those who were not sure what a
good death was, 'death with dignity' was used as the criterion for
both groups.

The second incident happened at the end of a four week multidisciplinary course at St. Christopher's Hospice, when an American doctor
remarked that a lot of the death considered 'good' at St. Christopher's, would be called euthanasia in America. This made me realise
that the lines drawn up for the battle between the two were not as
clear as I had originally supposed, and that what some people regard
as appropriate and therefore good medical practice, is already
embodied in medical ethical codes, whilst other people consider that
a change in the law is necessary to achieve good practice.

The paper aims to identify the similarities between the hospice
movement and the euthanasia movement and to speculate on where some
of the differences lie. It is suggested that in both movements a
death with dignity is death with control, but that the control serves
a different purpose in each. The underlying theme is 'what is human?'
that is what is it about human beings that makes a good death
desirable or possible, which leads on to considering what provisions
are in the 'best' interests of the dying. Using notions of communal-
ity and individual autonomy to understand different policies for the
two groups makes, perhaps, an awkward conjunction between philosophy
at its most abstract and daily practice for those involved. However,
as the observations evolved from the latter it is considered more
important to throw light on the dilemmas of practical policy making
than to tease out extreme philosophical positions. For this reason
discussion of the religious basis will be omitted, not because it is
not germane to the issue, but because it does not crucially explain
anything.

* Many thanks to Chris Wright for talking over the ideas with me,
and suggesting the categories.

The discussion will revolve round the examples of St. Christopher's Hospice representing the hospice movement, and Exit, the Society for the right to die with dignity, representing the euthanasia group. It should be noted that all hospices have evolved differently and have slightly different aims, and that although I shall be referring to the hospice as an institution in a building, most hospices either evolved from or have developed a domiciliary nursing team, so that a hospice is not just somewhere you go, it could come to your home. It should also be pointed out that there is some diversity between the euthanasia groups, varying from consciousness raising groups wishing to highlight inhuman hospital practices to those whose intention is to legalise the act of killing someone who has requested it. Therefore, any trends identified for either group have an ideal-typical rather than an empirical validity.

In sum then, this is to be a reflection on what each group is trying to achieve, and in particular what is the death with dignity that they are aiming for in their different ways.

A quote for Lisa Alther's 'Kinflicks' describes a bad death as measured by the criteria of both groups.

The plot so far:

Ginny is visiting her mother in hospital. Her mother has been there for several months suffering from internal bleeding from unknown causes, blood transfusions only work for 2-3 days before the condition deteriorates dramatically again.

'The next day Ginny's mother didn't answer her greeting. Ginny could not tell if she was asleep or just making herself unavailable. She sat and waited for a sign from her. Nothing happened. After a while she walked to her mother's bedside. She regretted interfering in her mother's efforts to sever her earthly connections, but she felt she had something significant to offer.

She began talking quietly as though her mother was awake and listening.

... some conversation....

Ginny ceased abruptly. Her mother didn't so much as stir. She was asleep. She hadn't even heard.

After a couple of minutes, though her mother smiled her familiar wry smile and nodded her head slowly and said with amused detachment at Ginny's earnest metaphorical efforts, 'Maybe'.

A few minutes later she added, 'Look after yourself, Ginny dear'.

'You, too, Mother,' Ginny replied in a choked voice.

Ginny got a phone call after mignight. She raced to the
hospital in the Jeep. Her mother had had a major motor
seizure beginning in her right hand and spreading through
the right side of her body. She was in a coma. Ginny
could scarcely see her round yellow face, now paralysed
on the right side, for the team of white starched
technicians who hovered over her making a pincushion of
her hip with injections - anticonvulsants and cortico
steroids. A bottle of fresh platelets hung dripping
into her arm. Dr. Vogel was lifting her eyelids and
studying her pupils with a small flashlight, pounding
her patellae with a rubber hammer, rubbing the soles of
her feet for Babinski reflexes. With huge syringes
laboratory workers were withdrawing blood samples, bone
marrow smears.

Ginny elbowed through these battalions to Dr. Vogel and
tugged his lab coat.

'Let her go', she said quietly.

'Please' he hissed. 'Can't you see I'm busy?'

'She's ready. Let her go'.

He seated Ginny in a chair and demanded rhetorically,
'Do you or don't you want your mother to live?' She
sat watching and listening to the low hum of consulting
technicians.

'We've done everything possible.' Dr. Vogel informed
her wearily five hours of injections later.

'I know you have, Dr. Vogel. And we appreciate it.'
Ginny assured him, trying to keep him from crying, which
he looked as though he might do at any moment.

An hour later, her mother died quietly, without regaining
consciousness.'

As was noted above, this narrative illustrates the sort of
circumstances which caused both the movements to evolve - the
intimidating, impersonal, painful and unnecessary prolongation of a
life that is no longer wanted. Both movements wanted to fill what
they perceived as an unmet need in the type of death possible in this
country - to provide some choice. In the 1976 report for St. Christopher's Hospice, Cicely Saunders mentions that the Hospice developed
to provide an alternative to the active treatments that were becoming
technically possible, but also an alternative to VES who were working
to 'make legal the option of a quick death'(1). Both groups are
agreed on the need to avoid a bad death and partly agreed on what
constitutes a bad death. Again to quote Cicely Saunders, 'both sides
in the debate have a vendetta against pointless pain and impersonal
indignity.' (2)

117

Both groups share in the ancient belief (3) that there is something special about human beings which makes their death highly significant and worthy of attention, as is shown by their considerable attempts to make proper provision for the death. Furthermore the groups consist of committed workers who see themselves helping people in need. It is easy to fall into the trap of suspecting Exit to be lurking eugenicists or parricides, wishing to impose non-voluntary euthanasia, but it is not so.

An important point of similarity is that both attempt to restore the individual's sense of control over their own death, so that for many death with dignity is death with control. The hospices try to do this by making the utmost of an individual's physical potential through control of symptoms, thereby allowing the patient freedom to control their mind, instead of having their mind controlled through physical incapacity and in particular, pain. The Exit group try to restore a sense of control by making provision for the individual to terminate life when it has become intolerable, and they claim that once this sense of control has been established, the individual is left freer to consider other things.

It is fairly obvious from what has been said already that they both agree that there is a 'right' time to die, an appropriate time, although they may differ over criteria for its assessment. An acceptable time may vary from the point at which an individual can bear his or her state no longer and wishes to end life immediately, to the fulfilling of social criteria which include trying to facilitate a bearable period after the death for those remaining.

Equally, the groups would both consider it inappropriate to 'strive officiously to keep alive' (4), when keeping people alive or trying to prevent their death takes no account of the physical and social circumstances of the person involved. Both groups accept that as humans we live, find meaning, work, die, despair of life or enjoy it within a specific social framework, and that this should be taken into account when assessing the value of life to a dying person and his or her relatives. However, whereas for some, loss of ability to control or take responsibility for personal behaviour necessarily heralds the end of dignity, for others a sense of human worth and dignity may be maintained by residing in a community which values individuals making optimum use of the control they have. Both groups would acknowledge the importance of social factors in making life of value, but the individually controlled sense of dignity is to be found in Exit, while the emphasis on a shared and sharing, community sense of dignity, is to be found in the Hospice.

The list of similarities is not exhaustive, but covers the most general areas, which I would like to round off by adding that the people involved in both groups have a fairly high degree of personal interest in their project, in that they tend to have arrived in either group as the result of some kind of personal experience.

Having briefly looked at the common ground, I would now like to mention where I think their main differences lie, which is in how they see the connection between the individual and society - that is the relationship between the two - and which has the priority. This aspect if worth discussing because it has implications for how we provide for the terminally ill.

Looking at the literature of both groups, it is possible to get some idea of what each regards as human dignity, and this can be used to get some indication of where they see the individual standing in relation to society.

To facilitate this discussion I shall employ the notion of ideal types to identify four general groupings of ideas on death and individual responsibility. Two of these groups are extremes and I am not particularly interested in them, they will be dismissed fairly rapidly to concentrate on the two groups into which I suspect most of us would fall.

The four groups to be considered are:

1. obligationists

2. possibilists

3. perfectionists

4. individualists

The obligationists and individualists are the two extreme groups. In the case of the obligationists the individual is entirely subsumed to the requirements of the community, and in the case of the individualists it is vice-versa - the requirements of the community are subsumed to those of the individual. If humans are considered to be a thinking, social species, total organisation on the basis of either of these groups would not be possible, but it is possible to note specific practices along these lines.

The guiding rules of the obligationists are utilitarian. It would not be necessary to assess individual needs as the welfare of the community would be paramount - so that a person might die if no longer required, as, for example in the now illegal practice of suttee, or if their death serves a greater purpose than their life, as in hara-kiri. For the obliganionists human dignity is centred round the fulfillment of an alloted task. By contrast individualist rules would expect individual needs and desires to be fulfilled without reference to the community, so that a person would die when, and how he or she chose, regardless of the effects their death may have on others. Here, human dignity is focused on individual assessment and control of life - and death. (5)

Now for the other two groups - the possibilists have the tendencies of the euthenasia movement and the perfectionists the tendencies of the hospice movement.

Each of them will be described as though they are distinct groups, but as was mentioned at the beginning of the paper such a division does not exist in real terms, and the models are just devices to try and illuminate the issues. The perfectionists and the possibilists note mutual obligations between the community and the individual and their differences lie in how they balance the legitimacy of one against the other.

The possibilists are the euthanasia group. They are called possibilists because they base their policies on what they observe to be happening and how it should and can be dealt with now i.e. based on the art of the possible. They are acutely aware of the pain and degradation people feel about the decisions currently being taken on how people die, they cannot justify the lack of positive steps to do something to alleviate it and so they press for effective action. For instance they observe that 'many must still endure the long drawn out and deeply distressing process of degeneration' (6) and that 'prolonged periods of pain are not the only distress some unfortunate patients have to suffer, feelings of suffocation, of nausea, of misery or of being desperately ill cannot always be relieved by pain killers and sedatives'. (7) Their policy for euthanasia encompasses provision for the needs they observe: 'When alternatives are death with dignity or death accompanied by prolonged pain and distress, common sense as well as compassion support the demand of the VES that choice whould be a legal human right of the individual.'(8) For this group of people death with dignity involves mental and physical control of their bodies and death is a bio-medical means by which to exert such control. 'For many people the loss of their ability to think, rationalise, communicate and serve their own basic natural needs is a situation which they cannot contemplate with equanimity. They there- fore live in fear. This fear is diminished when they know that they can decide for themselves how and when they will die.' (9) Thus, the fear of watching body and mind degenerate and not be able to do anything about it, may spoil the quality of the life that is led, as may the fear of being a burden to others. It is suggested that such fear can be overcome with the knowledge that something – induced death – can prevent progressive deterioration, thereby freeing the person to enjoy more fully the life that is left to them.

The policy of this group is to change the law so that if and when the individual decides he or she wants to die, they are able to do so and, moreover, expect that medical provision will be such as to enable them to do so. I will come back to this point a bit later.

Next to be considered are the perfectionist group, broadly the hospice movement. Like the possibilists this group observe that care of the terminally ill is inadequate, but unlike the possibilists they base their policies on more long-term development of choice. Compared with the possibilists they could be said to reach for ideals which may be very hard to realise, but in the meantime they tend to be averse to the possibilist emphasis on the individual right on when to take life.

For the perfectionists there is a strong community commitment to provide for the individual, but the individual also has responsi- bilities to the community and in particular to the family. To the best of his or her ability the individual is encouraged to remain part of the group - be it the hospice unit or the family - and to share in its life as a functioning human being, still giving and receiving.

The perfectionist feeling is that life ought not to be taken but it can be forfeited when certain criteria are fulfilled, which are as much social as medical. Death and dying take place within a set of social relationships, and relatives, friends, nurses, doctors and so on have to continue living after the death. Perfectionists take the post death period into account when considering what is a 'good' death, and therefore aim to make a death as easy and pain-free as possible, not only for the person dying, but for all those involved. Relationships are seen as worthy of consideration and attention throughout life, including when it is nearing it's end. For the perfectionists, the dignity of humans lies in their potential for creativity, and their ability to alter things. Thus, if the process of dying has meant a chance for growth, development and sharing, then dying itself has been dignified. Hospice policies aim to enhance the likelihood of dying being an integral and important part of living.

So, just to reiterate, in the two groups of special interest - the possibilists and perfectionists - dignity emphasises control of physical life in the former, and development and growth of potential in the latter. This is not to imply that the two are mutually exclusinve, rather that they place different emphases.

In practice, the aims of both groups carry with them some problems which are difficult to overcome for various reasons. Mentioning the euthanasia/possibilists first, one can detect some ambiguity between their demand for the individual's right to choose, and the obligations on the community to meet individual demand. There are two main, but connected areas of ambiguity - one of which relates to their desire to change the policy on euthanasia and the other in their expectations of modern medicine and its practitioners. Self-deliverance - the new word for suicide, which at the moment is considered less traumatic - is as complete control of the body as a human being is likely to achieve, and following the rhetoric of the group, the dignity of death lies in the individual decision to take life in circumstances of his or her own choosing, with certain safe-guards to themselves and the community. If physical inability is likely to become a problem in suicide, it is to be expected that someone might help the afflicted person if requested to do so. In England at the moment, the abettor - like Derek Humphrey (10) - is liable to 14 years imprisonment. Changing the law in this respect would enable the individual to remain consciously in control given limiting circumstances. (11) It might be supposed that a group like Exit, so concerned with individual control of circumstances would be pressing for a change in the law related to abetting suicide before concentrating on changing the law to authorise doctors to kill their patients - even though this is done on request, and subject to strict guidelines. Instead, the emphasis in Exit literature, seems to lie in waiting until the individual is no longer in conscious control and then requiring somebody else to act. In fact, it requires consider-able medical intervention. A sympathetic doctor has to 'give

euthanasia'. The 1969 Voluntary Euthanasia Bill was based largely on
a draft prepared by the Society.

> 'It's main provision was a form of written declaration
> requesting the administration of euthanasia to the
> declarant in the event of their suffering from an
> incurable – and distressing disease or disability, and
> in carefully defined circumstances ... The Bill
> aurhorised doctors to give euthanasia to a patient who
> had at least 30 days previously made such a written
> declaration before 2 witnesses.' (12)

Such an emphasis on professional outsiders may have more to do
with a desire not to kill oneself (13) – even though one wants to die –
than it has with protection against a brain and body becoming
obsolete before one has had a chance to do something about it. The
request for authanasia then, is based more on the individuals right
to choose (and imposes a duty on the community to carry it out)
rather than on the individuals right to physical control over his or
her own body.

The hospice/perfectionists aim is the creation of a good
environment in which to die, with the family as the unit of care,
rather than just the patient. Death with dignity is making a
positive experience out of dying, both for the person dying, and
those involved. The Hospice consider that there are mutual responsibilities between the community and the individual to make death as
meaningful and significant as possible. However, whilst it encourages
development of positive meaning, it may inhibit other, apparently more
negative individual characteristics such as anger and displeasure,
because they undermine the community – particularly when the hospice
is in an institution. One such incident concerned Len, a formerly
active and cheerfully beligerant cockney, now suffering from motor
neurone disease and progressively paralysed, who was yearning for a
good row. He was frustrated and angry with the world and wanted to
be a nuisance, and would behave deliberately badly. Instead of
treating him like a normally bad tempered human being and getting
cross with him, the staff tried to be patient and went to great
lengths to try to understand his distress at the loss of physical
control.

One of the other needs the community never seemed to cater for,
unless the need genuinely did not exist (14), were the sexual needs
of patients. Even a protracted kiss and cuddle seemed a bit hard to
come by. I suspect this is the result of some rigidity of interpretation of what care hospices should provide, but it is an individual
need that the community finds hard to manage. So, although the
hospices have adopted a commitment to assessing individual needs in an
attempt to maximise dignity through open communication and shared
thoughts, in practice this can soon become a sugary sweet acceptance
of the patients, which prevents the staff from showing emotions which
are very human, because they are thought to be threatening to the
community.

In conclusion, it has been suggested that the two apparently opposing groups of Exit and St. Christopher's Hospice, have a shared commitment to a better way of death, and that each has developed a policy which emphasises a particular view of what is human. Exit considers the problem as pressing and bases its policies on what is considered to be a practical option to currently inadequate ways of dying. Although the solution lies in future (except for those who are prepared to risk imprisonment by abetting suicide) changes in the law, once changed there would be the possibility of increased individual control over dying. For Exit, death with dignity means the termination of life when the individual no longer considers it of value. This implies an individualistic view of humanity in which the individual is fit to assess and choose the appropriate moment for death. The Hospice aim, through example and education, is to show that dying can be a positive part of living, so that death with dignity involves the relief of physical symptoms to encourage human potential for creativity, despite the formidability of the occasion. For the Hospice the emphasis is on humans as social beings able to make their lives meaningful through interaction with others. In practice it would appear that both groups are still struggling to balance the responsibilities of the individual and the community, to understand where they conflict, and how to deal with it.

NOTES

1. 1976-77 Annual Report from St. Christopher's Hospice, 51-53 Lawrie Park Rd. Sydenham, SE26 6DE.

2. As Note 1.

3. See H. Baker. The Image of Man (formerly the Dignity of Man) 1975 pub. Peter Smith.

4. From 'The Last Decalogue' - poem by A. Clough.

5. Such an approach could require euthanasia on demand. A Scottish Exit document is close to this when it states: 'Exit members believe in the total basic human right of all to terminate life on this planet (as they know it) as and when they will'. Whilst it is advocated that the person involved educate their family to avoid shock, it is nevertheless an individual decision to take their own life as they like.

6. P.4. 'The Need for Voluntary Euthanasia' - pamphlet from Exit, 13, Prince of Wales Terrace, London W8 5PE.

7. P.4 - as note 6.

8. P.5. - as note 6.

9. Confidential Exit document.

10. Derek Humphrey - Jean's Way - Fontana, 1976.

11. This is not to imply that Exit does not press for changes in the suicide laws, rather that the emphasis is on the administration of euthanasia by willing outsiders e.g. doctors.

12. P. 7 - as note 6.

13. See E. Stengel. Suicide and attempted suicide. Chapter 11 Pelican, 1977.

14. See Chapter 7 in Derek Humphrey - Jean's Way.

THE EVALUATION OF COMMUNITY CARE:
SOME GENERAL PRINCIPLES[*]

David Challis

Many studies which have attempted to demonstrate effectiveness
in the field of social intervention can perhaps be characterised by
their relatively modest results. Indeed, one review of major studies
of social work and allied caring services rather disarmingly concluded that '...the emerging picture of professional intervention is
far from clear. The evidence does not definitely indicate that such
intervention is effective or ineffective' (Mullen and Dumpson 1972).
However, a more recent review of work since 1973 undertaken by Reid
and Hanrahan (1980) suggests the emergence of a different trend from
which five points may be observed. Firstly, the newer caring
interventions tended to be more structured and clearly explicated
so that the experimental input was more clearly identifiable.
Secondly, the objectives of intervention were more circumscribed and
realistically attainable. Thirdly, there was a trend towards the
use of harder measures of outcome. Fourthly, and related to the
last three points, there was a greater degree of control by the
experimental investigators over the intervention which contributed to
the likelihood of a closer fit between inputs and expected outcomes.
Finally, it was noteworthy that most of the studies were able to
demonstrate positive outcomes. It would appear that the studies
cited by Reid and Hanrahan (1980) come closer than earlier work to
facing the critical question for effective evaluative research
formulated by Mullen and Dumpson (1972): 'On what basis and towards
what end will who do what to whom, for how long, with what effect,
at what cost, and with what benefits?'

This question is central to the evaluation of Community Care.
An evaluation of the care of the elderly has to be concerned with
the care that is actually provided, the milieu of that (or the way
in which it is provided), the personal attributes of the recipient,
and the effects of care upon them. The production of a welfare
model, drawn from the literature of Economics,(1) makes it possible

---

* I should like to thank Miss E.M.Goldberg for permission to refer
to the papers by Reid and Hanrahan (1980) and Hadley and McGrath
(1980).

(1) For examples of the application of this model to other care
settings see: Davies, B.P. and Knapp, M.R.J. (1980) Old People's
Homes and the Production of Welfare, Routledge and Kegan Paul; and
Knapp, M.R.J. (1979) 'Planning Child Care Services from an Economic
Perspective', Residential and Child Care Administration, 1, pp.229-
248.

examine these relationships in a systematic fashion, providing the structure to encompass the lengthy evaluative question earlier formulated. This framework clearly articulates the relationship between inputs (what is done), outcome (the effects of care or changes in the quality of life), how this relationship is mediated by other factors in the environment and organises the structure of data collection. Changes in a person's well-being or comfort can be related to such factors as the amount and type of care which they receive and differences in their personal and domestic circumstances such as health and housing.

It is this framework which is utilised in the evaluation of the Community Care Project,* a scheme to provide a more individualised and flexible system of care in their own homes for the most vulnerable elderly, whose needs would otherwise be normally met by more expensive institutional care. The essence of the scheme is the provision of a decentralised budget to field social workers who could both co-ordinate existing care and develop new forms of help for their clients. By utilising existing social service resources and with the budget developing resources locally, within an arbitrary ceiling of two-thirds of the cost of residential care, the workers could operate flexibly guided by a knowledge of the unit costs of existing services as a framework for making decisions about the appropriacy of different ways of helping their clients.

The following sections examine in more detail the individual components of an evaluative framework for care in the community.

(1) <u>Outcomes</u>

The measurement of effectiveness represents perhaps the most difficult and taxing area facing research, covering the vexed question of identifying quality of life and the need to link outcomes to the actual objectives of intervention. Outcome can be most easily understood in terms of the reduction in shortfall from a level of well-being, or the extent to which need is reduced. It is the net effect of intervention, constituting those results which can be attributed to that activity uncontaminated by other factors influencing the situation. In the simplest form outcome is the difference between subjects on a measure before and after intervention, $(t^2E - t^1E)$. The most sophisticated measure of outcome is that where measures are taken on both experimental and control subjects before and after intervention, and outcome refers to the change in the experimental group less that in the control group $([t^2E - t^1E] - [t^2C - t^1C])$.

In practice, well-being has frequently been conceived of as if it were synonymous with the provision of services, and therefore

----

*The evaluation is described in detail in Davies and Challis (1980) and the early operation and results discussed in Challis and Davies (1980)

outcome the receipt of these, rather than well-being the state of the person which itself justifies the provision of service. Such an approach, by confusing means with ends, tends to stultify the consideration of different means of achieving the objectives of well-being. Measures of outcome can properly be understood at distinct levels of generality or as stages in the causal process of achieving welfare. Davies (1977) has distinguished between three kinds of measure in the literature of outcome measurement, indicators based upon levels of provision, throughput and the effects of services upon the attainment of their objectives. It is at this third level that the concept of 'final outcome' is located, the objectives of care for the elderly representing those aspects of the quality of life which are more or less explicit within the social welfare paradigm.

In the Community Care Scheme an analysis of the literature of social administration, social work and government policy statements made possible the identification of seven broad dimensions of outcome for community care of the elderly, (Challis 1981). These have been defined as 1) Nurturance, or basic physical care; 2) Compensation for disability; 3) Independence, or the old person's degree of control over their own life; 4) Morale or life satisfaction; 5) Social Integration, referring to loneliness and social contacts; 6) Family relationships, predominantly the stress upon carers; 7) Community Development, referring to the more general effects within the local community of a caring intervention. Within the production of welfare model it is quite possible to distinguish between different dimensions as having different degrees of finality. Thus for example, the dimensions of 'Independence', 'Family Relationships' and 'Morale' are directly concerned with the effects of care upon the recipients, 'Morale' being the most general measure. The other dimensions, 'Nurturance', 'Compensation for Disability' and 'Social Integration' are concerned with experiences which when lacking in either quality or sufficiency are likely to be indicative of a dimunition in the quality of life, are more intermediate in their effect upon welfare and are closely related to the more modest objectives of services.

The analysis of the literature revealed very clearly that the development of techniques for assessment was in a very different state of development for each dimension, the availability of proven, reliable and valid measures in some areas being much greater than in others. Clearly the measurement of social contact and disability have experienced considerable research effort from the early studies of Townsend (1957, 1962), Tunstall (1906) and more recently from Wright (1974). In the USA life satisfaction and morale have been the subject of numerous papers and indices have been developed (Lawton 1975, Neugarten et.al.1961) which can be readily utilised in this country (Savage et.al.1977, Challis and Knapp 1980). Similarly, numbers of studies have examined the burden of care (Sainsbury and Grad 1971). However, in the measurement of 'Independence' or the old person's felt control over their own life, relatively little work appears to have been undertaken (Palmore and Luikart 1972, Kuypers 1972). Identification of effects upon the community of a caring scheme is the subject of a separate study examining the motivations and experiences of those who help. The Community Care Scheme has predominantly enabled field social workers to engage local people for specific payments, to undertake necessary tasks, often at times when other help was unavailable, for elderly people. Clearly the impact of such activity upon informal care within the community raises questions identified by Abrams (1977) as to whether public and community care can co-exist and whether it is possible to create a situation which may evoke latent caring potential. There is very little previous work which provides a substantial base for such work, (Qureshi, Davies and Challis 1979).

The substantial variations of development of different indicators of outcome is likely to be reflected in considerable variation in reliability and validity of measures. Often subjectively based indicators such as attitudinal measures have relatively low reliability due to factors such as mood swings in the subject or interviewer variability. Consequently, the lower the reliability of a measure the greater the observed differences which are required to demonstrate a significant effect. Measurement error makes possible the danger of a 'regression effect' (Campbell and Erlebacher 1970) occurring as repeated measures are taken. Thus, for example, if in a study comparing two presumably similar groups, one group appears worse than the other by the initial measures, then it is possible that the apparently worse group will show more improvement on subsequent measures as scores regress towards the mean.

Outcome measurement is more developed and presents less difficulty at a second, less general level related to the specific objectives of established domiciliary and day care services, and their adequacy and sufficiency for the recipient. At the most specific third level, outcome can be conceived of as very particular, concerned with the idiosyncratic needs and preferences of individuals such as the desire to retire to bed at a particular time rather than when the night nursing service is available. At all levels of measurement, but in particular these last two it is important that measures '... take into account, and assign a meaningful value to, the subject's own views of what benefits them as well as those of various caring agents' (Abrams 1977). However, low expectations may mean that elderly people sometimes find it difficult to conceive of judging the sufficiency of the help they receive, being habituated to 'making do'. An intriguing difficulty remains the different degrees of importance attached to outcomes by different actors. Some elderly people are likely to experience certain outcomes, such as 'independence' and 'nurturance' as inversely related, where the acquisition of greater security may cause the old person to relinquish control over their own life. That this is likely may be inferred from Blenkner's (1967) study of intensive preventative social work with the elderly, where it was found that intervention did not reduce but increased the likelihood of institutional care, as the social workers developed a concerned and protective response towards their clientele. Whilst the logic of determining relative preferences is lucidly described by Culyer (1976), a systematic method of recording such preferences would be likely to present difficulties with the frail elderly, as indeed it has in other situations (Davies 1977).

Finally, it is desirable that monitoring instrumentation link the process of need evaluation and provision of care in a fashion congruent with more general indicators of outcome, linking the input of fieldworkers with outcome. In the Community Care Scheme a version of the Case Review System (Goldberg and Warburton 1979) has been developed for work specifically with elderly people, (Challis 1979). Such a form of instrumentation is required in view of the loose and variable fashion in which information is recorded in the traditional form of case notes.

Similar indicators of outcome have been used in other studies of the care of the aged. The Triage scheme in the USA (Hodgson and Quinn 1980), which was concerned to provide a range of services both medical and social to the frail elderly, used measures of morale, independent living and family support. Goldberg (1970) in her study of social work help to the elderly, used measures such as 'Morale', 'Social Isolation' and 'Capacity and Mobility' although these were not derived from a priori theoretical but empirically defined from a pool of individual items by Principal Components Analysis. The Coventry Home Help study (Coventry 1978) used indicators of varying degrees of generality and incidence, including measures of self care and mental state, changes in the condition of accommodation, clients perceptions of the service and effects upon the community caring network and informal care.

However, the degree of finality of the outcome indicators chosen in any study will depend upon a number of factors, not least the difficulty and expense of data collection. For a number of studies, therefore, less general indicators of outcome have been chosen. The Hove Intensive Domiciliary Care Project (Dunnachie 1979) which provided both personal and household care to frail elderly clients, focussed upon indicators of the amount and frequency of help given, the receipt of other services and referral and admission rates for residential care. The ACCESS experiment in the USA (Eggert et.al.1980) which examined the effects of a single agency assessing and monitoring long-term care for the elderly was predominantly concerned with rates of admission to institutional care. This was the approach adopted in evaluating the Wisconsin Community Care Organisation (Applebaum et.al.1980) which attempted to provide an alternative to nursing home care, although organisational dynamics, issues and problems were also carefully monitored. Hadley and McGrath (1980), in an evaluation of 'patch-based' social services, noted the expense and time of a study of the degree of penetration of unmet need in the community of this organisational mode, despite the fact that such penetration is a major objective of patch work. Furthermore, the farther along the causal chain of outcomes, from service specific outcomes (like satisfaction with home care) to indicators such as life satisfaction the more difficult it becomes to specifically relate observed changes to experimental inputs rather than various exogenous inputs. In any study, the need must be for a range of inter-related outcome measures which are '...feasible to measure, given the constraints of time and budget, and more or less directly related to the goals of the program'(Rossi et.al.1979).

(ii) Inputs

In the production relations model, inputs can be divided into resource inputs and non-resource inputs on the one hand and endogenous and exogenous inputs on the other. This can be summarised figuratively below:-

	Resource	Non-Resource
Endogenous	A	B
Exogenous	C	D

Endogenous inputs constitute those factors which are the experimental input variables. Exogenous inputs are those factors which are likely to mediate between experimental inputs and their effects or outcomes. The dimension resource/non-resource is a distinction between the tangible and the less tangible, between such factors as the amount of care and the quality of care. In the diagram, cell A would refer to resource inputs such as staff, a day centre or aids, whereas cell B would refer to non-resource inputs, not the staff time involved in care but rather the quality of care, the way in which it is provided. Exogenous inputs, as resource inputs in cell C would be features such as the housing or income status of an elderly person, whereas at the non-resource end, cell D would refer to such factors as health status, and the personal history and personality of the person. These distinctions make it possible to examine the effectiveness of different combinations of inputs, to different clients in various situations by observing the precise way in which they operate to produce outcome in conjunction with one another.

Endogenous (or experimental) Inputs

Endogenous resource inputs constitute those factors conventionally described in the economic model of production and in the setting of community care may include staff, such as home helps, social workers, district nurses, physical capital such as day centres and goods such as aids and adaptations. Although in principle, these inputs present the least measurement problems, being readily defined, obtaining appropriate data may be much more problematic. For example the recording of the utilisation of services is very variable both in form and reliability both within and between local authority social service departments, relatively few having compiled the basis of a comprehensive data system which can answer these questions (Gateshead 1978). Similarly, the accurate assessment of social work input to clients is only possible from a careful diary based system

of recording which has to be sufficiently acceptable for sustained
use. Again, the collection of data about the services provided by
District Nurses is costly as information has to be sought from each
nurse individually.

Non-resource endogenous inputs represent those factors which
are the less tangible components of care. In the Community Care
Scheme, great emphasis has been placed upon the matching of helper
and helped, to provide the basis for a caring exchange that is both
instrumental and affective. In the Coventry Home Help Scheme
(Coventry 1978) the increased affective input on the part of the
home helps was noted. Much of this data can only be obtained from
a content's analysis of casenotes and in the case of Community Care
from an analysis of contracts given to helpers.

One of the characteristics of more recent evaluative studies
has been the more precise definition of experimental input (Reid
1980). Sometimes the definition of inputs categories may be the
prerequisite of more detailed evaluative work, such as the work by
Grunow (1980) in developing a typology of the 'sozialstationen' in
West Germany, which have emerged in the provision of domiciliary care.
At other times the nature of experimental input may be intrinsically
difficult to determine. Such a problem can arise when the central
features of the intervention involves close and frequent interaction
with informal carers, which may be extremely difficult to identify,
such as a locally-based care scheme.*

Exogenous (or quasi)-inputs

Exogenous or quasi-inputs represent those determinants of final
outcome which, at least in the short run, are not themselves modifi-
able as experimental inputs. They are therefore exogenous to the
model. Resource quasi-inputs would include such factors as the
elderly person's income or housing which are clearly quantifiable,
and may have a significant effect on any attempt to provide community
care for an individual. Non-resource quasi-inputs would include such
factors as Health status, Mental health, Personality, informal networks, life events and lifetime experiences of the client which can
clearly affect the outcome of provision of care, perhaps by making
an old person more or less difficult to help. For a number of these
dimensions, their operationalised measurement is quite well advanced
such as the work by Brown and Harris (1978) which has examined life
events, and the work by Bergmann et.al. (1975) in developing a
screening instrument for identifying psychogeriatric 'cases'.

(iii) Costs

Any scheme concerned with the care of the elderly in the
community cannot neglect the question of the costs of care and by
whom these are borne. Concern will be expressed naturally about cost

----

* See for example the work being undertaken by Bayley in Sheffield
and Hadley and McGrath (1980) in Wakefield.

flows to agencies such as the Social Services Department, the Local
Authority or the National Health Service, but also there are wider
questions about the costs to the community as a whole as well as to
individuals such as families. The careful articulation of cost flows
to different parties must take into account the relevant cost
criteria, the time incidence of costs, the probability of such costs
being incurred in any time period and the need to estimate costs
through time at present values.

Even the relatively unproblematic data collection may prove
onerous as was noted in Coventry (1978) where '...actual extraction
of the information from the various accounts was a very large undertaking, involving a careful scrutiny of every item'. Another
problem may be that data is more readily available for experimental
than control cases. However, in other areas difficulties of a
conceptual nature emerge. The valuation of informal and voluntary
help may well vary according to different assumptions about their
opportunity cost. It might be reasonable to postulate the opportunity cost of a carer at zero if they would otherwise remain at home
but for another who would otherwise go out to work, that of part-
time work. Again, the accurate estimation of costs borne by relatives in caring for elderly members presents difficulty, there are
travelling costs, loss of earnings, time spent visiting and odd
payments for goods and services which must be included, quite apart
from the psychological and social costs which have been considered
as outcomes. Indeed as Wright (1979) has noted the availability of
informal help is a substantial cause of variation in the public
costs of community care. In the Essex study of the cost of community
care (Wager 1972), it was notable that different assumptions about
the value to the community of housing occupied by an old person,
were sufficient to tilt the balance either for or against institu -
tional care.

Reid (1980) has noted the increasing trend for researchers to
be involved in the initiation as well as evaluation of new interventions. In such cases it becomes of even more importance to identify
which costs are incurred due to the normal day to day running of the
scheme, which are due to the early investment in development, which
may be discounted over the life of the scheme and which are directly
attributable to the presence of research itself, and additional data
collection. It is the first two of these categories with which an
evaluation must be concerned, with the comparison of a new scheme
against the costs of more usual forms of provision.

(iv) Unique Qualitative Factors

Just as the likelihood of an elderly person's admission to
hospital or residential care will depend in each district on variations in local provision, so likewise will the pattern of community
care for the elderly vary. Strategies of care which are observed
in an evaluation may only make sense in the light of an understanding about the relationships occurring throughout the whole network
of care. Thus particularly good care for discharged hospital

patients may arise through the efforts of a particularly energetic local geriatrician; again problems may arise due to poor communication between one set of care-giving agencies and another, perhaps due to local factors. The varied natures of local communities provide different opportunities for care while different strategies may occur as a result of the differing philosophies or leadership styles of staff as noted by Hadley and McGrath (1980). Without a clear understanding of such contextual factors and the historical background of exchanges and decisions that are made, an evaluation could be in danger of appearing over-mechanistic and too rational. Such an analysis is built into the Kent Community Care Scheme (Davies and Challis 1980), the Wisconsin Community Care Organisation study (Applebaum et.al.1980) and its importance is referred to in the ACCESS study (Eggert et.al.1980).

(v) Experimental Design

Goldberg (1970) identified five criteria for the effective evaluation of a field experiment in social work, which are relevant for any form of community care. These were:

1) There should be two samples of clients which are as equivalent as possible and representative of the population under study.

2) The treatment which is under examination will be administered to one sample, the 'experimental' group; whilst the other shall be a 'control group.

3) The treatment which is being evaluated must be clearly specified.

4) The criteria of success of the treatment must be clearly specified.

5) These criteria should be measured in both groups before treatment commences and again at the end of the experiment. The assessors undertaking the measurement should be independent of the providers of the treatment.

It is interesting to note that two of the changes noted by Reid (1980) in more recent studies, conform to 3) and 4) of these criteria.

In most evaluation studies the equivalence of the experimental and control groups has been achieved by the method of randomisation. In such a design, extreme care is taken that every person in a target population has the same chance as any other to be selected for the experimental or control group. The result of such a procedure is that in the long run, any systematic difference between the groups will be averaged out.

However, there are occasions when the randomised design may not afford the best solution to data collection. Firstly, the method only ensures the equivalence of the two groups in the long run, and may not work effectively for the relatively small numbers of a social experiment where due to random allocation the groups will never be exactly comparable in any single instance. Secondly, it is argued that the allocation of cases to treatments on a random basis is unethical and offends a sense of social justice, particularly in service providers. It is noteworthy here that such a situation may generate deliberate changes in referral patterns. The Wisconsin Community Care Organisation noted such differences between clients referred to the scheme during the random assignment phase and before and after, (Applebaum et.al.1980). Thirdly, there are political difficulties for a public agency such as a local authority in under-taking an intervention which denies a service to some potential recipients on apparently arbitrary and irrational grounds. Fourthly, randomisation in a scheme concerned with community care might enable existing agencies to divert their activities from experimental to control group clients, which would mean the comparison was no longer between usual provision and a new service but with a modified version of normal provision. Fifthly, although it may be argued in favour of the randomised design that the assessor is 'blind' as to whether a subject is in the experimental or control group, in practice it is likely that the subject is likely to reveal whether or not they are receiving a new scheme.

An alternative approach to evaluation which faces some of these difficulties is the 'quasi-experimental' method (Campbell and Stanley 1966), which uses an artificial method of approximating towards the equivalence of experimental and control groups achieved through randomisation. The evaluator attempts to identify and measure a group of individuals comparable in essential respects to those receiving the experimental treatment, and by means of 'matching' the selection of subjects resembling by major characteristics the experimental group may be achieved. This has been the approach used in the Kent Community Care Scheme (Davies and Challis 1980). Firstly, experimental and control groups are selected from adjacent but separate similar areas, so that at the aggregate level, differ-ences in area needs and need-meeting systems do not arise. Secondly, the initial equivalence of the two groups can be approximated by pairing individuals, matching a partner for each experimental case most similar by a set of circumstances likely to be predictive of outcome. In community care for the elderly these might be factors such as health, informal support and age. One study has shown that the use of matching by such criteria can procuce a considerable gain in the statistical efficiency of measures even with a small sample. (Bebbington et.al.1978).

A valuable gain from the 'quasi-experimental' approach is the increased facility for identifying 'systems effects' of an interven-tion, the effects of changes in demand for services due to the presence of a new scheme. Thus it is possible that a new pattern of referral may emerge as a response to a new service which is dealing with previously unmet needs. The detection of such an effort would be simpler with the quasi-experimental design although matching of cases might prove difficult if a similar process did not occur in the control area. The randomised design might only be able to solve this problem at some political cost, perhaps placing the experiment itself in jeopardy.

It is notable that the quasi-experimental design has been adopted by several recent studies as offering the more manageable response to evaluation than the randomisation model. Thus, the derivation of a similar 'comparison' group in this way has been used by Hadley and McGrath (1980) in evaluating patch-based social services, in the Coventry Home Help Project (Coventry 1978) and in the Hove Intensive Domiciliary Care Project (Dunnachie 1979). The choice of experimental design ultimately must rest upon what is possible within the political and organisational constraints of evaluative research and the nature of the research questions themselves.

Conclusions

This paper has briefly examined, in the light of earlier imprecise findings from evaluative research, an approach which offers a more structured form to data collection and analysis in such studies and has examined the problems of choice of experimental design. The use of concepts from the language of another discipline can at times evoke unease in the reader but .... there is nothing about the approach that encourages the researcher to perceive complex human relationships as simple and mechanistic. In fact, the opposite is quite the case, for the approach more nearly matches the complexity of reality than any of the alternatives so far developed. The production perspective encourages us to be precise about issues which might otherwise be fudged and forces a more comprehensive account to be taken of the factors at work...' As long as we remember that we are arguing by analogy, that we are discussing a 'quasi-technology' based substantially on perceptions and assumptions of actors and not a true technology based on machines, nothing but good can come from the fresh insights that the perspective can offer'. Knapp (1979). Like any approach it must be tested against the insights that it can produce.

BIBLIOGRAPHY

Abrams, P. (1977) 'Community Care: Some Research Problems and Priorities' in Barnes, J. and Connelly, N. (eds.), <u>Social Care Research</u>, Bedford Square Press.

Applebaum, R., Seidl, F.W. and Austin, C.D. (1980) 'The Wisconsin Community Care Organisation: Preliminary findings from the Milwaukee Experiment' <u>Gerontologist</u>, 20.3. pp.350-55.

Bebbington, A.C. (1978) 'Improving the power of an experimental investigation in social work by the use of matching and covariance analysis'. <u>Discussion Paper 84</u>, Personal Social Services Research Unit, University of Kent.

Bergmann, K., Gaber, L., Foster, E.M. (1975), 'The development of an

Eggert, G.M., Bowlyow, J.E. and Nichols, C.W. (1980) 'Gaining control of the Long Term Care System: First returns from the ACCESS erperiment', Gerontologist, 20, 3, (1), pp.356-63.

Gateshead (1978) 'Social Services Real Time Computer System', Gateshead Metropolitan Borough.

Goldberg, E.M., Mortimer, A. and Williams, B. (1970) Helping the Aged, Allen and Unwin, London.

Goldberg, E.M. and Warburton, W. (1979), Ends and Means in Social Work, Allen and Unwin, London.

Grunow, D. (1980) 'Sozialstationen: A new model for Home Delivery of Care and Service', Gerontologist, 20, 3, (1) pp.308-317.

Hadley, R. and McGrath, M. (1980) 'Evaluating Patch-Based Social Services Teams: a pilot study'. Paper given at workshop on Recent Trends in Evaluative Research in Social Work and the Social Services, Stroud. (Policy Studies Institute).

Hodgson, J.H. and Quinn, J.L. (1980) 'The impact of the TRIAGE Health Care Delivery System on Client Morale, Independent Living and the Cost of Care', Gerontologist, 20, 3, (1), pp.364-71.

Knapp, M.R.J. (1978), 'Cost functions for care services for the elderly', Gerontologist, 18, pp.30-36.

Knapp, M.R.J. (1979) 'Planning child care services from an economic perspective', Residential and Child Care Administration, 1, pp. 229-248.

Kuypers, J.A. (1972) 'Internal-external locus of control, ego functioning, and personality characteristics in the old', Gerontologist, 12, pp.168-73.

Lawton, M.P. (1975) 'The Pheladelphia Geriatric Centre Morale Scale: a revision', Journal of Gerontology, 30, pp.85-9.

Mullen, E.J. and Dumpson, J.R. (1972) Evaluation of Social Intervention, Jossey Bass, London.

Neugarten, B.L., Havighurst, R.J. and Tobin, S.S. (1961) 'Measurement of life satisfaction', Journal of Gerontology, 16, pp.134-43.

Palmore, E. and Luikert, C. (1972) 'Health and social factors related to life satisfaction', Journal of Health and Social Behaviour, 13, pp.68-80.

Qureshi, H., Davies, B.P. and Challis, D.J. (1979) 'Motivations and rewards of Volunteers and Informal Care-Givers', Journal of Voluntary Action Research, 8, (1-2), pp.47-55.

instrument for early assertainment of psychiatric disorder in elderly community residents: a pilot study', Gerontopsychiatric, 4, pp.84-119.

Blenkner, M. (1967), 'Environmental change and the ageing individual' Gerontologist, 7, pp.101-5.

Brown, G.W. and Harris, T. (1978), Social Origins of Depression, Tavistock, London.

Campbell, D.T. and Stanley, J.C. (1966), Experimental and Quasi-Experimental Designs for Research, Rand-McNally, Chicago.

Campbell, D.T. and Erlebacher, A. (1970) 'How regression artifacts in education look harmful' in Helmuth, J. (ed), The Disadvantaged Child, vol.3, Education: a national debate, New York.

Challis, D.L. (1979) 'A case-review system for work with the elderly' KCCP Paper 45, Personal Social Services Research Unit, University of Kent.

Challis, D.J. (1981) 'The measurement of outcome in social care of the elderly', Journal of Social Policy, (forthcoming).

Challis, D.J. and Davies, B.P. (1980) 'A new approach to Community Care for the Elderly' British Journal of Social Work, 10. pp.1-18.

Challis, D.J. and Knapp, M.R.J. (1980),'An examination of the PGC Morale Scale in an English Context' Discussion Paper 168, Personal Social Services Research Unit, University of Kent.

Coventry, (1978) 'Coventry Home Help Project: Costs and Benefits', One day workshop-report of proceedings, Coventry Social Services Department.

Culyer, A.J. (1976) Need and the NHS, Martin Robertson, London.

Davies, B.P. (1977), 'Needs and Outputs' in Heisler, H. (ed), Foundations of Social Administration', Macmillan, London.

Davies, B.P. and Challis, D.J. (1980) 'A production relation evaluation of meeting needs: the Community Care Project', paper given at workshop on Recent Trends in Evaluative Research in Social Work and the Social Services, Stroud. (Policy Studies Institute).

Davies, B.P. and Knapp, M.R.J. (1978) 'Hotel and dependency costs of residents in old people's homes', Journal of Social Policy, 7.

Davies, B.P. and Knapp, M.R.J. (1980) Old People's Homes and the Production of Welfare, Routledge, London.

Dunnachie, N. (1979) 'The Hove Intensive Domiciliary Care Project' Social Work Service, 16.

137

Rossi, P.H., Freeman, M.E. and Wright, S.R. (1979) <u>Evaluation: a</u>
<u>systematic approach</u>, Sage, Beverley Hills.

Reid, W.J. and Hanrahan, P. (1980) 'The effectiveness of social work:
some recent evidence'. Paper given at workshop on Recent Trends in
Evaluative Research in Social Work and the Social Services, Stroud.
(Policy Studies Institute).

Sainsbury, P. and Grad, J. (1971) 'The Psychiatrist and the geriatric
patient: the effects of community care on the family of the geriatric
patient'. <u>Journal of Geriatric Psychiatry</u>, 4, pp.23-41.

Savage, R.D. Caber, L.B., Britton, P.S., Bolbon, N., Cooper, A. (1977)
<u>Personality and Adjustment in the Aged</u>, Academic Press, London.

Townsend, P. (1957), <u>The Family Life of Old People</u>, Routledge, London.

Townsend, P. (1962), <u>The Last Refuge</u>, Routledge, London.

Wager, R. (1972), <u>Care of the Elderly</u>, Institute of Municipal
Treasurer's and Accountants, London.

Wright, K.G. (1974) 'Alternative Measures of the Output of Social
Programmes' in Culyer, A.J. (ed.) <u>Economic Policies and Social Goals</u>,
Martin Robertson, London.

Wright, K.G., Cavins, J.A., and Snell, M.C. (1979) 'Research Project
on Alternative Patterns of Care for the Elderly' University of
York, Institute of Social and Economic Research.

THE IMPACT OF PSYCHOGERIATRIC DAY-CARE ON THE PRIMARY

SUPPORTER OF THE ELDERLY MENTALLY INFIRM

Chris Gilliard and Glenda Watt

While there have been several descriptions of day hospital
services for the elderly infirm, and various suggestions regarding
their role in the provision of care for the elderly, very few studies
have been reported which have tried to evaluate this type of service,
and none have concerned themselves with their effect on those who
bear the responsibility of providing the primary support of such
patients in the community. Our aims in this paper are threefold: to
describe the factors which led up to the creation of a day unit in
one Scottish hospital, to outline the purposes of the service and
show how these have developed since the unit started, and to present
some data that has been collected in order to try and measure the
impact of the service through the eyes of the supporters.

One of the major advances in the provision of services for the
elderly in the past 25 years has been the development of day care.
However, we do not have a society where the elderly can take part in
normal social intercourse and because the proportion of 'older'
elderly will be increasing in the next two decades, day care provision
needs to be developed further. What is day care? Confusion has
arisen over the terminology. Few people outside geriatric medicine
realise that there is a difference between the service and support
of day hospitals and that of day care centres. There is also
considerable variation in the uses to which the day hospital is put,
so that the term means different things in different areas of the
country. Despite this variation it is generally agreed that the day
hospital should be reserved for people with disabilities and not be
used simply as a refuge for the socially deprived and lonely, however
desirable that may be. It should not become a creche for the elderly.
Among the advantages of day hospital care is the fact that it conser-
ves hospital beds, the units are easier to staff, as they are not
open during unsociable hours and they are economically viable compared
with full time admission. Great flexibility regarding frequency and
period of treatment and attendance is also an asset. Psychological
stimulation and motivation for patients and support and relief for
the relatives are important products of day hospital attendance. By
contrast, day centres act mainly as socially oriented 'holding units'
run by voluntary organisations, social services or health authorities.
Clients may attend as long as socially desirable and as frequently
as vacancies occur.

Reasons for the Hospitalisation of the Elderly Mentally Infirm

Greene and Timbury (1979) have shown an increase in the proportion of dementia patients attending their day hospital from 46 per
cent to 90 per cent over a five year period. In their study, the

majority of patients were admitted to day care from the community, with the commonest reason for attendance - at least in the dementia patients - being, 'Family unable to cope'.

Why is the family unable to cope and what factors lead to their reduced coping abilities? We have recently completed a preliminary analysis of the responses of 65 supporters of day hospital attenders, the majority of whom are suffering from dementia. We used a 25 problem check list. Six dimensions have been identified through factor analysis. The first dimension is made up of the following problems which seem to represent a factor of impared self-care. This dimension is often apparent in analyses of disability amongst elderly patients, and is seen by many as the core of dependancy.

9 per cent unable to dress without help.
10 per cent unable to wash without help.
33 per cent need help at meal times.
23 per cent cannot be left alone for more than 1 hour.
16 per cent unable to communicate.

The second dimension represents social disturbance which is often apparent in analyses of disability, and appears here to be the second most important 'problem' area for the supporters.

35 per cent demand attention.
13 per cent physical aggression.
12 per cent temper outbursts.
 1 per cent wandering at night.
27 per cent noisy, shouting.

The third dimension represents physical infirmity. It emphasises physical infirmity not directly dependant upon mental impairment, but more on the physical health status of the patient.

30 per cent physically too heavy to move easily.
33 per cent need help at meal times.
 6 per cent falling.
20 per cent not safe if outside the house alone.
 3 per cent incontinence - wetting.

The fourth factor represents deterioration in personality, separate from the dimension of social disturbance. It is sex-linked, in so far as more men than women present with these sort of problems.

15 per cent bad language.
38 per cent vulgar habits.

The fifth factor appears to be a specific 'mobility' factor. It suggests that faecal soiling, in this population, is more associated with physical mobility problems, than either impaired self-control or overall physical infirmity.

7 per cent unable to get in or out of bed without help.

4 per cent incontinent - soiling.
18 per cent unable to manage stairs.

The sixth factor appears to be one of 'emotional demandingness'.
It seems unique to the problems of caring for the elderly mentally
infirm, and presumably affects the perception of 'burden' on close
relatives.

32 per cent disrupting personal social life.
36 per cent create personality clashes.
20 per cent not safe if outside the house alone.
23 per cent cannot be left alone for more than 1 hour.
29 per cent always asking questions.

These six dimensions have been identified as factors which lead
to the relatives seeking professional help and subsequently day care.

A Day Hospital for the Elderly

The hospital at which the study was done provides a psychogeriatric service for approximately two thirds of a Scottish city, covering
a population of 283,000 of 65 and over. During the last five years
there has been an obvious need to extend the psychogeriatric facilities
and, if possible, relieve the pressure upon the hospital beds. A few
elderly patients attended the wards as day patients, but this arrangement proved unsatisfactory due to shortage of space, staff and slow
recognition of the special needs of day patients and their relatives.
The inpatient population demanded most staff time and expertise,
leaving day patients to fend for themselves. The idea of a day hospital was conceived five years ago when plans for a new psychogeriatric
wing were initiated, but again due to shortage of space and facilities
accommodation was not found until the Easter of 1979. An obsolete
acute admission ward was commandered to accommodate the new interim
day hospital. The facilities proved to be excellent but one main
disadvantage prevailed - a second floor situation and the use of a
very temperamental lift.

The functioning role and aims of the new unit were based upon a
collection of ideas pooled by the Consultant Psychiatrist, Occupational Therapist and the Ward Sister. The main aim was to provide
an alternative form of treatment for the elderly mentally infirm and
maintain them in the community for as long as possible. In order to
achieve this aim it was obvious we had to provide an economic support
system for the primary carers of these patients.

The Supporters of Day Hospital Patients

The majority of patients attending the Day Hospital are supported
by relatives and professionals within the community. Of 54 day
patients, 43 per cent were married with the primary supporter being
the spouse, 31 per cent lived alone but were supported by visiting
relatives or professionals, i.e. home helps, wardens, 13 per cent
lived with their offspring, 9 per cent lived with a sibling, and

141

4 per cent lived with a professional helper. It was felt that such supporters had a need for discussion and support, therefore it was decided to hold a regular monthly relatives meeting. An invitation to meet in an informal group and discuss common problems was sent to all primary supporters. The first meeting took place three weeks after the opening of the unit and since then an average of fifteen supporters have attended each month. As time progressed, more skills were acquired and assessment of patient and relatives needs led to the introduction of many new group activities, most of which provided an excellent medium for assessment. During the weekly referral meeting, each new patient was allocated to a trained member of the nursing team. This nurse then undertook to assess the patient in his total environment, to make a plan of his care in conjunction with other team members, and to implement that care and evaluate the results. This task was made easier by the use of problem oriented notes.

The unit has now been functioning for over one year. Many ideas have been introduced, some have failed and have been disregarded, others have grown and developed. The Day Hospital is now regarded as a family oriented assessment unit, liasing with the primary care team to give an effective form of treatment and support.

Assessing the Impact on Supporters

The principal method by which the assessment data has been gathered is through questionnaires. Two questionnaires were employed copies of which are available. Very briefly, one has been concerned with the attitudes and feelings of the supporters at the point when their relative, neighbour, or tenant has been accepted for day care. The second refers to the changes that the supporters have observed following day care attendance for a period of between three and nine months. The data is very much provisional pilot study data, and subject to criticism on that count. It is hoped that, while not providing the ultimate answer to questions regarding the effectiveness of day hospital care, the results will be seen as raising useful questions regarding the development of services in this area, and also as providing some justification for the 'family orientation' of the day hospital.

The sample concerned refers primarily to a group of thirty patients and their supporters attending the day hospital. In some cases, only a proportion of these 30 patient supporter pairs have sufficient data to be described. In other cases, data obtained from two other daycare facilities will be introduced, gathered in a similar manner for comparative purposes. One of these units (where the sample size is ten) represents daycare with the minimum of input-in terms of the physical setting, fairly low level of activities, and minimal contact with relatives. The other (where the sample size is 15) represents a more comparable dayhospital service, with activity programmes and a relatives group, although with perhaps, less emphasis on specialised counselling.

142

The data to be presented from the questionnaire has also been supplemented with 'outcome' data, gathered from 45 patients for whom there is at least six months follow up information. This includes the thirty patient-supporter pairs, together with an additional 15 patients who had either been discharged or institutionalised or died before the questionnaire data was gathered.

The results of these pilot studies fall into five main categories. Firstly the results of outcome six months after patients began attending the day hospital. These results are concerned with the relationship between the type of support available, the diagnostic status of the patient and the extent to which the patient continued to be maintained in the community. Secondly, data will be presented regarding the estimated helpfulness of day hospital attendance, as far as the supporter him or herself felt it helpful and also as far as they felt it helpful to the patient. Thirdly, the advantages and disadvantages described by the supporters ensuing from day hospital will be outlined. Fourthly, the supporters' judgements of the changes occurring in the patient following day hospital attendance will be presented and comparisons made between the three day units. Finally, the results from a small longitudinal follow up of patients attending the day hospital will be presented to indicate the sort of subjective changes occurring in the supporters perceptions of their burden and in their feelings about looking after the patient.

In relation to the issue of outcome, the most important questions are, does the maintenance of the patient in the community seem a reasonable goal, and is the support offered by the day hospital related to who the primary supporter is?

Thirty four patients with clincial dementia and ten with functional illnesses have been followed up for six months.

TABLE 1

Outcome at 6 Months

Dementia Patients

	'n'	Still attending %	Died/in care %
Living with spouse	(16)	81	19
Living with children	(7)	43	57
Living alone, but supported (relatives, neighbours)	(11)	64	36

Functionally Ill

	'n'	Died/In care	Still Attending %	Discharged (Community) %
Living with spouse	(1)	0	0	100
Living with children	(3)	0	67	33
Living alone, but supported (relatives, neighbours)	(6)	0	67	33

143

As is clear from Table 1, more than two thirds of the dementia
patients were continuing to attend some six months later, and forty
per cent of the functional patients were successfully discharged.
It is apparent that for the dementing patients, living with a spouse
was an important factor in determining continued community life,
whilst living with a child or children was much less likely to lead
to such successful maintenance. It is also apparent that living
alone - even though regular support was generally available from
relatives, wardens etc. (only one woman was felt to be without a
'primary supporter') - is more commonly observed in the functionally
ill. This no doubt contributes in part to their emotional vulnerability.

On objective grounds therefore, it would seem from the outcome
data that the day hospital was having an important effect. How do
the supporters view the situation? Part of the second questionnaire
asked the supporters to judge how helpful they had found the patients
attendance at the day hospital some three to eight months after the
patient began attending. They were asked to judge the units' helpfulness from both their own and from the patient's point of view.
Data was gathered from the day hospital and the two other city units
to yield the following comparative results.

TABLE 2

Evaluation of Overal Helpfulness, by 3 'Units'.

	Unit 1 (28) %	Unit 2 (10) %	Unit 3 (15) %
V. helpful to self	81	40	63
Helpful to self	19	40	37
Unsure/no help	0	20	0
V. helpful to patient	39	20	38
Helpful to patient	36	10	38
Unsure/no help	23	70	25

The first point to be noted is that while day hospitals
are seen as helpful to both supporter and patient, generally they
are seen as most helpful to the supporter. The diagnostic composition in all three units was between 70 per cent and 80 per cent
dementia patients. Secondly, there is a strong suggestion that the
unit with the least facilities was seen as least helpful - despite
the fact that the relatives had of course no reason to be aware of
the alternatives. The day hospital with which we are mainly
concerned comes out rather favourably from the comparison, and seems
to justify the approach of the unit to the problems of both patient
and supporter. We have gone on to enquire what particular advantages and disadvantages the supporters of the patients at the hospital have obtained from day hospital services. Since this involved
an open-ended set of questions, we have had to group some of the

answers into a set of categories on rather arbitrary lines.

In general, the advantages reported are seen primarily in terms of the benefits experienced by the supporters. This has been our principal focus at this stage in data gathering. But it is apparent that the supporters often experienced some ambivalence about the respite that they now received. Relinquishing part of the role of caretaker, particularly for wives and husbands, involves mixed feelings .... One lady stated, 'At first I had a guilt complex about leaving him at the hospital, but now I realise the free feeling I have and somehow that has helped me to come to terms with his disability'. In all, 6 categories of advantages were reported. The most frequent (56 per cent) was describing a sense of relief, peace of mind, the opportunity to relax.... 'the strain has been lifted,' wrote one lady, 'and there is a feeling that some real help is being given.'.... another described, 'A feeling of less pressure and a thankfulness that you are standing by.'

The next most frequent advantage (34 per cent) reported referred to a feeling of time, typified in such responses as....'There is a great sense of freedom on those days he attends and I can go about with hardly a thought about my wife - but with the knowledge that she is being looked after and is well cared for....' or 'Knowledge that on two days a week my time is my own, I can shop and see to financial matters while he is out....' Other advantages reported include; advice and support from staff, patient's enjoyment in attending, supporter gaining more knowledge and patient getting extra stimulation. Few (3) supporters mentioned disadvanatges, and only one described any disorienting effect on attending day hospital. Certainly there is no evidence to assume that the change of environment one day after the other during the week brought any untoward effects.

But despite these advantages, did the supporters feel that there were any significant changes in the patients resulting from their attendance? Part of the questionnaire asked the supporters to describe what changes in the patients had occurred since they began attending day hospital. This data was also obtained from our own day hospital and from two other day units. While most supporters in all three units reported continuing deterioration in cognitive function, there was no general deterioration in the patients emotional state and behaviour. However there were interesting differences between the units. There was no change in our own sample very little change in the third unit and it was only in the second unit, where activities were more limited, that emotional-behavioural change continued to follow cognitive functioning in a deteriorating pathway. Such inter-unit variance is interesting, since it seems to demonstrate that difference in input and care do, in turn, produce differences at least in the eyes of the supporter. It argues against simplifying day hospital care into simply a 'granny sitting' service.

145

So far these rather piecemeal results have given only a cross-sectional view of how day hospital is seen by the supporters and how they feel they have been affected. At present, ten respondents from the overall sample have been given the first questionnaire and also had it repeated some two to three months later (together with sections from the cross-sectional questionnaire). The results are encouraging, though not of a nature whereby one can attach judgements of their statistical significance.

TABLE 3

Changes in 'perceived' burden - n = 10 supporters of dementia patients

Rated 'burden'	Initial	2/3 months
	%	%
None	0	10
Occasionally	60	80
Great	20	0
Intolerable	20	10

Self-description	Initial	2/3 months
(adjective check-list)	%	%
Optimistic	0	30
Managing	10	30
Irritable	50	50
Tired	60	40
Sad	60	30
Despairing	20	10

As may be seen from Table 3, there is some reason to assume that at least in the first months of attendance, relatives/supporters do report a slight lessening of the burden, and a reduction in the negative emotions that they experienced when day hospital care was first offered to the patient.

Our general conclusions are threefold; day hospital care can make a significant contribution to relieving the strain on relatives, it can provide an alternative service to the hospital at least for a time, and it is seen in a positive light by the supporters of the elderly mentally infirm.

How much the lifting of the burden and improved morale suggested here actually adds to the number of days that they continue to care is of course a further question, at which the present data can only hint. We hope to be able to go on to investigate such questions more thoroughly.

REFERENCES

Ussher, C.W.J. (1979) 'If Day Care was a Drug, You'd Never Stop Prescribing It', Geriatric Medicine: August 1979.

Fuller (et.al.) 'Dementia: Supportive Groups for Relatives', British Medical Journal: June 1979.

Arie, T. (1979), 'Day Care in Geriatric Psychiatry', Age and Ageing: 1979.

Green and Timbury, 'A Geriatric Psychiatry Day Hospital Service, A Five Year Review'. Age and Ageing: 1979.

ENGAGEMENT: AN IMPORTANT VARIABLE IN THE
INSTITUTIONAL CARE OF THE ELDERLY

Malcolm McFadyen, Tony Prior and Kathleen Kindness

Until recently, as (Miller, 1977) points out, 'psychologists who have looked at dementia have almost universally confined themselves to the problems of assessment, and the analysis of functional deficits'. Such assessment has naturally emphasised aspects of behaviour considered most central to the disorder, such as cognitive functioning, self care, communication etc.

More recently there has been an increasing interest of clincial psychologists in the care and management of the elderly confused. Here again there is often an emphasis on these central functional deficits. For example, Reality Orientation (Folsom 1967, 1968) which has perhaps attracted the most interest from clinical psychologists, postulates that many functional deficits are secondary to the central deficit in orientation, and that R.O. Therapy, by improving orientation will have a more general effect of reducing deficit in other areas.

This can be seen as a culmination of a quasi-medical approach of identifying the disorders of the patient and attempting to put these right. In other words while the terms and techniques of this kind of clinical psychologists are psychological, the basic approach is still a diagnostic/curative one.

An alternative model is currently developing where the psychological perspective can be seen as complimentary, rather than supplementary, to the medical perspective. At its simplest, the most useful psychological view of the patient is a person who is handicapped in leading a normal independent life. The goal of care becomes that of providing such help and conditions as required to allow the person to lead as normal and independent a life as possible consistent with his abilities. The approach thus emphasises the need to attend to all the persons behaviour and not just to that construed as illness.

If the goal of continuing care institutions is to maximise independence and normality of life, we need some operational definition of normality. To this end Kushlick and his colleagues have introduced the concept of engagement (Blunden and Kushlick, 1975) in an attempt to focus on an aspect of behaviour which relates to normality or quality of life. A person may be said to be 'engaged'.. if he is reacting with materials or with people in a manner which is likely to maintain or develop his skills and abilities. Conversely, a person can be said to be 'non-engaged' when he is 'doing nothing'. The person can be seen to be 'engaged' or not, and engagement can therefore be assessed by observation.

The advantage of focusing on engagement, as well as functional impairment, lies in the possibility of improving the quality of life of the institutionalised elderly, even if we cannot substantially reverse the behavioural consequences of their brain pathology.

Aim of Study

The suggestion that maximising engagement is a realistic goal with the institutionalised elderly demented patient, implies that engagement is, at least to some extent, independent of degree of dementia. We found some scepticism from colleagues on this point... 'They don't do anything because they are demented'. The first aim of the study was therefore to investigate the relationship between measures of engagement and measures of dementia-associated impairment.

A second problem is knowing what to expect in any attempt to maximise engagement - how engaged are normal old people? On informal visits to a particular Old People's Home we had the impression that the residents were generally more active than residents of most psychogeriatric wards, and we had noted a general atmosphere among staff of encouraging, but not imposing activity. We therefore made a comparison between Old People's Home residents and psychogeriatric ward patients, on measures of engagement.

Populations and Settings

The first population consisted of 30 patients in a modernised psychogeriatric unit. Almost all were diagnosed as 'globally demented'. All were women with an age range 68-86 (Mean 80). The care staff was 1 to 6, plus domestics.

The second population consisted of 24 residents (randomly selected from a total of 71 residents) in a modernised Old People's Home. A few were considered to be demented. There were 19 women and 5 men, with an age range 74-95 (Mean 84). The care staff ratio was around 1 to 11, plus regular volunteers (average 3 between 9 a.m. - 5 p.m.), plus domestics.

Method of Observation and Measures of Engagement

Each subject was observed once, approximately every half hour. 30 seconds of observation was allowed, if necessary, to clarify what the subject was doing. The observed behaviour was coded as follows: firstly, location; secondly, 'General Behaviour', whether sitting, standing, walking or lying down; thirdly, social interaction, whether one way or two way, and with whom; and finally, specific behaviour into the following categories:- Self Help Independent (SHI), Leisure (any non-deviant active behaviour engaged in for the person's occupation or amusement (L), Walking (WK), Other Active Non-deviant Behaviour (O), Self Help Dependent (SHD), Watching (showing interest in some aspect of the person's environment - physical or social) (W), Deviant Behaviour (DB), Asleep (A), Doing

149

Nothing (IN), plus a 'can't say between IN and W category (IN?W).(1)
The observer also recorded a brief written description of the specific behaviour and social interaction. In this paper location and
general behaviour will not be reported (there is little difference
in the two populations on general behaviour, and location is, of
course, largely specific to the setting). The total observations per
subject averaged 60 for the psychogeriatric group and 54 for the Old
People's Home group. The total period of observation was 2 days from
9 a.m. to 8 p.m., and one day 9 a.m. to 12 noon, for each population.

Three observers were involved for each group. Regarding observer reliability, after training, there was greater than 90% agreement on coding of specific behaviours and of social interactions,
between any 2 observers, on pre-experiment joint simultaneous
observations of 20 patients.

Measures

Two 'engagement' scores were calculated for each subject. The
first, 'Non-engagement', consisted of the number of observations
coded as A (Asleep) and DN (Doing Nothing). These scores were
expressed as a percentage of the total of observations for each
subject (Total numbers of observations varied slightly as subjects
were occasionally out of the ward or Old People's Home). This score
can be seen as a measure of the amount, or frequency, of 'engagement'.
The second score – 'Active Engagement', consisted of the number of
observations coded SHI (Self Help Independent), L (Leisure Activity),
WK (Walking), and 0 (Other Active Behaviour); here again they were
expressed as a percentage of the number of observations for each
subject. This score reflects, not only frequency, but the quality
of the engagement.

This second measure was selected to test whether quality of
engagement might be more related than amount of engagement to
dementia-associated impairment.

Since conversing is a particularly relevant form of engagement
in any group living situation, an additional score was calaulated
for each subject, reflecting the number of two way social interactions observed.

Impairment Measures

All subjects were rated by a charge or staff nurse, in the case
of the psychogeriatric ward, and by the warden, in the case of the
Old People's Home, on a scale developed by the investigators and
others for assessing deficits in orientation, memory, self-help,
mobility, communication and sociability, and physical handicap.

The reliabilities of the items, (calculated as the agreement
between 2 raters on 18 patients), varies from 0.50 to 1.00 (The Mean
is 0.69).

150

The orientation and memory items were combined to give a 'Cognitive Impairment' score, the Self Help items were combined to give a 'Self Care Impairment' score, and Communication and Sociability items combined to give a 'Communication and Sociability Impairment' score, all with ranges 5-25. Combining these three scores gave the 'General Impairment' score with range 15-75. (A high score reflects high impairment). Reliabilities (calculated as the agreement between 2 raters on 18 patients were, 0.94, 0.70, 0.86, and 0.96 respectively).

A factor analysis of the scale (Varimax rotation) give support for these item combinations. 3 main factors were identified from an analysis of ratings on 59 psychogeriatric patients. The first factor, (accounting for 65 per cent of the total variance), can be interpreted as a General Impairment Factor. Cognitive Impairment and Communication do not separate from the General Impairment factor. The second, (accounting for 12.5 per cent of total variance) can be interpreted as a Self Care Impairment Factor. The third, (10.7 per cent of total variance) as a Sociability Impairment Factor.

In an analysis on 54 residents from the Old People's Home, there were again 3 main factors. The first factor, (accounting for 52.6 per cent of the total variance) being again a General Impairment factor, but with Communication items coming out as the second factor, (19.7 per cent of variance). The third factor, (accounting for 12.7 per cent of the total variance) is again identifiable as a Sociability Impairment Factor. Self Care did not separate from the General Impairment Factor in this group.

In addition to the staff ratings, M.S.Q. scores (Wilson and Brass, 1973) were obtained for the Old People's Home population. The M.S.Q. is a brief questionnaire of 10 items concerning Orientation, Personal, and Current information.

RESULTS

Relationship between Engagement and Functional Impairment

Table 1 shows the intercorrelations between the Engagement scores; including the Social Interaction score, with the main Functional deficit scores from the ratings. Table 1a gives the correlations between M.S.Q., rated Deficit scores, and engagement for the Old People's Home population. All probabilities are 1-tailed.

The M.S.Q. is considered to tap a central cognitive impairment typical of dementia. It can be seen that the correlations between M.S.Q. scores and engagement scores fail to reach significance.

The correlation between Non-engagement scores and rated Cognitive Impairment is also non-significant for both populations.

The correlation between Non-engagement and Self Care Impairment is

151

TABLE 1

INTERCORRELATIONS: RATED FUNCTIONAL IMPAIRMENT AND ENGAGEMENT SCORES

		Self Care Impairment	Communication/ Sociability Impairment	General Impairment	Non-Engagement	Active Engagement	2-way Social Interactions
COGNITIVE IMPAIRMENT	HOME	0.60***	0.65***	0.89***	0.14	-0.24	-0.29
	WARD	0.66***	0.84***	0.90***	0.11	-0.34	-0.25
SELF CARE IMPAIRMENT	HOME		0.44*	0.86***	0.17	-0.35*	-0.10
	WARD		0.81***	0.90***	0.56***	-0.65***	-0.34*
COMMUNICATION/ SOCIABILITY IMPAIRMENT	HOME			0.76***	0.46*	-0.51**	-0.42*
	WARD			0.96***	0.35*	-0.46**	-0.32*
GENERAL IMPAIRMENT	HOME				0.27	-0.41*	-0.28
	WARD				0.38*	-0.55*	-0.32*

TABLE 1a

		Cognitive Impairment	Self Care Impairment	Communication/ Sociability Impairment	General Impairment	Non-Engagement	Active Engagement	2-way Social Interactions
M.S.Q.	HOME	-0.77***	-0.50**	-0.55**	-0.68***	-0.30	0.34	0.30

```
  * p 1   0.05
 ** p 1   0.01
*** p 1   0.001

   one - tailed tests
```

moderate and significant for the psychogeriatric group, but is not significant for the Old People's Home group. There is no obvious explanation of the difference in correlation between groups.

The correlation between Non-engagement and Communication/Sociability Impairment is low and significant for the psychogeriatric group and moderate and significant for the Old People's Home group. These correlations are not surprising in view of the overlap between Engagement and Social Interaction measures.

In both groups there is a low correlation between Non-engagement and General Impairment (significant only for the psychogeriatric group).

The intercorrelations between Social Interaction scores and Impairment scores are very similar to those between Non-engagement and Impairment scores.

The correlations between Active Engagement and Impairment scores show a fairly similar pattern to those between Non-Engagement and Impairment scores, but the level of correlation is higher throughout, with more of the correlations reaching significance.

The results indicate that the amount of engagement, as defined here by the Non-engagement score is, to a considerable extent, independent of dementia-associated impairment. However, the quality of engagement, as defined here by the Active Engagement score, is slightly more related to such Impairment; that is less impaired persons, when engaged, tend to be more actively engaged than passively engaged. More impaired persons tend to be passively rather than actively engaged.

Comparison of Groups

Table 2 shows how the two groups compared on rated functional impairment. It can be seen that the Old People's Home residents are minimally impaired, and the engagement pattern to be described for them can therefore be considered a 'best estimate of the engagement pattern of a 'normal' elderly population in an (enlightened) institution.

Table 3 shows the pattern of engagement observed in the two populations. The Old People's Home population spends, on average about 70 per cent of the time actively engaged, 10 per cent passively engaged and 20 per cent not engaged. About 50 per cent of the time is spent on 'leisure' activities, such as chatting, reading, watching T.V. etc. There is virtually no deviant behaviour.

The psychogeriatric population spends, on average 30 per cent of the time actively engaged, about 30 per cent passively engaged, about 35 per cent of the time not engaged, and about 5 per cent engaged in 'deviant behaviour'.

TABLE 2

RATED FUNCTIONAL IMPAIRMENT SCORES

		POSSIBLE RANGE		MEAN	s.d.	SIGNIF. OF DIFFERENCE (t-test)
COGNITIVE IMPAIRMENT	HOME	5–25		7.00	3.09	
	WARD			16.07	5.10	p. .001
SELF CARE IMPAIRMENT	HOME	5–25		6.88	3.65	
	WARD			14.80	5.48	p. .001
COMMUNICATION/ SOCIABILITY IMPAIRMENT	HOME	5–25		7.00	2.06	
	WARD			14.27	4.88	p. .001
GENERAL IMPAIRMENT	HOME	15–75		20.88	7.46	
	WARD			43.13	14.20	p. .001

154

TABLE 3

SPECIFIC BEHAVIOURS (% ages OF TOTAL OBSERVATIONS)

	ACTIVE ENGAGEMENT				PASSIVE ENGAGEMENT		NON ENGAGEMENT			
	DHI	L	WK	O	WA	SHD	A	IN	W?IN	DB
WARD	10	15	1	4	24	5	12	23	◁4	6
	30%				29%		35%			
HOME	15	48	5	1	9	1	8	13	◁1	0
	69%				10%		21%			

KEY:

SHI = Self Help (Independent)
L = Leisure
WK = Walking
O = Other
WA = Watching

SHD = Self Help (Dependent)
A = Asleep
IN = Doing Nothing
W?DN = Watching? Doing Nothing
DB = Deviant Behaviour

155

Table 4 shows the pattern of social interaction in the two populations. The frequency of social interactions did not differ in the two populations, and interactions in each recorded on about 12 per cent of all observations.

TABLE 4

SPECIFIC BEHAVIOUR: SOCIAL INTERACTIONS

% ages of total number of social interactions

	R <---> R/V	R ---< R/V	R -> S	S -->R	R<--->S	TOTAL as % of all observations
WARD	57	15	4	12	12	12%
HOME	82	5	1	1	11	13%

KEY: R – Resident
       V – Visitor
       S – Staff

156

There is **no** difference in frequency of two way interaction with staff, but the psychogeriatric group have more 1 way interaction from staff (usually instructions), more 1 way interactions generally, and fewer two way interactions between residents.

Obviously the normative value of the engagement observations are limited. However, in the relative absence of other date on 'engagement', the data presented here offer some guide for comparison with other populations and settings.

Discussion

If degree of dementia-associated impairment does not account for the variation in engagement, both within and between these populations, what does? Some of the variation is likely to be due to individual differences – some people tend to be more active than others. Some, however, is likely to be due to situational or nevironmental factors, the physical layout of the institutions, and the, for want of a better word, regime of the institution. Obviously, it is this potential for improving quality of life by change in the physical and social environment of the institution which is the most promising feature of this approach.

Returning to the earlier point of the need for a move away from the concentration on cognitive impairment to a consideration of 'quality of life' variables, it is suggested that, if the effects of such 'treatment' packages as reality orientation on quality of life variables e.g.'engagement', had been assessed, rather than the effect on cognitive functioning, there might be less pessimism about the effectiveness of such changes in regimes.

Conclusion

Reviews of literature (e.g. Woods and Britton 1977, Hodge 1977) show that there have been other attempts to assess, and modify, non-deficit behaviours, particularly social interaction. However, it seems likely that Kushlick's concept of 'engagement' could provide a more consistent and useful 'quality of life' variable in studies of behaviour change following changes in methods of care in institutions, and in comparative studies of 'quality of life' in different wards or institutions.

NOTES

1. Definition of engagement categories:

    SHI = SELF HELP INDEPENDENT: Any self care activity carried out without staff assistance.

    L = LEISURE: Any non-deviant active behaviour judged by 0 to be for the person's amusement or occupation. Watching television included here.

    WK = WALKING

O = OTHER ACTIVE NON?DEVIANT BEHAVIOUR: Active behaviours not falling into the above categories.

SHD = SELF HELP DEPENDENT: Any self care activity carried out with staff assistance.

W = WATCHING: Showing 'passive' interest in some aspect of the physical or social environment.

D.B. = DEVIANT BEHAVIOUR: Behaviour judged to show delusional, hallucinatory or unwarranted aggressive quality, e.g. physical aggression, talking to self, undressing inappropriately.

A = ASLEEP

D.N. = DOING NOTHING: Showing no involvement or interest in the environment.

W?W? = Observer unable to decide between categories DN and W.

2. Blunden, R. and Kushlick, A. (1975) 'Looking for Practical Solutions,' Age Concern Today, 13, pp.2-5.

3. Folson, J.C., (1967) 'Intensive Hospital Therapy for Geriatric Patients', Curr. Psychiat. Ther. 7, pp.209-215.

4. Folson, J.C. (1968) 'Reality Orientation for the Elderly Patient', J. Geriat. Psychiat. 1, pp.291-307.

5. Miller, E. (1977) 'The Management of Dementia: A Review of Some Possibilities', Brit. J. Soc. Clin. Psychol. 16, pp. 77-83.

6. Woods, R.T. and Britton, P.G. (1977) 'Psychological Approaches to the Treatment of the Elderly', Age and Ageing, 6,pp. 104-111.

7. Wilson, L.A. and Brass, W. (1973) 'The usefulness of the Mental Status Questionnaire', Age and Ageing, 2, p.92.

8. Hodge, J. (1977) 'Psychological approaches to the Management of Dementia'. (Paper presented to the Group for the Psychiatry of Old Sgem November, 1977, Gartnavel, Glasgow).

ATTITUDES OF RESIDENTIAL CARE STAFF IN
HOMES FOR THE ELDERLY

Gerald Evans, Beverley Hughes and David Wilkin

The emphasis placed on care of the elderly in the community at this conference is to be welcomed. However, the term 'community care' is commonly interpreted as excluding care in institutions. We feel that local authority residential care for the elderly should be seen as a vitally important part of the resources available to a community, rather than a separate and undesirable alternative to care in the community. Residential homes, situated in communities, provide 24 hour supervision for many elderly people who are unable for one reason or another to manage in their own homes. The staff of these establishments deserve far more attention than they usually receive as the providers of a basic community service for the elderly. In this paper we shall report some of our findings concerning the roles and attitudes of staff who find themselves caring for an increasingly disabled population in residential care. This paper is based on a small part of a major study of the management of physical and mental impairment in homes for the elderly, (Evans, Hughes and Wilkin,1981). However, before discussing staff roles and attitudes it is important to set the scene by providing a brief account of the characteristics of the resident population in homes as compared to long-stay hospital wards.

For the past 5 years a research team based in South Manchester has been conducting annual assessments of levels of functioning among the elderly populations of local authority residential homes, geriatric wards and psychogeriatric wards (Wilkin and Jolley, 1979, Wilkin, Mashiah and Jolley 1979). A modified version of the Crichton Royal Behavioural Rating Scale (Robinson, 1968), has been used to assess physical dependence and mental disturbance, the most recent data having been collected in July 1979. Table 1 presents data from selected items on the scale, comparing the populations of the homes and hospital wards.

Not surprisingly, the geriatric wards contained the highest proportions of non-ambulant elderly people (59 per cent) but there was a total of 70 (14 per cent) bedfast or chairfast people in the 14 residential homes surveyed. Despite the fact that none of the residential homes studied were designated as specialist homes for the mentally infirm, we found that they contained almost as high a proportion of disoriented people as the geriatric wards. In terms of total numbers, the homes were providing accommodation for more severely confused people than the long-stay hospital wards. Regular

Table 1. Mobility, Orientation, and Continency by Type of
Institution

| | Type of Institution | | | |
	Residential Homes n = 514 (100%)	Geriatric Wards n = 222 (100%)	Psychogeriatric Wards n = 56 (100%)	Total n = 792 (100%)
Mobility				
Independent	286 (56%)	24 (11%)	23 (41%)	333 (42%)
Mobile with aids	157 (31%)	68 (31%)	26 (46%)	251 (32%)
Bedfast or chairfast	71 (14%)	130 (59%)	7 (12%)	208 (26%)
Orientation				
Completely oriented	257 (50%)	73 (33%)	0	330 (42%)
Oriented in institution	159 (31%)	97 (44%)	20 (36%)	276 (35%)
Completely lost	98 (19%)	52 (23%)	36 (64%)	184 (23%)
Continence				
Fully continent	308 (60%)	82 (37%)	8 (14%)	398 (50%)
Continent if regularly toileted	128 (25%)	40 (18%)	28 (50%)	196 (25%)
Regularly incontinent	78 (15%)	100 (45%)	20 (36%)	198 (25%)

incontinence is commonly regarded as sufficient reason for admission
to hospital, but although the hospital wards were coping with
substantially higher proportions of incontinent people than the homes,
15 per cent of residents were incontinent and a further 25 per cent
were only continent if regularly toileted. The evidence, therefore,
suggests that non-specialist homes for the elderly are playing a vital
role in caring for many physically dependent and mentally infirm
individuals. This is in marked contrast to the view expressed in
the Report of the Royal Commission on the National Health Service
(1979)

> "Residential homes cannot care for those who
> are physically dependent and need nursing
> care or those whose behaviour is more than
> mildly disturbed".

160

An intensive study of the problems encountered in six residential homes with varying proportions of able and disabled elderly people was mounted by the research team with funding from DHSS. The study employed a variety of observational and interviewing techniques to examine the situation from a number of different perspectives. We were particularly concerned to examine the effects of managing a mixture of confused and lucid residents, from the point of view of its effects on the social environment, the residents and the staff. We shall concentrate here on the background role and attitude of staff, since these are largely ignored in the literature on residen - tial care of the elderly. It is indicative of the status accorded to care staff in homes that they are classified as manual workers. This and the lack of any recognised training or qualifications make it relatively unattractive as a possible career. However, the fact that homes are now providing a level of care which might formerly have been associated with nursing, suggests that more attention should be paid to the care providers.

The research team interviewed a total of 106 (78 per cent of the total) supervisory, care and domestic staff in the six residential homes studied. The questionnaire covered background, training, role perception, attitudes to residents and attitude to management. No major difficulties were encountered in obtaining the agreement of staff to be interviewed, and most were prepared to discuss problems and make criticisms of various aspects of the homes.

RESULTS

Background and Training

91 per cent of staff were female and 62 per cent were married. Their ages ranged between 18 and 62, care staff being slightly younger on average than domestics. 76 per cent belonged to social classes IV and V based on the occupation of the primary wage earner in the household. Domestic staff were not asked about their educational background, but 73 per cent of care and supervisory staff had left school with no qualifications.

In-service training following entry into residential care work was extremely limited and 51 per cent of care and supervisory staff reported having no training for the work they were doing, other than on-the-job instruction.

45 per cent of care staff had attended in-service training courses organised by the Social Services Department, although these commonly included little more than instruction in the basic techniques of home nursing and first aid. Three of the officers in charge were, at the time fieldwork was conducted, attending part-time courses for the Certificate in Social Services. All three found the course stimulating and of considerable value to them in their work.

Nature of Staff Work

We used data obtained from interviews and from observational

161

studies to compare staff perceptions of their roles with how they actually spent most of their time. When asked which tasks consumed most of their time, 72 per cent of supervisory staff mentioned administration 65 per cent of care staff mentioned physical care of residents and 97 per cent of domestics mentioned domestic duties. The fact that a third of care staff found that domestic duties consumed most of their time suggests that there was considerable ambiguity in the roles ascribed to care staff. Lastly, only 2 (both supervisory) members of staff reported that a majority of their time was devoted to tasks which might be classified as social care.

Observational evidence largely confirmed staff's own perceptions of their role (Table 2). A total of 628 observations of members of staff were made at all times of the day. The majority of supervisory staff time was devoted to administrative duties and domestic staff time to domestic duties. As suggested above, the care staff role was more diffuse and they spent equal amounts of them on domestic and physical care activities. In general, it is worth noting how little of total staff resources appeared to be devoted to physical and social care in comparison to domestic duties and administration. The 'other' category of activities consists largely of tea breaks, excluding meal times, which accounted for 16 per cent of the total number of observations.

Table 2.   Observed Staff Activity

| | Category of Staff | | | |
Nature of Duties	Supervisory	Care	Domestic	Total
Domestic	1 (1%)	62 (28%)	128 (66%)	191 (30%)
Physical Care	5 (2%)	63 (28%)	10 (5%)	78 (12%)
Social Care	11 (5%)	33 (15%)	9 (5%)	53 (9%)
Administration	140 (64%)	2 (1%)	–	142 (23%)
Other	57 (27%)	61 (28%)	46 (24%)	164 (26%)
Total	214 (100%)	221 (100%)	193 (100)	628 (100%)

Attitudes to Residents

Using data obtained from interviews with supervisory and care staff, we shall concentrate here on staff preference for working with different categories of problems. Staff were asked which types of resident they found easy/difficult to care for, and which they particularly liked/disliked working with. They were also asked to identify individual residents whom they felt presented various problems. Where possible their classifications were compared with behavioural ratings of the same individuals conducted by the research team. In the main, the labels applied by staff matched the behavioural

assessments. Thus, for example, those residents described by staff
as 'confused' usually scored 6 or more on a confusion sub scale
(range 0 - 11) derived from the total behavioural rating.

Before discussing the findings, a note concerning the use of
response categories is necessary. The questions put to staff were
open-ended, and they were, therefore, able to define categories of
residents in their own terms. Since many residents presented a
variety of different problems (e.g. mental infirmity combined with
physical disability) there was considerable scope for overlap in the
use of categories. In presenting the material we have used
categories which reflect the labels applied by staff, since our main
concern was with their perceptions of categories of problems. This
means that a category of 'non-physical management problem' may include
physically disabled individuals as well as those who were fully
ambulant, where the problem identified by staff was not the physical
management but the resident's 'awkwardness','uncooperative behaviour'
or 'ungratefulness'.

Although a total of 76 care and supervisory staff were inter -
viewed, response rates to questions concerning attitudes towards
caring for residents who presented different categories of problems
were variable. Of those who responded, 41 per cent described the
confused as 'easiest to care for' and 71 per cent said that they were
the group they 'most liked working with' (Table 3). In contrast, only
33 per cent found the physically disabled 'easiest to care for', and
nobody said that they particularly liked working with this group.
Some staff mentioned only specific individuals, feeling unable to
identify categories of residents. Most of the individuals mentioned
suffered some degree of confusion.

Table 4 analyses responses to questions concerning which categories of residents they found 'hardest to care for' and with whom they
'disliked working'. It should be noted that only 22 (29 per cent) of
staff felt able to identify categories with whom they 'disliked
working'. Nevertheless, it is clear that most of these disliked
working with residents who presented non-physical management problems
(excluding confused behaviour) and they also found this group
difficult to care for. They referred, in the main, to lucid residents
who were 'awkward' or 'ungrateful', most of whom were not heavily
dependent on staff for physical care. In other cases, although
residents were physically disabled, it was their attitude to the
staff rather than their dependence for physical care which presented
problems. A significant minority of staff found severe physical
dependence a particular problem in itself, but relatively few
identified confusion as a problem.

Discussion

The background and training of staff working in residential homes
for the elderly reflects the relatively low status and financial
rewards attached to this type of work. We feel that the virtual
absence of training for most care staff is cause for considerable
concern, in the light of the fact that homes are providing care for

Table 3.   Category of Residents Selected as Easiest to Care for
and with whom Staff Liked Working

	Easiest to care for	With whom staff liked working
Confused	25 (41%)	32 (71%)
Physically able	20 (33%)	0
Lucid	6 (10%)	0
Individuals	7 (11%)	9 (20%)
Other	3 (5%)	4 (9%)
Total (100%)	41	45

Table 4   Category of Residents Selected as Hardest to Care for
and with whom Staff Disliked Working

	Hardest to care for	With whom staff disliked working
Non-physical management problems (excluding confused behaviour)	36 (60%)	19 (86%)
Physical management problems	14 (23%)	3 (14%)
Confused	7 (12%)	0
Other	3 (5%)	0
Total (100%)	60	22

an increasingly disabled population of elderly people who might
formerly have been considered appropriate for admission to hospital.
However, despite their lack of formal training most staff are providing
a high quality of care under difficult circumstances. Any attempt to
improve standards through improved training should begin with an understanding of existing staff roles and their attitudes towards residents.

Interview and observational data from the present study suggests
that, whilst the roles of supervisory and domestic staff are clearly
delineated, those of care staff are more diffuse and open to interpretation. Respondents themselves identified a number of problems
arising from role definitions. Supervisory staff often felt that they
spent too much time on administrative duties and too little time 'in
contact' with the residents. Care staff felt that too much time was
devoted to domestic duties and insufficient to social and recreational

activities with residents. What was most evident from the observational data was how little of total staff time was devoted to social activities with the residents, and we have reported elsewhere the consequences of this in terms of low levels of engagement and communication among the residents (Evans, Hughes and Wilkin, 1981). These problems were only partly a result of poor staffing ratios which meant that resources had to be concentrated on the 'essential' aspects of daily life. The lack of an appropriate training encompassing social care, and the attitudes of social services management, which appeared to place more emphasis on cleanliness, order and book keeping than on the quality of the social environment, helped to reinforce existing patterns of behaviour.

Responses to questions concerning attitudes towards caring for different categories of residents produced some surprising results. Whilst confused residents are commonly acknowledged by policy makers as a problem in residential homes, the majority of staff found them easy to care for and preferred working with them. In contrast, they found many lucid residents, some of whom were physically able, difficult to care for and demanding. Physical care is accepted as part of the job, but coping with the 'moods' 'whims' and 'awkwardness' of those who could help themselves was unacceptable to staff. In short, they appeared to make a distinction between those who deserved to be cared for and those who did not.

There seemed to be four possible interpretations of staff attitudes to caring for different types of resident. Firstly, they appeared to find confused residents less demanding than lucid people.

'The confused are easier - not quite as demanding.
They're more dependent but less demanding'.

A distinction was made between demands of a physical nature and those of an emotional or psychological nature. Whilst the confused were physically demanding to work with, the demands of lucid residents placed psychological burdens on staff. However, it should also be noted that some staff found continuous work with the confused emotionally strenuous, and they welcomed the opportunity to have a conversation with lucid residents.

A second possible explanation of attitudes, which was referred to by a number of the officers-in-charge, was that staff found the confused more malleable than the lucid. One care assistant said:

'The confused - they're like children, you get
more out of them if you make it a game - you
can get round them'.

The analogy between dependent elderly people and children has often been referred to in the literature on geriatric nursing. May Clarke (1974), for example, in her study of long-stay psychogeriatric wards, suggested that the child analogy was regularly used by them and that, in order to achieve compliance, staff often adopted the role of teacher. It is interesting, in this context, that one of the

165

confused residents referred during an interview to being in school and to the teachers being 'bossy'.

A third possible interpretation is related to the child analogy in that the confused were seen as a substitute family by some care staff. In some cases this constituted a reason for entering employment in residential care:

> 'The family had grown up and I felt that I had
> to have someone to care for'.

Whilst these interpretations help to explain the attitudes of care and supervisory staff, we feel that a fourth possible interpretation, which arises from a desire to clarify staff roles and achieve higher status for care work, is important. Work with lucid, physically able residents is perceived as akin to being a servant rather than acting in a professional caring capacity. Even among those who were physically disabled, staff often felt they could do more to help themselves and consequently tended to view them as undeserving. In contrast, the confused were wholly dependent upon staff and therefore the legitimate recipients of professional care. Caring for such people enabled staff to adopt a role closer to that of the nurse with the implied increase in status and job satisfaction. They felt more confident in defining and meeting the needs of dependent people for physical care. Such an interpretation was substantiated in comments made by care staff about residents and by the widely expressed view that they should be relieved of chores, such as bed-making. Domestic duties were not perceived as consonant with aspirations to a professional status comparable with that of the nursing profession.

In conclusion, it seems likely that, for the foreseeable future, most local authority residential homes will continue to care for elderly people with widely varying levels of physical and mental impairment. Whilst those residents who are physically disabled and those who are severely confused require substantial amounts of physical care, we do not accept that this is necessarily best carried out by nurses in a hospital environment. Most physical care does not require the expertise of a trained nurse and it can usually be performed by care staff in residential homes with the support, when necessary, of the community nursing services. There is, however, a danger that care staff in homes will increasingly see their roles and their needs for training as closely akin to nursing, partly because this offers the prospect of an improvement in status through a process of professionalisation. We feel that a move in this direction would be a retrograde step for residential care, since it would tend to result in a neglect of other aspects of the environment which are important determinants of the quality of life in institutions. To the extent that the role of care staff requires development through training programmes, great emphasis should be placed on the acquisition of the skills necessary to manage the social environment. This is a key factor which distinguishes residential social work from nursing. Development along these lines would offer a potentially better quality of life for all residents as well as increased job

166

satisfaction for staff, who would be more able to see their role in broader terms than the provision of physical care for disabled people.

References

Clarke, M. (1974) <u>Working with Elderly Patients: Nurses Expectations and Experiences</u>, Unpublished research report.

Evans, G. Hughes, B. and Wilkin, D. (1981) The Management of Mental and Physical Impairment in Non-Specialist Residential Homes for the Elderly, Research Report No. 4, Research Section Psychogeriatric Unit, Withington Hospital, Manchester.

Robinson, R.A. (1965) The organisation of a diagnostic and treatment unit for the aged. In Psychiatric Disorders in the Aged, Report on a Symposium, Manchester: Geigy.

Royal Commission on the National Health Service, Report (1979) Cmnd 7615, London: HMSO.

Wilkin, D. and Jolley, D.J. (1979) Mental and Physical Impairment among the elderly in hospital and residential care, <u>Nursing Times</u>, Occasional Papers, pp 74,30,117-20.

Wilkin, D. Mashiah, T. and Jolley, D.J. (1979) Changes in the behavioural characteristics of elderly populations of local authority homes and long-stay hospital wards, 1976-7 <u>British Medical Journal</u>, 2, 1274-76.

PARTICIPANT OBSERVATION IN A HOSPICE

Geoffrey Sparks

Introduction

In the past dying was a familiar and public act with appropriate rituals governing the behaviour of the dying and those interacting with them. Death was seen as a collective destiny and led to a simplistic and unproblematic acceptance. (1) In contrast the structural and cultural changes associated with industrial society has led to a very different perspective on death. Contemporary culture has been portrayed as death denying with death replacing sex as the major taboo. (2) This has resulted in death and dying being associated with anxiety, fear and isolation. Death now occurs predominantly in hospitals and related institutions and, as a result, it has become 'hidden' and 'segregated' from everyday social settings and experiences. (3)

Sociological research carried out in American hospitals (4) has drawn attention to the problems faced by both medical staff and dying patients and their families, that have resulted from the institution- alisation and bureaucratisation of death within the hospital. Such research has highlighted the social and psychological processes associated with dying and has shown that terminal care is deficient at the socio-psychological level. The research also suggests that hospitals whose ideologies and organisational routine are oriented towards 'cure' do not provide the most suitable locale to meet the needs of dying patients. Similarly, psychological research (5) into the experience and processes of dying has aided our understanding of the psycho-social factors involved. The research and subsequent development of death education and training programmes stresses the need for openness about death and dying and suggests that if certain procedures are followed 'the experience of dying' can be less negative and painful. (6)

The increased knowledge and understanding of the dying process together with greater mass media coverage of the topic can be seen as a trend towards a less death-denying culture. Writing on the American context Kastenbaum (7) suggests that in the last decade we have seen the development of a 'death awareness movement' and an increasing quest for 'healthy dying'. The British inspired Hospice Movement has been at the forefront of such developments. The hospice approach to terminal care emphasises the inadequacy of the 'cure' model (the characteristic orientation of most hospitals) as being inapplicable to the needs of the majority of dying patients. It focuses on the 'care' of the dying patient, concentrating on pain control and the patients psychological, social and spiritual needs. The need for an appropriate model of care for terminally-ill patients is increasingly being recognised by health policy makers (8) the health professions and the general public. The hospice movement has played a significant part in this.

The major aim of the research now to be discussed was to investigate what has been portrayed as the 'ideal dying trajectory' - the hospice model of care. Utilising Glaser and Strauss' concept of awareness context it was anticipated that the hospice would be characterised by a commitment to 'openness' about death and dying and that communication and interaction patterns would not reflect the stress and problems depicted in previous studies of dying in hospitals.

The Hospice and its Care System

The hospice in which the fieldwork took place was established by an International Charitable Foundation in 1974. It is more commonly known as one of the Foundation's homes rather than a hospice, and was the first unit to be specifically established by the Foundation to provide 'care' for both terminal and convalescent cancer patients. Originally designed for 10 patients a new wing was opened in 1978 so that the home now cares for a total of 20 patients. The overall work of the Foundation is 'devoted to the relief of suffering on the widest scale'. It is particularly concerned that its homes never become 'institutional' nor the individual 'instutionalised'. The central philosophy is to try and give those resident in the foundation homes a 'family sense of being at home, each with something to contribute as an individual to the common good'. The Medical Director defined the purpose of the hospice as 'to provide support for those with terminal illness and their families/closest friends'. This support includes:

1. Medical and nursing care to relieve symptoms.

2. Truthful personal attention to the spiritual, psychological and social needs of each individual patient and family.

3. Flexible routines to allow for individual patient needs.

4. The skills of all staff working in a hospice must be concentrated on terminal care, so that an expertise develops in dealing with the problems of patients with terminal disease and their relatives.

5. An ability to attract and to work with volunteers in all stages of caring.

6. A sensitivity to the needs of individual patients and relatives. (9)

These stated aims have been outlined because they constituted the hospice concept in operation at the home and the day to day patterns of life within it. As with other hospices, the nursing staff have a clear commitment to the humanistic approach to patient care; care for the patient as a whole and attending to social, psychological and spiritual needs not just medical and physical needs.

169

The decision to accept a patient for care in the home is based on the following criteria:

1. Patients whose malignancy has entered a terminal phase,(10) and has changed from the curative to the palliative and require skilled terminal nursing care and/or medical control.

2. Those whose social conditions or isolation prevents adequate terminal care being given at home.

3. Short term planned period of care to enable a family or neighbours to have period of relief.

4. Supportive care and recuperation either between or at the completion of intensive treatment programmes of chemotherapy and radiotherapy.

In addition, a small number of patients are admitted at the instigation of General Practitioners, often to solve a 'crisis' in the patient's home situation.

The majority of patients are referred by consultants from district general hospitals and the regional cancer hospital. In the six years up to 1979, 409 patients had been admitted, drawn from a large geographical catchment area served by five different area health authorities. With the opening of further hospices (including another home for cancer patients provided by the foundation in one of the largest urban centres in the region), the majority of patients are now admitted from three area health authorities, and competition for beds is now lessening. The new wing, opened in 1978, has increased the number of admissions to an average of around a hundred in each of the last two years. Thus in 1978 there were 105 admissions, 4 patients were still resident at the end of the year and 101 patients had an average stay of 49 days. In 1979, 92 patients were admitted, 14 were still present at the end of the year and 78 patients had an average stay of 37 days. During the main period of observation the admission decision was made by the Medical Director and Director of the Regional Cancer Centre, since then the policy has changed and admissions are now decided upon by the Medical Director and Matron. While the home is not part of the national health service the fees (which in April 1980 were £147 a week) are primarily met by the patients area health authority. Patients are also invited to pay towards their costs although this is not a criteria for admission. There is a shortfall in running costs of over £40,000 which has to be met by the foundation. This is raised by the Foundation's fund raising activities including those of the home itself.

As indicated above not all admissions to the home are for terminal care, although these constitute the majority. Thus, most of the patients have reached the 'nothing more to do' stage and are at different phases of a progressively downward sloping 'lingering trajectory'. One important consequence of this situation noted during the observation period was that there was a continual focus on the needs of the individual patient, and this focus helped prevent

routinised procedures for dealing with dying patients from becoming
dominant.

As anticipated, and in accordance with the hospice concept, the
home has an open communication policy about death and dying. Some
of the structural conditions which it has been suggested contribute
to the existence of and maintenance of closed awareness contexts are
absent in the home. The dominant medical professional practice of
non-disclosure is absent. A necessary feature of the home's philosophy involves a preparedness to be open and frank about death and
dying and not to conceal the nature of the patient's true condition.
A commitment to open awareness is therefore seen as a necessary
feature of humanistic care. There is no explicit attempt however to
manoeuvre patients into open acceptance of dying. The stated
practice is that 'it depends on the individual patient'. The
orientation, including denial, which a particular patient takes
during his terminal trajectory is respected as a feature of that
patient's dignity, though everything is done to ensure the patient
does not experience anguish and stress. It is felt that even if
patients do not wish to explicitly discuss their condition they must
know they are dying. The medical staff look for any cues that imply
the patient might want to discuss the issue. Most of the patients
are admitted from hospital either to receive specialised terminal
care, or for care to overcome the effects of intensive therapy. Some
patients have not been told they have a malignant disease (ie cancer)
and many do not know the true nature of their prognosis. This does
create problems for the staff, for they then have to build-up not
only the patient's well-being but also their confidence and trust,
before making the appropriate disclosure.

Pain control is an important feature of patient care and the
medical staff of the home have developed expertise in this area. This
is a particularly important aspect of enabling patients to lead as
'normal a life as possible'. The home has found that pain control in
some of the hospitals from which patients are admitted is inadequate,
especially the problems associated with the management and specialised
care of patients who have cancer involving the head. Each patient's
pain is investigated in depth and 'managed' according to the needs
and pain threshold of the individual patient. Once the pain is
controlled and the appropriate drug regime developed these are
administered at four hourly intervals to ensure, as far as possible,
permanent relief from pain.

A further problem the home faces with some first time admissions,
especially those from hospital, concerns the patients experience of a
definition of the patient role. This has been based on hospitals and
wards geared up to the model of cure rather than care, with the
appropriate sick role, social structure and patient-staff relationships which maintain this role. The home does not look like a
hospital, and there are no resident doctors. The nursing staff have
to reassure patients that they are professionally competent, wearing
uniforms helps signify this. The patients soon realise this, and
find the home is capable of caring for them. Subsequently they tend

to identify with the home and their affinity changes from the hospital to the home.

The home is located in a former private house set in large and beautiful grounds on the edge of a village overlooking a valley in the Yorkshire Pennines. As a former family house it has all the characteristics and appropriate architecture which signifies a 'family home'; bedrooms (there are single and double), bathrooms, a lounge, dining room, kitchen and also a small chapel. All the rooms have large windows which overlook the gardens and view across the valley. Thus the architecture and structure contribute to the sense of 'homeliness', and being a member of a 'family' is an important feature of the home's philosophy.

Being fairly isolated the home is different from many other hospices. Most of its patients, homes, and therefore relatives and friends, come from anything up to 35-40 miles away. Therefore visiting is difficult, especially if it has to be undertaken by public transport, and tends to take place at weekends, although several volunteers visit and spend time with the patients. The isolation and distance from most patients' homes, makes the involvement of relatives in patient care, and contributions to the community/ family ethos more difficult to achieve. Similarly, there isn't a home care programme or day patient facility, though this has been tried. Therefore, unlike hospices in large urban centres with such facilities, many newly admitted patients (especially those who are terminal) have no prior knowledge or conception of the different model of care to which they are to be subjected.

As with many of the other smaller hospices there is no full-time hospice doctor. The Medical Director is a full-time consultant at a local hospital and normally visits the hospice twice a week, his work is supplemented by two local general practitioners who have two sessions a week at the home. The vast majority of care therefore is undertaken by full-time nursing staff under the day to day supervision of the Matron and her deputy. As yet, training facilities in terminal care for other health professionals are limited, but the programme is increasing. The ethos is not predominantly religious though there is a chapel in the new wing, and local clergy do visit. A Christian ethos does underly the Foundation's philosophy but religious conviction is not a necessary pre-requisite of employment or of admission. Finally, the services of a psychiatrist do not feature in the home's programme of care.

Methodological Framework

The major aim of the research was to 'catch the process' of life in a setting explicitly committed to the hospice concept. The concepts 'awareness context' and 'dying trajectory' were used as sensitising concepts. It was anticipated that the hospice model of terminal care would provide a normative framework for communication and social interaction within the home. To overcome the problem of feelings of marginality which is often associated with observation it was agreed that the author would be a 'known participant observer' and act as volunteer nursing assistant. This was aided and facilitated by sharing and acting as far as possible in accordance with the hospice model of care underlying the work activities in the home. The patients were not told of the research and interaction with them took place on the basis of nursing care. Talking and communication with them was facilitated by the fact that such practices with patients are an important feature of the care programme and humanistic nursing role. The main observation period took place over a two week period in the summer of 1979 followed by a further visit in 1980, most of the discussion centres on the earlier period.

The Nursing Role

The majority of nurses had developed a prior interest in and commitment to working with dying patients. Most of the qualified nurses had experience of working in hospitals prior to their present role; they had received their training and professional conception of their role within the context of the ideology and philosophy of hospitals centred on the 'acute care' and 'life saving' approach. When nurses were interviewed for a post, a commitment to terminal care nursing was emphasised and the model of care and the problems and difficulties involved in such an approach were made clear. Initially most new recruits were taken on for a probationary period, so that they could become oriented to the home's approach to nursing care.

The nurses were clearly committed to the hospice concept of care and the associated 'humanistic nursing role'. This approach, to which the home was especially committed, served as the 'model'/ideal type against which the observations of the nursing role were compared. The commitment of the home to 'enhancing the quality of life' entailed relationships with patients which were not highly structured and an overall preparedness to get 'involved'. In fact the matron stressed that nurses should get involved. The emphasis on the home being a 'community' and a 'family' was a reflection of this approach to relationships. Patients were referred to by their Christian names, their special likes and dislikes, and idiosyncracies, were catered for. This contributed to the family atmosphere and sense of community and reflected the nurses commitment to the patients. Patients got to know about the nurses and their families, what they were doing in non work time etc. Thus, there was a two way flow of involvement. 'Distancing tactics', used to prevent involvement and maintain a more detached nurse-patient relationship, were not in evidence.

The home had a commitment to an open communication system and disclosure of the real nature of the patient's condition. As indicated, not all 'short term care patients' had been told they had cancer, neither were the terminal patients told of their impending death. In such cases the doctors and matron undertook the major responsibility for disclosing the appropriate information, though all nurses had a contribution to make. The nurses accepted the emphasis on 'openness' and were prepared to discuss and broach the topic with patients. Conditions which contributed to the 'non-accountable of terminal care', which could lead to the avoidance of interaction with terminal patients were absent. Not all the nurses found talking about dying with patients unproblematic, especially when they were looking for the appropriate time and situation to broach the topic. As one nurse explained, 'it's a question of being able to find the right words'. The fact that many patients had not been told of their condition prior to entering the home did create difficulties and the maintenance of complete open awareness was at time problematic. However, this didn't appear to lead to stressful situations because the nurses were prepared to be open about the topic. Many patients were aware that they were dying, the nurses experience being that 'most people are'. However if the patient didn't want openly to discuss it and prepare for death in his/her own way then this was respected by the nurses. This was seen as an important aspect of maintaining patient autonomy and control of the situation.

Most of the nurses had not received specialised training in the psycho-social aspects of terminal care. Though committed to enhancing these features of the hospice concept, many were unfamiliar with the literature in the area. The more experienced staff had developed the appropriate strategies and skills for implementing this approach to terminal care and to a certain extent they acted as role models for younger and less experienced nurses.

The model of care in operation contains a model of acceptable dying; living as fully as possible until death, and being able to accept and face death without pain, anguish and distress. Though nurses respected and enhanced the identity and individuality of their patients and the ways in which they individually approached death and managed their dying trajectory, they did have typifications of 'acceptable dying'. Thus, the 'cheerful patient' contributed much to the ethos and community spirit of the home and set a standard for other patients.

Because of the home's admission policy patients were at differing stages of their illness careers. Although, as suggested earlier, this was a factor which helped to focus on the needs of the individual patient, a degree of routinisation of care was inevitable. Carrying out the nursing role in accordance with the hospice concept and in humanistic terms was still work; activities had to be planned for and they had to be scheduled, hence the shift system. A great deal of the nurses' work was concerned with the basic technical skills associated with terminal care, and managing the daily routine. Therefore, a considerable amount of time was spent on activities such as getting patients up, supervising meals, toilet care, the drug round, etc. When patients were confined to bed the work could be even more exacting, whether the patients were recovering from intensive therapy or in the last stages of their trajectory.

Though an element of routine was inevitable this was not bureaucratically rigid, and there was plenty of time available for interaction with the patients during these basic task-oriented routines. Helping patients to become mobile and as independent as

possible was an important feature in enhancing the quality of life
and contributing to their self-confidence and morale. Patients
autonomy and preferences were respected and not swamped into a
routinised system of care and pattern of work. If patients wished to
stay in their rooms rather than, say, eat in the dining room or
sit in the lounge, then that was accepted. If they wanted to go out
into the garden, or summer house, visit the pub or shops, then,
whenever possible, such activities were encouraged. The patients were
therefore less subject to routinised processing than tends to occur
in the hospital situation.

The argument suggested here is that there is a crucial difference
between hospice work routines and the routinisation of systems of
care which result in collective people processing. The observations
also suggest that much routine work takes place as a necessary feature
of terminal nursing care. It is further suggested that some accounts
outlining and advocating the hospice concept are rather romanticized
in that the routine, more mundane and perhaps problematic features
are glossed over.

Relationships between the nurses were characterised by a high
degree of informality, the more formal bureaucratic status hierarchy
of the hospital being absent in the home. Seniority did have an
important role in the care programme, such tasks as the drug round
and some specialised technical care being the responsibility of the
more senior, experienced and qualified staff. Good working relationships and a strong sense of camaraderie were important sources of
satisfaction for the nurses and contributed to the 'community ethos'
and the 'high morale'. This was outlined by one of the nurses in the
following way, 'We all rely on one another and each shift knows that
the previous shift will have completed all the work it is supposed
to have done'.

The colleague group provided mutual support in helping each
nurse to cope with the grief experienced when a patient who they've
known well and loved dies. Each nurse, including juniors and
nursing auxiliaries made a contribution to 'conferences' at the start
of each shift and at other times. Relationships with auxiliary staff
were also informal and facilities were shared. Their observations
and relevant comments on the patients were also welcomed.

The humanistic approach to the care of terminal patients was the
other main source of job satisfaction. 'I can do proper nursing here',
was a view expressed by many of the nurses. The commitment of nurses
to the patients and to the home was reflected in their giving up spare
time to engage in fund raising activities. Some of the nurses found
that they talked far more about their work when they got home than was
the case when working in hospitals. The emotional involvement with
patients did generate problems though; the colleague group helped but
some of the nurses stressed the need to be able to 'switch off',
particularly at home, in order to be able to cope. One feature of
their work that seemed strange, at least initially to some of the
nurses, was working with volunteers. However they soon got used to

175

it and the volunteers work was seen as a necessary and important part
of the home's philosophy of care.

The Patient Role

During the main period of observation there were 19 patients,
the majority elderly, resident at the home.

There were twelve women and five men. During this period two
of the patients died, a 51 year old man and a 68 year old woman.
They were replaced by two new terminal admissions, both men, one 49
the other 61.

As pointed out above, the patients were at varying stages of
their illness careers, reflecting the differing admissions criteria.
For the majority of newly admitted patients it was their first
contact with the home and the model of care was different to their
experience of the 'patient' role in hospital. The more loosely
structured and person-centred approach seemed strange at first,
especially to those patients coming from hospital. The nurses had
to convince them they were 'professional' and competent to care for
them. Often in the early days at the home patients behaviour was
more compliant and dependent, with expressions of gratitude for
everything that was done for them. In other words they saw control
of their role resting with the medical staff. Gradually as they
adjusted to the new situation with its different ethos and model of
care, they began to join in and become part of the community.

Control of symptoms, especially pain, gradually becoming
mobile (if previously confined to bed), getting to know the staff
and other patients led them to identify with the home and to feel
confident in the staffs' ability to care for and help them adjust
to as full a life as possible. Central to this confidence and
community ethos was the home's reassurance that they could return
after a period of discharge. This was demonstrated one afternoon by
the return of Jane from a period of radiotherapy who exclaimed 'I'm
glad to be home again'.

Great efforts were made to maintain and enhance the patients'
self confidence, autonomy and control over their illness/dying
trajectories. When seen from this viewpoint what might appear in
the outside world as 'mundane activities', for example getting out
of bed and dressed, take on a new significance. Such an activity,
with the assistance of a nurse, might take half an hour or more.
To Cecil, a terminal patient with cancer of the spine, it signified
another day, a day to be 'lived' not spent in bed. Though the act
of dressing demanded great concentration and effort, it meant that
he wasn't confined to the 'sick role', but able to join in the daily
routines of the home. This was important to him because it
emphasised his (albeit limited) control of the situation. Alfred,
a retired railwayman with a terminal malignancy primarily centred
in the mouth, had had the unpleassnt side effects of this cleared
by skilled care. As a result he had the self-confidence to visit

176

the local railway museum - an event that he greatly enjoyed.

The importance of the patient subculture and patient self-help has been noted in previous research. Four of the male patients who had been there some time, formed such a group. They visited one another's rooms and maintained each other's morale when feeling 'down!. The men and women in the home did interact, especially in the lounge and dining room, but friendship patterns and closer informal relationships appeared to be on a sex specific basis. During the observation period the patients' terminal condition and their own impending deaths were not significant topics of conversation, only one patient openly discussed it. This doesn't mean that a closed awareness context was in operation. Most of the patients knew of their condition and apparently accepted it but in their own way. Clearly the existence of a culture that is still not completely open about death creates difficulties and problems. Supporters of the hospice movement however, argued that such problems had been eased for patients dying under its framework of terminal care.

It was difficult for patients to avoid the 'phenomenon' of death for the signs were ever present. The death rate was high, for example there were 15 deaths in both June 1979 and 1980, although as mentioned above, only 2 in the main observation period. It was therefore a familiar phenomenon and patients often felt sad when one of their 'friends' died. The male group were saddened when one of the members, Joe, died and were still talking about him a few days later. Patients noticed when someone no longer came to the lounge. Furthermore, patients learned to read the 'signs' which indicated a change (downwards) in their trajectory. Not eating or being unable to keep one's food down was interpreted as such a 'sign' by the informal male group. They had observed that this was a feature of the last stages of Joe's demise and Sid pointed out that Ken was getting a bit worried because he hadn't eaten very well for a day or two.

'Death'

We have seen then that death and dying were not taboo subjects in the home; death was not 'physologically hidden'. The commitment to openness and hospice informed terminal care prevented this. The death of a member of the community was experienced as a sad event and was reflected in the 'mood' of the home. Certainly the nurses grieved over someone they had become involved with and had to give each other mutual support. However the 'sentimental order' was basically cheerful and convivial, interspersed with periods of sadness especially when large numbers of deaths occurred in a short period of time. The staff consoled themselves with the observation that things quickly returned to 'normal'. This did not reflect a cynical or psychological distancing stance, it was merely a necessary feature of the hospice concept of terminal care.

Patients weren't necessarily moved into a single room or 'hidden away' during the last phases of their dying. Eric, commenting on the death of his room mate, thought what a nice, dignified, peaceful death it was compared to the 'horrific' sights he'd seen during the war. He said, 'As far as I'm concerned there is no necessity to close the door when someone dies'. However, it was the practice to remove bodies as unobtrusively as possible. Hearses came to the side of the home and the coffins were taken out through the store.

Glaser & Strauss note that after the dead patient had gone from the ward the final disposition involves the staff bringing to a close the story of the patient's death and dying in their minds. Some patients' stories were more unusual or significant than others and seemed to be a major topic of conversation. A similar process was noted amongst both staff and patients at the home. The death of one old man who had been a terminal patient for several months was a matter of some concern. He had become 'anaemic' and it was suggested to him that a small blood transfusion might help his situation. He was very reluctant but finally agreed. However afterwards his mood and disposition changed and he progressively deteriorated and died. It was only after his death that it was discovered that his wife had died after a transfusion and that he had received his about the time of the anniversary of her death. In contrast, the death of a female patient who had been planning a trip to Lourdes was significant to the staff because she died a 'peaceful death'. What was of concern to the nurses was that she appeared to have no relatives, only her 'family' at the home.

The situation observed in the'home' indicated support for the view that the hospice approach to terminal care can lead to a less painful and stressful dying trajectory for many terminally-ill patients.

Conclusions

A number of difficulties and problems associated with implemen-ting and maintaining a policy of open communication by the home have been noted. One major difficulty was associated with the fact that prior to entering the home some patients had not been told of the true nature of their condition. Doctors and/or nursing staff then had to attempt to disclose such information. Some of the nurses found this a difficult task. Not all patients talked about or apparently 'openly' accepted their impending death. It was pointed out that such a patient definition of the situation was accepted by the home and seen as reflecting patient autonomy.

The limited evidence from the 'home' suggests that there are varying degrees of 'openness' in relation to the 'ideal' of complete openness. Thus, the portrayal of hospices reflecting open communica-tion policies, in contrast to those closed policies which are assumed to operate in many hospitals, is too stark and simplistic. The practices and difficulties of nurses and patients associated with 'openness' which have been outlined were interpreted as being in accord with the hospice concept and model of care.

178

But it is also possible to interpret the difficulties of achieving openness in the home as a reflection of wider cultural values surrounding death and dying. Most nurses find working in the home a rewarding experience but, as indicated earlier, the emotional costs are often fairly high. Thus, an alternative interpretation of the practice of 'respecting' a patient's non open stance towards dying is also possible: some nurses adopting it in order to maintain some 'distance' from patients. Some hospices use psychiatric support services for specialist counselling of both patients and staff. Such a service at the home, especially on the use of counselling techniques with patients, could give useful guidance and help in coping with the difficulties experienced.

The evidence concerning the capacity of the hospice approach to alleviate the distress and anguish often associated with dying from malignant diseases in particular, is positive rather than negative. However, there have been few sociological studies of patients in hospices of receiving hospice care and a number of features need further investigation. In particular, more longitudinal studies of illness careers may give further insight into the processes and problems involved in the transition from a sick to terminal patient role within the context of lingering dying trajectories. Finally, there have been few, if any, studies of admission decisions. It is suggested that it would be useful to have more systematic information about the processes involved and how such factors as conception of social need and the social location of patients effects such decisions.

REFERENCES

(1) P. Aries, Western Attitudes to Death, John Hopkins, 1974.

(2) P.Aries, op. cit., and H. Feifel, The Meaning of Death, McGraw Hill, 1959.

    G. Gorer, Death, Grief and Mourning in Contemporary Britain, Doubleday, 1965.

(3) R. Blauner, 'The Bureaucratisation of Modern Death Control' in H.D. Schwartz and C.S. Kart (eds) 'Dominant Issues in Medical Sociology, Addison Wesley, 1978.

(4) See the Glaser and Strauss trilogy -
    B. Glaser and A. Strauss, Awareness of Dying, Weidenfield and Nicholson, 1966.

    B. Glaser and A. Strauss, Time for Dying, Aldime Publishing Co., 1968.

    B. Glaser and A. Strauss, Anguish, Martin Robertson, 1977.

    and

    D. Sudnow, Passing On, Prentice Hall, 1967.
    U. Brim et.al. (eds) The Dying Patient, Russel Sage, 1970.

B.W. Buckingham, Living with the Dying, Canadian Medical
Association Journal, Dec. 18, Vol.15, No.12, 1976.

(5) J. Hinton, Dying, Pelican, 1975.
C. Murray Parkes, Bereavement, Penguin, 1973.
E. Kubler-Ross, On Death and Dying, Macmillan, 1969.
H. Feifel, New Meanings of Death, McGraw Hill, 1979.
E. Schneidman, Death: Current Perspectives, Mayfield, 1976.
A. Wiseman, On Dying and Denying, Behavioural Publications,1972.
C. A. Garfield (ed) Psychosocial Care of the Dying Patient,
McGraw Hill, 1978.

(6) See L.S. Shusterman, Death and Dying in Nursing Outlook, Vol.21.
1973.

(7) See R. Kastenbaum 'Healthy Dying', A Paradoxical Quest Continues
in Journal of Social Issues, Vol.35, No.1. 1979.

(8) St. Christophers Hospice and St. Joseph's Hospice, London.
Personal communication.

GROWING OLDER: ISSUES IN THE USE OF
QUALITATIVE RESEARCH
Eileen Fairhurst and Roger Lightup

In this paper we consider four issues. Firstly, we want to
identify differing methodological approaches to the study of age
and ageing, which allow us to distinguish between the notion of
chronological age as a correlate of behaviour with our notion of age
and time as a matter to which individuals orient themselves. Then we
discuss the approach used to get people to talk about growing older in
our study on the menopause and leading on from this to the ways in
which individuals do interpret and talk about this topic. Finally,
we suggest that tapping the meanings of growing older appropriately
calls for a particular theoretical perspective which, whilst in
itself not new (Johnson 1976 and Marshall 1978-9) has been largely
ignored in gerontological literature.

1. Age - Researchers and Actors Constructs

Without being simple-minded, a cursory glance through gerontological journals alerts one to the importance with which the notion
of age and ageing is endowed. The point is that this is done without
conveying the nature of the experience from the perspective of
individuals themselves. On the one hand chronological age is seen as
a category around which behavioural patterns are clustered. Age is
cast as an independent variable which is located within a search for
explanation requiring the postulation of causal relationships. Hence
a concern with memory performance and chronological age. On the other
hand an interest in ageing, as opposed to age, is expressed but this
seems to be with little recognition of a theoretical concern for
process which is implicit in its usage. (Johnson 1976b) A focus on
age as a variable provides a snap-shot which temporarily freezes
social life: the former is endowed with a pervasive explanatory
quality to the exclusion of recognising the contextual features of
social action.

Addressing social action in contrast to behaviour calls for an
alternative theoretical and methodological view of social life.
Within this perspective, matters of meaning and more specifically,
actors constructions, unfettered by those of analysts, are paramount.
Thus, while age is often used as a resource, in our approach, it
becomes a matter for scrutiny: how do individuals interpret an
abstract notion like 'age'.

One way of understanding individuals own experience of ageing
is to utilise longitudinal studies. Although this method has some
currency in American research on ageing, (Palmore 1974) there is
an important difference in that approach and the one we would
advocate. Though both are concerned with questions of subjective

meaning. We would argue, however, that tapping meaning demands a suspension of the researcher's hierarchy of relevance in favour of that of the individual being interviewed. For example, in the case of our research project, on the menopause, several individuals expressed concern about feelings of uncertainty about what would happen to them during this time. Though others did not voice such concerns we cannot say they were untouched by such considerations. The point is that some people saw this as a relevant matter for discussion while others did not. In contrast a more traditional approach would have asked individuals if they had experienced any feeling of uncertainty. In these circumstances it would be assumed a priori that this matter is of importance and the respondent would have been presented with the issue by the researcher. The answers given would allow presentation of material in terms of X per cent experienced uncertainty and Y per cent did not. In a thematic interview, the onus is on a particular individual to tell a researcher as much, or as little, as they want about a specific theme. In this way, our approach is akin to one of omission if a matter is not raised then it is assumed it is not of importance to the individual concerned.

2. Life History, Thematic Interviews and Talking About Growing Older

So far, we have identified two different approaches to the study of growing older. Now we want to look at some aspects of our own work in an attempt to suggest one way of approaching this topic. This is not to suggest an alternative cookbook approach but merely to focus upon some of the findings of our own research project which addresses individual's interpretation of age and ageing. Indeed this matter of growing older came to light in the course of using a life history approach rather than as a result of any preconceived ideas we may have had on the subject.

Our use of life histories has rested on interviews where the intention is to cover a number of areas but their precise order and formulation varies from context to context. It has not been unusual for individuals to talk about matters which we wanted to cover without prompting from us. The way we compile life histories is to move people through events in their lives and ask them for their thoughts and feelings about them.

A cornerstone of our approach is that we see the interview as a conversation, an opportunity to talk with people about what they think. Since most people are unlikely to be familiar with this type of interview we always stress that we will not be presenting them with questions expecting answers of the form 'yes', 'no', or 'never'. Rather we emphasise that we will be talking about such matters as children leaving home, the work they do, how they spend their spare time, as well as discussing health and the menopause. Instead of focussing upon one important issue menopause, incidence of arthritis, or whatever, we are able to locate the issues raised in the broad spectrum of individual experience and are able to assess the importance attached to a particular event by the people concerned. (cf. Stimson 1976).

A crucial ramification of this conversational approach is that it entails the researcher giving of him/herself in the encounter. Thus, rather than just taking from individuals, ideas are presented to the interviewees so that they can reflect upon them and either give their view or note that they had never thought about the matter previously. So, in contrast to the type of approach we have mentioned above, we talk with people about ageing in an attempt to locate its experiential aspects. In doing this we try not to put people on the spot and are careful to avoid formulating our themes in terms of why questions: in our culture, why questions demand because answers.

Organising an interview as a conversation allows people to talk at great length and depth about themes without the researcher being conscious of the necessity to fit material into the constraints of preconceived categories. But a conversational format may not be without its difficulties for those being interviewed. For example, one individual thought our approach was 'oblique'. He had not expected a life history approach but rather exclusively a consideration of matters relating to the menopause.

It may be that our experience of peoples' willingness to talk is an illustration of a 'Hawthorne effect': once the spotlight is put on an individual they grow to like it and continue to talk. Moreover, though there is a discrepancy in age between the researcher and the researched we do not find this a barrier to getting people to talk. On the contrary, life is seen as a shared experience. Individuals make this apparent when discussing matters of which they believed we would have little or no knowledge. Thus, references by them to educational qualifications would be in terms of School Certificate or Matriculation with the explanation 'We didn't have GCE's and such like in our day'. Similarly, when referring to National Service, men often remarked, 'but that would be before your time'.

We have, then, indicated the approach adopted by us to get people to talk about the meaning of growing older. Though we would argue a life history approach has served us well it is not without its problems which, in turn, raise issues for analysis. Firstly, people may be seen as straying from the point and one has to ask what is relevant and what is not. Secondly, and more pertinently for our argument, how does the analyst interpret the significance of material. As we will show in the next section, this is just as much a problem for actors as it is for analysts. This matter will be linked to our concluding remarks on the type of approach called for in studying individual's perspectives on growing older.

3. Individual's Orientation to Age and the Passing of Time

Before considering the way the people we spoke with viewed age and the passing of time, we should note that, whilst all were aware of themselves growing older, some had never thought about themselves as middle-aged: it was an age bounded category which did not apply to them. We would argue that this emphasises the problematic usage

of the term age as an explanatory device in gerontological literature.
Whilst age can serve well to pinpoint areas for exploration, the use
to which individuals put it must be contextualised in order to shed
light on the experience of growing older.

Clearly, people make interpretations which have recourse to
unique features of their biography, but, nevertheless, there are
discernible patterns in this process. Nor do we see it as part of
our task to apply measures of life satisfaction to what individuals
have told us. For the purpose of this paper, we are considering the
way four individuals viewed ageing and the passing of time.

Clearly, the selection of examples from this interview data
may raise the issue of validity, but we can return to this matter
in discussion.

It seems to us that while all four individuals interpret age and
the passing of time in terms of present experiences, two restrict
their concerns to the present and two relate present events to the
future. For the individuals we spoke with, the passage of time, and
especially attaining age 50, frequently referred to as a milestone,
is clearly signalled in terms of an awareness that friends and
relatives of a similar age are dying. In addition, a recognition of
declining physical power is met with a general slowing down of
activity. Mr. Sharpe put these notions into context when he said:

> 'They made quite a fuss of me when I was 50 last year,
> and I think it is being looked on as some sort of
> milestone - it's not all that wonderful, but on the
> other hand, this year I've lost two friends - one 49
> and one 50 - so there's a tendency to feel as if you
> get over 50 then you have achieved something.....
> I'm 50. I've tended to slow down a little bit. I
> can't do as much as I used to be able to do but I do
> what I want to and take a little more time over it'.

and Mrs Fletcher added her own perspective:

> 'I don't think you have all sorts of fears when you
> get older that you don't have when you're younger. I mean
> I can remember my father many many years ago saying that
> he dreaded looking at the paper at night, "there's
> always somebody that I know that's passed away" and it's
> getting like that with us now'.

Mr. Sharpe's and Mrs Fletcher's analysis provide an illustration
of Roth's (1963) notion of nench-marks as a way of structuring time.
For them, their age as it relates to the possibility of dying acts
as a reference point in assessing the passing of time.

Mr. Chapman's views on the physical manifestations of ageing
reveal his interpretation of the passing of time:

'I think it's sad but it's probably true that you
don't look closely at your partner day by day and
you tend to carry in your mind a sort of stylised
view of your partner that may be 20 years younger
than the present age. I think you'll find yourself
that you reach a stage where you don't grow any older
inside. Outside you do, but inside you're perpetually
28 or something....wherever you stop. But..... this is
really quite interesting and I wonder if this goes on
into old age. I hope I'll find out.....You get more
philosophical as you grow older and what you do realise
as years go by is how finite time is. I remember just
after I was 35 waking up one night, I normally sleep
like a log, and thinking, "Heavens, half my life has
gone. It's all down hill from now".... you realise
that time is finite, that when you're 20 you can look
forward to 50 years and at 50 you can only look forward
to 20 years, even assuming that you're going to have
the Biblical 3 score and 10'.

In talking about ageing and the passing of time he makes a clear
distinction between ageing of a physical body and ageing of a social
being. Nicholson (1980) reports that rather than fearing death,
people are interested in what is going to happen in later life and
they do not want their 'passing' to cause any trouble to those who
survive them.

Just as Mr. Chapman ponders on the possible ramification of the
passage ot time, so does Mrs Heath. When reflecting on past events
she notes:

'In your thirties you just have that confidence that
people treat you better really. I suppose you're more
mature and you've more sense.....nothing in the 40's
was exciting for me. Maybe when I'm 60 I'll probably
think my 40's were a good time, but at the moment I
don't really. I don't think they're bad, but I don't
think they're wonderful'.

Whereas Mr. Chapman homes in on the notion of an inner self and
changes which may or may not become apparent, Mrs Heath is concerned
with how the passage of time will affect her judgement of past events.
So, for both Mr. Chapman and Mrs. Heath, growing older is far from
an abstract notion. Rather it is a process, the interpretations of
which calls for assessment of the present in terms of the past and
future events. As McHugh (1968:24) puts it, 'This is because the
past influences the symbolic definition of the present, the
definition of the present is influenced by inferences about the
future, and the events of the future will reconstruct our definition
of the past'.

Mr. Chapman and Mrs. Heath explicitly acknowledge the problematic
nature of the passing of time and age. Given our approach which

emphasises actor's rather than researcher's definitions, then analysing such matters must also be problematic for researchers. Within the constraints of one interview we attempt to discern the processual nature of people's links but this can only be possible up to the present time. The significance of many of the things people tell us can only be appreciated retrospectively, by them as well as us.

Concluding Remarks

A predominant theme of this paper has been an emphasis on actor's rather than researcher's constructs in mapping out existential matters of growing older. We related our discussion to the ways this is done. We presented the teasing out of the significance of such meanings as a tantalising matter for analysis. We would argue that ascertaining such significance is appropriately done by a career analysis, which is explicitly geared to the notion of change. Much of our material calls for a 'second look', both by the researcher and the individual. A number of different methods could be adopted for handling this. One way could be to use data from a previous interview and ask for their feelings about them. Ageing is a process and assigning relevance to past events is not a once and for all matter. Practical problems, such as tracing people, may well be associated with longitudinal studies but we would argue that this should not deter people from embarking upon them.

BIBLIOGRAPHY

Johnson, M. 1976(a) 'That Was Your Life: A Biographical approach to later Life' in J.M.A. Munnicks and W.J.A. Van Den Heuval (eds) Dependency or Independency in Old Age. The Hague: Martinus Nijhaff pp.148-61.

Johnson, M. 1976(b) 'Medical Careers: A Biographical Approach'. Paper presented to B.S.A. Medical Sociology Conference, April.

Marshall, V.M. 1978-9 'No Exit: A Symbolic Interactionist Perspective in Ageing'. International Journal of Ageing and Human Development. 9(4): pp.345-357.

McHugh, P. 1968 Defining the Situation, New York: Bobbs-Merrill.

Nicholson, J. 1980 The Prospect of Dying, New Society, 53, 928: pp.399-401.

Palmore, E. 1974 Normal Ageing II Durham, North Carolina: Duke University Press.

Roth, J. 1963 Timetables NewYork: Bobbs-Merrill.

Stimson, G.V. 1976 'Biography and Retrospection: Some Problems in the Study of Life History'. Paper presented to the BSA Medical Sociology Conference, April.

THREE TRADITIONS IN LIFE-STYLE RESEARCH

Rex Taylor and Graeme Ford

In this paper we are concerned with the nature, usage and potential of the concept of life style. We are going to concentrate on usage and specifically on the way in which it has been used by three teams of American research workers.

Before we look at these American studies it is probably useful if we begin by explaining how and why we first became interested in the concept ourselves. In the first three months of this year we interviewed a sample of 619 men and women aged 60 and over living in their own homes in Aberdeen City. We intend to re-interview them on at least two further occasions over the next two years. Our main focus is on their coping behaviour and adjustment and we hope to be able to distinguish between successful and unsuccessful copers. In searching for the social correlates of success of adjustment we will, of course, begin with single variables like age, sex, marital status, living arrangements, and so on. But since most of these variables have already been cross-tabulated with adjustment, we have always been attracted by the possibility of using more composite variables. We were initially attracted by the idea of life style because it seemed to offer a supplement to social class. There are, as you will know, a number of practical difficulties in assigning an elderly man or woman to his or her appropriate social class. Thus, in our sample in which most of the men had already retired and almost half of the women had never worked, it did not make much sense to rely solely on a classifactory scheme which was based on occupation. We had a sample of consumers rather than producers and therefore it seemed more appropriate to try and classify members on the basis of their differential use of time - the only commodity they all had in abundance.

The concept of life style to which we were initially attracted was therefore 'nominal' rather than 'real'. For us it represented a preliminary classifactory device which might prove more or less useful and we were not at that stage interested in whether it also constituted some sort of existential reality for the people we were studying. This is now a major question for us and we are inclined to the view that it is only when life style is defined in 'real' terms - as a member's as well as an analyst's category - that it can make a useful contribution to social gerontology. This conversion from a nominalist to a realist view of life style was not instantaneous, there was no blinding light on the road to Damascus, but resulted from a careful consideration of previous attempts to utilise the concept.

187

We think it is useful to start with the Lowenthal, Thurner and Chiriboga (1) study because it adopts a clear-cut nominalist approach. Their typology is derived from simple counts of the number of activities a person regularly engages in and the number of separate roles he performs. This produces two pairs of opposites - the Complex and Simplistic pair represent hyperactivity and withdrawal respectively, and are virtual embodiments of the Activity and Disengagement theories of ageing. In the second pair the Focussed type posits someone with a wide role scope but narrow range of activities (eg. a man with a large family and nominal membership of many clubs but who spends all his time playing golf) while the Diffuse type posits someone with few roles but very active nevertheless (eg. a childless widow with few close friends who spends most of her time in various church and voluntary organisations).

Like other structural typologies of its kind, and we would mention Bott's distinction between those involved in open and closed networks (2) and Merton's distinction between cosmopolitans and locals, (3) this four-fold typology only has a preliminary classificatory function. It identifies four categories of individual on the basis of a crude or minimalist style and invites the analyst to go on and see if they have anything else in common. Given our own interest in 'successful' ageing we might, for example, want to go on and ask if those with simplistic styles are more or less successful than those with complex styles? However, once we ask such a question it is immediately apparent that there are many ways of acting out each of the four styles. For example, those classified as having a simplistic style could include a bedfast senile dement and a retired professor writing his magnum opus - both have few roles and engage in a limited number of activities, yet the content of their lives is very different. It is in short, a typology of <u>structure</u> rather than <u>content</u>. The authors acknowledge this limitation and suggest that it would be possible to elaborate on their four types by examining within each the differential salience given to the three domains of work, family and leisure. There is a paragraph in the 1976 book promising further analyses of this kind, but as far as we are aware nothing has yet appeared in print. While the Californian group have not extended the analysis in this way, others have. Perhaps the best known recent example comes from the Rapoports', whose approach is based on the premise that 'individuals develop their lives along three lines - work, family and leisure... (and) combine them in characteristic ways to form whole life style patterns! (4)

But while this may be the best known example we think it falls far short of the much more sophisticated approach taken by Maas and Kuyper in their remarkable longitudinal study <u>From Thirty to Seventy</u>. (5) We have characterised their approach to life style as one based on <u>content</u> but this is a relative rather than an absolute designation. Their typology includes structural variables similar to those employed by the Lowenthal team but the resulting types are mainly derived from the differential salience given to twelve domains of daily living. Collectively, these domains - they call them arenas - represent an elaboration of the family/work/leisure triology. Family - is disaggregated into marriage, parenting, grandparenting and family of origin. Leisure - into home and visiting, friendship and informal relations, clubs and other formal groups, church and politics. Work - constitutes a single arena, and the list is completed by the inclusion of health and preoccupation with death. In each of these twelve arenas Maas and Kuyper assess interaction, involvement, satisfaction and perception of change. It is an elaborate structure containing 88 separate life style components in all. They obtained scores and ratings for each variable and then used factor analysis to identify four life style clusters for males and six for females. Their method of working is complex and is perhaps best illustrated by looking at two of their life style clusters. Briefly, for husband-centred wives life style focusses on the marriage arena, their only high involvement is as a marriage partner and they do most things with their spouses. Their intimate circle is somewhat circumscribed - particularly with family members - and their core living area seems to be in and around the home. By contrast, for group centred mothers, life style extends beyond family into the arenas of clubs, church and politics. None of their satisfactions lie in either the marriage or the family arenas and they spend most of their time outside the home. Similar analyses are available for each of the remaining life styles but taking only the examples at hand, there is an obvious relevance for our interest in successful ageing. Consider reactions to widowhood. We could analyse these in terms of single variables like age, duration of marriage, education, social class, and so on, but it is highly likely that none of these would have the same predictive power that we might get from an analysis in terms of life style. If we turn our attention from reactions to widowhood to reactions to physical impairment or retirement the utility of their approach is equally apparent: a husband-centred wife being unlikely to perceive and react in the same way as a group-centred mother.

In defining their types mainly on the basis of content, Maas and Kuyper run the risk of assuming that equivalence of content means equivalence of function. There are many instances where this is patently not the case. For example, one woman goes to an Over-60- Club because she is lonely and depressed and the club provides her with daily company, another goes because she feels the need to help those she defines as less fortunate than herself, and the club provides her with opportunities for this work. Both spend lots of their time at the club for each woman it serves a different function and has a different meaning.

And so we move to the third approach we want to consider. Williams and Wirths' Lives Through the Years (6) comes from a re-analysis of panel data from the Kansas City Study of Adult Life. We have characterised their approach to life style as one based on meaning, but again this is a relative rather than an absolute designation. Like Lowenthal et.al. they are interested in the volume of activities and the number of roles held, like Kuyper and Maas they are interested in the kinds of things people do to fill up their lives, but their primary focus is on the meaning and value people attach to these things. For Williams and Wirths what finally determines a person's life style is not whether he spends most of his time with his grandchildren or his wife or playing golf or doing voluntary work but whether his basic orientation to interaction is diffuse or specific, affective or neutral and whether his long term relationships can be described as particularistic or universalistic, instrumental or expressive. Utilising these Parsonian criteria it is hardly surprising that their procedure for deriving life style types is based on their own ratings of interview material and not on the statistical manipulation of a large number of variables.

In the time available we cannot even begin to do justice to their rich and complex analysis, anyone seriously interested in ageing should read the book in its entirety, for present purposes we should restrict ourselves to two of the most relevant features, one methodological, the other substantive.

Methodologically, the most important aspect of their study is their attempt to go beyond behaviour to incorporate meaning and values into the definition of life style. For most of the cases they analyse there is an overall consistency between behaviour and value orientation but there are many examples of discrepancy, and in some cases value orientations take precedence in the final allocation to types. For example, one of their cases was a married 78 year old man living with his second wife but allocated to the Living Alone type because he wouldn't let her come near him either emotionally or physically. Another case involved a retired business man who sat around doing nothing but was allocated to the World of Work type because work had been his whole life, and despite his failing health he still hoped to be able to work again. Throughout the book there are many examples of this discrepancy between behaviour and values, between what people are able to do and what they would like to do. While Williams and Wirths provide no systematic treatment we feel that this discrepancy between behaviour and values has major implications for our understanding of social ageing. If we follow Thomae, (7) as we are inclined to, and define the real developmental task of old age as 'the continuous restoration of the balance between desires and achievements in a situation of increasing potential for imbalance', the process of social ageing can be viewed as an attempt to maintain an earlier or valued life style. With increasing frailty and various forms of deprivation this becomes progressively more difficult: some people cope by changing the behaviour components, others by changing the value components of their style. To the extent that they are unable to do so - and to maintain a balance between achieved and desired styles, they can be described as ageing successfully. It will be clear that our conversion from a 'nominalist' to a 'realist' view of life style is almost complete. Human beings, as Lazarus has recently argued, (8) are self-interpreting... they struggle to make sense of the content of their lives with their current self definitions'. Williams and Wirths come nearest to this view but even they do not give to self definitions the importance we now think they deserve. In none of the three studies we have reviewed has there been a systematic attempt to identify the subjects' self-characterisation. Both the California studies rely exclusively on constructs imposed by the analysts, and even in the Williams and Wirths study it is almost impossible to distinguish between their own and their panel members' definitions of the situation.

In terms of substantive results Williams and Wirths main contribution lies in their demonstration of the relationship between styles of life and 'successful' ageing. Each panel member's success was rated on two dimensions - autonomy/dependence and persistence/ precariousness, to yield four success categories: autonomous/persistent, autonomous/precarious, dependent/persistent, dependent/precarious. When style and broad success categories are combined the authors show that while it may be easier to achieve success in some styles - notably Living Fully and Couplehood - it is possible to be both successful and unsuccessful in all six styles. Thus, Williams and Wirths provide an effective refutation of both the Activity and Disengagement theories of successful ageing. Success, as they have defined it, is neither guaranteed by sustained activity not by gradual withdrawal. Moreover, and this is their main conclusion, each style has its own and somewhat different prerequisite for success. Their findings provide a clear pointer to the kind of research which social gerontologists should be doing, and we are amazed that so little progress has been made along these lines.

In our own approach to life style we have drawn on all three of the studies we have summarised. Overall, we have tended to adopt a 'real' rather than a 'nominal' view of life style but we have retained a strong interest in the more normalist and structural approach exemplified by Lowenthal, Thurner and Chiriboga. We have collected extensive data on primary group contacts, interests, hobbies and associational life and typical daily activities. The first data set will provide us with a number of quantitative and qualitative dimensions of interaction, eg. high contact/low contact, distant/intimate, close-knit/loose-knit, and so on. The second data set will allow us to classify sample members on such dimensions as active/passive, solitary/group and self-improving/utilitarian, time-filling/hedonistic. The third and most extensive data set, consisting of fairly detailed accounts of social activities in the four days prior to the interview will give us the opportunity to classify sample members in terms of the Complex/Simple and Focussed/Diffuse typology suggested by Lowenthal et.al.

This interest in structure notwithstanding our main effort has been directed towards eliciting our respondents' self-characterisation. We started by collecting together all the different life styles identified by previous workers. We found that there were around 15 and, after discounting those which were not sufficiently distinct and those which seemed inappropriate for a British sample, we finally arrived at 11 separate life styles. Our next task was to characterise these 11 styles in simple two or three line vignettes. This was not easy and our final agreed versions only emerged after

much piloting with ad hoc samples of old people. The 11 life styles
were defined along the following lines:

A. TAKING LIFE EASY

'Someone who feels she/he has earned a bit of a rest and
fills her/his time without doing anything in particular'.
(cf. Williams and Wirths' Easing Thru' Life with Minimal
   Involvement)

B. GREGARIOUS

'Someone who is very sociable. She/he spends as much of
her/his time with other people as she/he can and she/he
avoids being on her/his own'
(cf. Maas and Kuyper's Group Centred Mothers)

C. SOLITARY

'Someone who describes her/himself as rather a solitary
person. She/he spends most of her/his time doing things
on her/his own rather than with other people'
(cf. Williams and Wirths' Living Alone)

D. CHURCH-CENTRED

'Someone who describes her/himself as a religious person.
She/he spends a lot of time on church and religious
affairs'

E. SPOUSE-CENTRED

'Someone who shares everything with her/his spouse. They
have similar interests and when they are together they
don't need other company'
(cf. Williams and Wirths' Couplehood and Maas and Kuyper's
   Husband-Centred Wives)

F. INVALID

'Someone who feels unwell a lot of the time and her/his
health stops her/him from doing many of the things she/he
would like to do'
(cf. Maas and Kuyper's Unwell and Disengaged)

G. ALTRUIST

'Someone who spends most of her/his time doing things for
other people and feels this is the best way to spend
her/his time'

H. HOBBYIST

   'Someone who has a serious hobby or interest. It takes up
   a lot of her/his time and she/he would feel lost without it'
   (cf. Maas and Kuyper's Hobbyist)

I. FAMILY CENTRED

   'Someone who spends as much time with her/his family as
   she/he can and she/he prefers being with them to doing
   anything else'
   (cf. Williams and Wirths' Familism and Maas and Kuyper's
   Family Centred)

J. WORK CENTRED

   'Someone who describes her/himself as a 'doer' because
   she is busy doing some job or other most of the time.
   She/he doesn't often sit doing nothing and feels she/he
   should be using her/his time profitably'
   (cf. Williams and Wirths' World of Work and Maas and
   Kuyper's Work Centred Mothers)

K. FULL LIFE

   'Someone who lives a full life. She/he is an active
   person and is involved in a large number of outside
   interests and activities'
   (cf. Williams and Wirths' Living Fully)

   Our 619 sample members are currently being presented with
these vignettes and they are asked to rate each in terms of it
being very like, a bit like, rather unlike, and very unlike themselves, both as they are now and as they were when they were 50 years
old. We hope that this second rating will provide us with an indication of personal change and, in turn, an opportunity to explore
Thomae's suggestion that the attempt to maintain an earlier life
style constitutes the main dynamic in the process of social ageing.

   Turning our attention from the definition of life style to the
steps involved in the derivation of types, we do not expect our
sample members to do all the work for us. On the basis of early
returns we can only expect that a small proportion will define themselves as 'very like' one of the 11 vignettes and 'unlike' the ten
others. The majority see themselves in a number of our vignettes.
Moreover, our four point rating style for each vignette gives us an
overall matrix of 44 cells. Our analytic task will therefore take
us beyond the identification of differential salience to involve us
in the search for patterns or clusters, a la Maas and Kuypers. We
hope that some of the preliminary analysis will be available for
presentation at next year's conference.

REFERENCES

(1)   Lowenthal, M., Thurner, M. and Chiriboga, D. (1976), <u>Four Stages of Life</u>, Josey-Bass, San Francisco/London.

(2)   Bott, E. (1957), <u>Family and Social Network</u>, Tavistock, London.

(3)   Merton, R.K. (1949), <u>Social Theory and Social Structure</u>, Free Press, Illinois.

(4)   Rapoport, R. and R.N. (1975), <u>Leisure and the Family Life Cycle</u>, Routledge and Kegan Paul, London.

(5)   Maas, H.S. and Kuypers, J.A. (1977), <u>From Thirty to Seventy</u>, Josey-Bass, San Framcisco/London.

(6)   Williams, R.H. and Wirths, C.G. (1965), <u>Lives Through the Years</u>, Aldine-Atherton, Chicago.

(7)   Thomae, H. (1976), 'Bonn Longitudinal Study of Ageing', <u>Contributions to Human Development</u>, vol.3, Karger, Basel.

(8)   Lazarus, R. (1979), 'The Stress and Coping Paradigm', mimeo, privately circulated.

THE KENT COMMUNITY CARE PROJECT: PROBLEMS
OF REPLICATION ON ANGLESEY

Elizabeth Tarran

Essentially the Kent Project attempts to mobilise or generate extra help in the community to adequately meet the needs of the very vulnerable elderly clients requiring residential care. Aims formulated include the improvement of services to elderly clients by providing more flexible individually tailored services in conjunction with those currently available and more effective utilisation of resources either by postponement or reduction of need for residential care. To achieve these aims experienced social workers were provided with a decentralised budget allowing them to buy in local community services to supplement existing services the client was receiving from formal and informal support networks. This creative and resourceful response operated under three constraints:-

(a) clients accepted into the scheme had to be eligible for admission to residential care while preferring the option of continued residence in the community;

(b) an arbitrary weekly limit on expenditure for all departmental services per client was set at two thirds of the marginal cost of a place in residential care, so that limited resources should not be too narrowly focused upon relatively few clients and

(c) the workers could use knowledge of the unit costs of existing departmental services for decision-making about the relative appropriateness of different means of helping clients.

Fieldwork commenced in May 1977 with three experienced social workers working alongside a generic social work team in Ramsgate. Widely ranging activities were undertaken by the social workers to improve the quality of life of their elderly clients. To complement existing services, locally-based helpers were recruited to perform tasks for clients. These helpers worked for relatively small payments thus enabling project workers to provide practical services together with a good degree of personal contact. Potential helpers were recruited mainly by local press advertisements and they were inter-viewed carefully by project workers. Client and helper were matched on the basis of shared interests, compatability, skills and proximity, on the assumption that if helping was mutually satisfying for client and helper, then the possibility of either party 'giving up' was likely to be reduced. Financial rewards for helping were seen primarily as enabling, removing disincentives to helping, rather than acting as an incentive in itself.

The research tasks and objectives

From its inception, KCCP fieldwork was monitored and evaluated by research officers from the University at Canterbury. The research was based on a 'before and after' experimental design, whereby clients in the experimental area (Ramsgate) receiving project services for twelve months were matched, after selection, with similar clients receiving conventional services in a control area (Margate).

The main research aims were to:

(1) Identify benefit and outcomes accruing to the experimental clients after receiving project services for a year and compare them with those for clients in the control group;

(2) to identify and compare the costs to the Social Services, other statutory agencies and the community of maintaining clients in both groups in their own homes using project type and conventional services, and comparing these costs with the costs of the residential care that clients would have required had the project been unable to support them at home;

(3) to identify the motivations and rewards of persons recruited and used as 'helpers', and their experiences of the helping task, and

(4) to study the benefits to and experiences of those families who were supporting clients of the project providing additional and often indirect support.

All experimental and control clients were interviewed twice, firstly at the beginning of the twelve months, before the experimental group had started receiving project services, and then again after a year. The interview schedule gathered information about the client's current level of functioning and formal support being received, it also included well-tested measures of morale and depression. Services provided to clients were costed by carefully computing the marginal and actual costs of services received by each client from a wide range of services provided by statutory and voluntary agencies, the client, his family and the community.

Replication of the KCCP in Gwynedd

By mid 1978 preliminary evaluations in Kent indicated that the objectives of the schemes were being successfully met, the new packages of care were working satisfactorily and there was a substantial supply of paid and unpaid helpers willing to undertake the often arduous tasks. But since it was still undergoing develop-ment and refinement, in both practice and research, it was impossible to say how successfully such a scheme could be operated in an area with very different conditions, needs and resources. Further testing was necessary.

The reasons for a replication study on Anglesey can be summed up as follows. Firstly, to permit Gwynedd SSD to extend their ways of working with their frail elderly population in a way that was likely to be effective in terms of the clients' welfare and cost to the department. Secondly, to test the feasibility of putting the concepts

196

of the KCCP into practice in an area with contrasting geographic and
demographic characteristics. Thirdly, to establish the feasibility
of implementing the scheme within a different Social Services Department, where organisation, services and priority needs were different
from those in Kent. Fourthly, to contribute to the body of knowledge
on community care schemes, by adding to Kent data and finally, to
allow consideration of the problems and issues involved in replication.

By October 1979 the Project Organiser was in post in the Anglesey
Area Social Services office in Llangefni, the island's county town.
The research officer was based in the Social Services in Rural Areas
Research Project team of the Department of Social Theory and Institutions at the University College of North Wales (UCNW) in Bangor,
within easy reach of Anglesey. Plans were made for representatives
from the Social Services management and the UCNW research team to meet
regularly as a monitoring group to ensure that the basic principles of
the scheme were maintained and to make the necessary adaptations for
successful implementation of the scheme in a totally new environment.
At about this time the Anglesey scheme was given the name 'Gofal'
which is the Welsh word for 'care', thus giving it something of its
own identity.

General issues involved in replication

Any research that is a collaborative venture with a service-giving
agency is likely to encounter problems, be it a new project or a
replication of a previous or existing one. It is of great importance
that the welfare of the individual clients is not affected detriment-
ally by super-imposing on the agency a programme of research. To
minimise such problems, and yet maximising the value of the research,
it is important that there is close co-operation and understanding at
all times in the planning and implementation. To achieve this, time
spent in developing good working relationships and understanding is
unlikely to be wasted.

The original reasons for undertaking a replication rather than a
completely original project in Gwynedd have already been discussed.
However, in the early stages the advantages of replication were
perhaps more obvious to the management staff of Gwynedd SSD than to
the project organiser and the research officer, (hereafter termed the
project workers). The KCCP was seen as a package that had been tried
out and tested in one area, providing the basic idea of community care
for the elderly, the main concepts and principles which it embodied
and the documentation required for both practice and research purposes.
The inputs required from the SSD to replicate the scheme were finance,
the appointment of a project worker, a considerable degree of flexibility in social work method and its administration and, above all, a
sense of commitment. For the project worker and the research officer
having the core-elements and some documentation of the scheme already
worked out made a superficial understanding of it relatively easy,
but to absorb the concepts and principles to a degree that would allow
for further development or adaptation to the individual needs of
Anglesey seemed particularly difficult. These feelings remained for
some months with both workers and were only overcome gradually through

197

considerable contact with Kent personnel. Gofal benefitted from the experience and mistakes of the KCCP and we hope that the Kent workers have gained by seeing their advice and suggestions working satisfactorily in Anglesey.

Although not necessarily advantageous or disadvantageous to the outcome of the replication, the difference in baselines in Anglesey and Kent must be realised. In both areas the scheme had to an extent already been in existence on an informal level, in terms of people acting in a helpful and neighbourly manner to elderly people. Despite this, there were differences in community attitudes towards caring for the elderly and in the potential helper reservoir in terms of social class, mobility, age, time to help and type of tasks that would be undertaken. The rural/urban nature of the comparison also made for differences. The policies of social service, health and social security departments vary between Kent and Anglesey, thus affecting issues such as bed-blocking in non-geriatric hospital wards, the admission policies relating to Local Authority residential homes and the use of private residential homes. The policies and resources of the two Social Services departments differ as do the staffing levels and team composition. Skills, experience and expectations vary not only between the Ramsgate and Anglesey teams, but also within each team, so this affects the ease with which a replication is managed as well as its eventual outcome. It is perhaps worth stressing again that such differences do not make for an inherently better or worse replication, but rather force a replication project to develop its own momentum and identity.

As a response to the particular needs and resources of Anglesey, both Project Workers began to develop methods of work and focii of interest that were a little different from the original project in Kent. For example, the Project Organiser began to recruit helpers through the informal network, often using the client as a starting point, rather than recruiting all helpers by newspaper advertisements. He also developed a register of available helpers, recruited in a variety of ways, thus providing an immediately possible source of help in emergencises. Rota-working for two or three helpers assisting one client, and a considerable number of family support cases (i.e. where they get project support to continue caring for the client) are also features receiving greater attention on Anglesey. Likewise, the research officer for Gofal has developed some focii of interest and methods of work that are a little different from those in Kent. Lack of research manpower has meant that less can be evaluated in Gofal than in the KCCP. The degree of detail and breadth of focus in the costing of the scheme is likely to be less, and time may not permit interviews to be undertaken with families of clients. In the KCCP interviews with helpers, the main focus was on their motivations and rewards, for Gofal helpers it is hoped that a broader picture of their experiences can be gained.

To focus more clearly on the problems of replication three main types of problem will be considered, namely those specific to the persons responsible for putting the replication into practice, those inherited from the original project and those specific to the

198

replication project. Each type will be examined in turn with examples
given as experienced in Gofal.

Person-specific problems and issues

These are perhaps not so much problems as issues which may affect
the work being done by the replicators, and its outcomes. Any previous
experience of the original project or a similar one or a similar role
will be important. The previous training, experience and personality of
the individual will naturally influence his current methods of work,
expectations and attitudes. Previous knowledge of the geographical
area and its personnel and language will affect the workers in the
initial stages. In Gofal the experiences and training and background
of the Project Organiser and the Research Officer have been quite
different both from each other and from Kent personnel. This has
introduced new perspectives, methods of work and interests to the
Project, some of which were perhaps difficult to reconcile initially,
but have enabled Gofal to develop its own distinct identity. For
example the Project Organiser's previous experience in community work
has influenced his method of recruiting helpers through the informal
contacts of the client rather then through advertisements as in Kent.
Likewise the Research Officer's previous experience as a research
social worker was useful and perhaps compensated to some extent for
her lack of familiarity with the needs and problems of the very frail
elderly.

Problems and issues inherited from the original project

Within the group of problems inherited from the original project
three merit attention, the first of these being areas where the policy
and practice was still under development. For example it gradually
became clear that there was no particular level of physical or mental
functioning that indicated a person's need for residential care, but
rather a varied combination of factors, including social ones, that
were different for each individual. Without an established set of
operational criteria, the Gofal workers found it very difficult to
establish what sources of referral, other than SSD, might exist once
the scheme was publicised. Ascertaining the likely number of referrals
to Gofal was also difficult for not only was it likely to depend to an
extent on the numbers referred to the SSD team for the elderly, but
also on what was an unknown quantity, namely the extent to which
clients would agree to act as 'guinea-pigs'. This problem, which has
also been experienced in Kent, was gradually overcome as referring
agents became more familiar with the operation of the scheme. Another
issue which has caused some problems in Gofal has been that of costing
the scheme. Detailed costing of the KCCP and conventional services
has been important in ascertaining the relative costs of different
types of care. In the Gofal replication it was initially difficult
to ensure that the cost-data gathered would be on the same basis as
that for Kent. The main areas requiring greater specification were
to establish what components make up the costs of community care,
to ascertain how regional differences in prices and wages can be
accounted for (particularly important at the level of inter-project
comparison) and to establish how certain costs can be derived, for

example the cost of the travel element in the cost of a Social Worker visit. Discussions with and documentation from the Kent team have led to greater clarification of these issues both in Kent and in Gofal, thus reflecting the stages of development in the costings procedure in Kent, rather than a real problem of replication.

A second type of inherited problem is that which the practice and methods used in the original project indicate that refinements are desirable and/or possible. An example of this was the interview schedule for use with the elderly clients. It had been put together hurriedly in Kent, so Gofal shortened it a little and slightly amended it to make it more comprehensive and suitable for persons whose first language was Welsh.

A third group of inherited problems were those in which practice problems have remained unresolved or have recurred, despite attempts to resolve them in the original project. Several such problems came to light in Gofal. One of those experienced by the Gofal research officer arose out of the difficulty of obtaining sufficient and suitable control clients. As in the KCCP social workers had no motivation to refer apart from a lengthy interview (although clients usually enjoyed this). The demands of the research programme required a change of practice by social workers and met opposition from their protective attitude towards clients and their general lack of understanding of the need for research control. Despite being recognised in both the KCCP and Gofal this continued to be a problem for both projects, although sheer persistence in explaining the need for control clients and the need for periodic review of caseloads reduced it somewhat.

Administrative problems occurred in the KCCP and similar ones, especially regarding the payment of helpers, have been experienced in Gofal. In both situations the Treasurer's Department of the Local Authority have been unable to respond with the promptness and accuracy demanded by the nature of the community care projects. Retrospectively, a more localised financial administration, closer to the setting of the project organiser, would have been more appropriate to the needs of the scheme.

A problem affecting both the research and practice elements of Gofal, also inherited from Kent, was the detection of all suitable control and experimental clients, as some always managed to slip through into residential care, without being brought to the attention of the project workers. On detection, this problem was minimised but not completely overcome by attendance of the project organiser at meetings for the allocation of beds in Homes for the Elderly (part III). An unfortunate side-effect of using the same social services area for both experimental and control purposes was that the reduction of admission to residential care in the experimental area created more beds for take-up by clients in the control area, thus enabling them theoretically, to enter residential care at a lower level of need than would have occurred prior to the implementation of the scheme. This has been offset to an extent however, by using some of these beds for short-stay purposes, rather than allowing them to be

200

filled by persons barely requiring them.

Problems specific to the replication study

As has been indicated earlier, a replication study is likely to
be undertaken in an area with a very different baseline in terms of
geography, demography, resources, needs and policies and practices of
the different statutory agencies. Given these differences, certain
problems and issues are likely to arise because of the particular
environment within which the replication is taking place and within
the particular replication project, regardless of its environment.
Within this group of problems specific to the replication study are
four areas of concern.

Firstly, there are the problems encountered by the project
workers in accurately maintaining the core elements of the original
in the replication study. The way in which the concepts and philosophy behind the scheme are internalised greatly affects how it is put
into practice in a new area. The Gofal project workers had not been
involved in the initial concept developing stages of the original
scheme so their understanding was limited as to how it would work in
practice and exactly what type of client it would cater for. This
made it difficult, both for explaining the scheme to others, who
might make referrals or become helpers, and also in defining the type
of client it could serve and the type of service it could provide.
Naturally this problem was also experienced to some extent by the
Kent personnel, but their proximity to the hub of the community care
scheme development was much greater achieved by the Gofal workers.
For replication purposes this presented considerable problems in
ascertaining whether Gofal was accepting similar clients. Initially
there was a high number of inappropriate referrals, some too early
to make a Gofal input cost-effective, while others were too late to
be able to develop care packages suitable to prevent admission to
residential care.

Another problem specific to the replication study was the
development, shortly after the pilot project (which had lasted for
about 6 weeks of the pre-implementation phase), of some tensions
between the research and practice elements of the replication. The
project organiser was naturally keen to move ahead with the main
project while the research officer was still needing to comprehend
and internalise the research requirements and refine the research
recording instruments. An element of 'creative tension' was
experienced by both project workers as they gradually internalised
concepts of the scheme and sought to develop out from these, without
being sure of the parameters.

A third problem experienced by the replication study were the
expectations of others. The arrival of the 'Kent scheme', long and
eagerly awaited on Anglesey led social workers to expect the project
to provide a valuable additional resource and to relieve them of the
more difficult very frail elderly clients. The resulting pressures
experienced by the Gofal workers exacerbated their feelings of
unfamiliarity with the basic concepts and how they could be developed

on Anglesey. Prior to accepting clients, the project workers had to clarify several issues. Uncertainty had been expressed about the adequacy of numbers of suitable clients likely to be generated if Anglesey were to be divided into a control and experimental area as originally proposed. An attempt to make a more accurate prediction was undertaken by careful examination of the numbers of existing residents in local Homes for the Elderly, the waiting lists, and those on social worker caseloads who might shortly make application for residential care. Such a prediction proved more difficult to make than originally anticipated, and again it begged the question of what were the operational criteria for eligibility to enter residential care for the elderly.

Because workers had expected a fairly rapid development of the new project, since it was replicating something that already existed, the credibility of the project workers began to diminish with time as the new service did not come into sight. As a result, a small pilot project, involving only six clients, was started within the first two months of the pre-implementation period. This enabled some of the anticipated problems to be tested out, notably those relating to eligibility criteria, suitability of referrals, the locating of helpers and administration of the research interview schedule. The pilot project proved more successful than anticipated; some of the above problems began to diminish and a feel for the type of client and possible helpers gradually developed. The credibility of the project workers improved and social workers were able to see the scheme in operation and thus contribute their ideas to the development of the replication exercise.

Lastly, the fourth type of problem specific to the replication study was where external unexpected developments and changes occurred which influenced the development of the project. Outlined above are the difficulties experienced in predicting accurately the probable numbers of clients likely to be referred to the project, basing the predictions on extrapolation of past referral patterns. To complicate this an unexpected change was that actual referrals to the social services team for the elderly dropped by roughly a third over the late winter months, probably as a result of the relatively mild weather. Contingency arrangements had to be made to extend the whole scheme into another area of Gwynedd SSD should the required number of referrals be unforthcoming. After six months of implementation, a firm decision was made to extend the project to the adjacent social services district in Arfon.

A final unexpected development to affect Gofal was the large cutback in expenditure by Gwynedd SSD as a response to the worsening national economic situation. Although the Gofal budget was not reduced, it became crucial to ensure that the scheme was not only being cost-effective, but also providing a service demonstrably different from the Home-Help and Good Neighbour services that were experiencing drastic reductions in their budget. It became essential that clients receiving Gofal services were really on the borderline of requiring residential care and that it was not just a glorified Home-Help service that was being offered. It therefore became increasingly important that helpers should gradually interweave with existing support networks. Also, where a home help was already involved, she was offered the possibility of Gofal work in addition to home help duties, thus minimising any possible relationship difficulties that might occur. That this was practicable at all was only made possible by the fact that the SSD employed a large number of casual and part-time home helps who represented a substantial pool of available Gofal helpers.

The extension of Gofal into the Arfon area SSD has allowed many of these problems of replication to be considered. Some of those experienced in Anglesey, recurred, such as inappropriate referrals from social workers, and administrative difficulties regarding payment of helpers. However, eliciting suitable referrals for control and experimental groups was achieved much more quickly in Arfon as the project workers had six months experience in Anglesey on which to draw. Unfortunately difficulties regarding payment of helpers has persisted.

SOME PROBLEMS IN THE EVALUATION OF A
NEW PSYCHOGERIATRIC DAY HOSPITAL

Gilbert Smith

Introduction

This paper discusses some of the practical, conceptual and
methodological problems of research design which have been encountered during the early phase of planning and launching a study of the
developing services of a new psychogeriatric day hospital. The study
originated as an 'evaluative' exercise but the distinctive features
of the research have derived from the fact that it is apparent that
the most usual 'rationalistic' ways of thinking about evaluation in
health care may have major weaknesses in this context. This is
because there are a range of different views about specific service
objectives, criteria of success and defined relevant outcomes,
because the controls of the 'experimental method' are not possible
and because much often remains to be done in describing the precise
nature of the service itself. Thus rather than attempting a priori
specification it is first necessary to establish empirically the
nature of the service and the range of different objectives, notions
of success and outcomes that are in fact being pursued.

The study described here therefore has a dual focus. By
describing the way in which one new hospital is operating, the
research seeks to contribute to our understanding of the nature and
development of psychogeriatric day hospital services. Through this
description the research also explores the problems of embarking upon
evaluative research in this field. In summary, these aims may be
described as, first, to provide an account of the services of a new
psychogeriatric day hospital and suggest what factors may be most
influential on the course of this development and, second, to explore
some of the conceptual and methodological problems of evaluating new
health services with particular reference to 'defining objectives',
'measuring outcomes' and 'determining criteria of success'. This
latter aim will entail describing the different purposes for the
hospital, held and acted upon, by different groups, at different

---

* The project described here is supported by a grant from the
Scottish Home and Health Department to the Department of Social
Administration and Social Work, University of Glasgow, where the
research is based. I am particularly grateful to the hospital
staff who are co-operating in the research.

times, in different contexts, for different reasons and with different effects. It is a basic premise of this research that without the empirical study of these differences any attempt to evaluate a service the nature of which has not been established, on the basis of criteria the relevance of which is debatable, is entirely premature.

History of the Research Design

Just as medical institutions change over time, depart from ideal blueprints and are subject to extraneous variables, so also the same is true of research designs. The plans for the research described here represent the outcome of several months of discussion between the various parties to the research enterprise. It may be useful to review briefly some features of the sequence of events during the early part of the research both because the activities of launching and commissioning a project have an important bearing upon the design of evaluative research and because this project probably has much in common with other evaluative studies in this respect. In particular, although strictly speaking the project is not a commissioned piece of work since it is supported as the result of a research proposal from a grant applicant to a funding body, it did arise in part at the initiative of the relevant Health Board and through discussions between representatives of the Health Board and a government agency. These initiatives were largely responsible for the timing of the research, its location and the research problem in embryonic form.

In the autumn of 1979 one of the Health Board's Community Medicine Specialists responded to the funding body's publicly expressed interest in 'naturally occurring experiments' in the health service, by indicating considerable local interest in the evaluation of a new psychogeriatric day hospital which became operational in October 1979. I then began to explore the possibilities for an evaluative study. I visited the hospital and Health Board Offices in December and prepared a discussion note which served as the basis for a small grant in support of preliminary research.

Throughout this first phase of the negotiations a number of points were widely shared. There was a sense of urgency; the research should start as soon as possible. Otherwise there seemed little point in having selected a new hospital in the first place. Ideally the research would have started when the hospital opened. This is often the case with evaluative studies. The designs that first come to mind often require the research to be established in advance of the service being evaluated yet typically this does not occur. It was also clear that the hospital might serve a rather wide range of different objectives and any research would need to take account of this as an important part of the hospital's development. This, too, is typical of new organisations. Finally, because of both practical and methodological difficulties the controls of an experiment or clinical trial were quite out of the question. Any research would have to find other ways of 'evaluating' the service and thus any study was bound to differ substantially from a traditional piece of evaluative research. Much evaluative research appears to encounter this difficulty yet it is not always confronted face on.

With these points in mind I prepared a fuller research design which met with considerable criticism. Although scholars do not usually report the alleged weaknesses of research proposals that fail to attract support it is instructive to note the reasons given for criticisms at this stage insofar as they shed light on the process of setting up evaluative research.

In general practitioners and administrators saw evaluation as, in principle, a straightforward exercise. A research project would collect the data and deal with technical complications that might arise through data collection and analysis. Support for evaluation which did not approach the task in this way was muted on several counts. The study was seen as introducing unnecessary complications. There was a straightforward question, 'Has the impact of this day hospital upon the community proved beneficial?' and what was required was research which would measure that. The study was seen as failing to specify what objectives of the hospital were to be evaluated and how. Furthermore the study failed to specify any 'outcome' measures. In general it was felt that the study did not fit that rational model of research which the term 'evaluation' tended to suggest.

Again with these points in mind I prepared a revised research design (which did attract support). I had learned that a particular mode of health service 'evaluation' is so deeply embedded in administrative and professional (and some academic) practice that any study which departed from this mode would have to treat the term 'evaluation' with considerable caution and might even have to be cast in other terms. Thus insofar as 'evaluative' research rests on a presumed rational relationship between means and ends in service provision and a requirement to specify in advance of the research the service objectives, etcetera, then this study is not an 'evaluative' study but rather a study of some of the problems associated with evaluative research. The distinction is drawn throughout in this research between 'topic' and 'resource'. The objectives, etcetera, of the day hospital are seen, at least initially, as topics for research investigation rather than as resources to be defined in advance and used as tools of research. Thus the task of specifying objectives and outcomes is seen as dependent upon the results of the research proposed here. These results might facilitate that task. On the other hand they might indicate that the task was, in any case, a misguided one.

Aims and Approach

As several methodological tests have pointed out, evaluative research often begins with a deceptively simple format: define service goals, specify service outcomes as measures of goal achievement, define criteria of success, isolate the effects of the service from other possible causes, measure achievements, and adjudicate on the success (or otherwise) of the service. The simplicity is deceptive because, as a good deal of research in hospitals as well

206

as other organisations has shown, objectives vary between and
within significant groups, are complex, multiple, conflicting, change
over time and context, are variously interpreted, are notoriously
ambiguous and sometimes are difficult to locate at all. Moreover,
in policy studies the presumed rational relationship between goals
and outcomes has been questioned and described as an ideological
gloss rather than an accurate description of the development of new
services. Pluralist models direct our attention to several consti-
uencies of service organisations and incrementalist theories point to
ambiguity and confusion as typical rather than unusual features of
most agencies.

An alternative approach to what has been termed 'rationalistic'
analysis, is therefore, to expect that generally the objectives of
new health and welfare organisations will be presented in different
ways by the different groups involved (or else they will be presented
in such general terms that they can be and usually are interpreted
for practice in different ways by the different groups involved) and
then study these differences. There may be no single criterion of
success but rather what shall count as success will be itself a part
of the organisation's growth and development. Research may then turn
this feature of health service organisations to advantage by using
a study of the various interpretations of service objectives and the
way in which different groups pursue what they see as important
outcomes and notions of success, as a way into studying the underlying structure and functions of the operation of the service.

As a new psychogeriatric day hospital, the particular hospital
being examined in this research, is an especially good location for
this type of study. First it is a new organisation and it will be
possible for the research to take advantage of that. Of course few
organisations are entirely stable over time and, as historical
studies of hospitals have shown, the goals and objectives and
influences of different groups are continually altering. However,
change in the early months is often particularly clear and, most
important for present purposes, debate and conflict about hospital
objectives is often quite explicit at this time and thus most readily
observable. So research attention is drawn to issues which might
otherwise pass unnoticed. Second, the activities of diagnosis and
prognosis in geriatric psychiatry are sufficiently flexible to allow
for a wide range of interpretations on the part of nursing staff,
paramedicals, social workers, relatives and others, of the nature of
the 'problem' as well as the nature of a suitable solution. We
might thus expect perceptions of the services of this kind of hospital
to be particularly characterised by divergence and ambiguity. Third,
the hospital involves a particularly wide range of different kinds
of staff with social work services playing a more significant role in
this hospital than is usual within the health service. And precisely
because patients attend only in the daytime and for a variable number
of days in the week, the perceptions of 'community based' professionals - home-help organisers, general practitioners, area team social
workers, community nurses, occupational therapists - may have a
direct bearing upon the way in which the hospital operates.

207

The aims of the research, stated earlier in summary, can thus now be spelled out a little in the form of a series of questions. Firstly, what are the different and significant groups involved in the operation of the day hospital? Initial study suggests, at least, the following list: consultant psychiatrist, day hospital nurses, ward nursing staff, social worker, area team social workers, residential social workers, community nurse, occupational therapist, chiropodist, physiotherapist, medical officer, home-help organisers, general practitioners, relatives, patients and hospital administrators. Of course, these groups vary in significance and there may be others. Secondly, what are their conceptions of the objectives of the hospital, of relevant measures of the outcomes of its services and of criteria for judging success? Thirdly, in what ways do the different groups implement these objectives as they see them in the part that they play in the hospital's operation and how does this experience, in turn, influence their conception of the hospital's services and the problems of its patients? Fourth, what factors might explain why the hospital is viewed in particular and different ways? And finally, what are the implications of such an analysis of the hospital for the way in which evaluative research should be conducted?

One or two brief examples may serve to illustrate the approach.

A review of background papers to the planning of the hospital indicated that much of the initial impetus arose from a concern amongst health service administrators and consultant psychiatrists at the high level of demand which could not be met in the area, at least in the immediate future, for hospital beds in psychogeriatric in-patient wards. Thus for some groups there was the immediate and relatively limited task of reducing numbers on the waiting list for hospital admission.

However, this was not a problem for all groups involved. Social work managers, for example, have a waiting list problem of a different kind and might well view the day hospital as a way of relieving demand for the services of hard pressed area teams or freeing places in residential institutions which may be coping with psychogeriatric patients for which they were never designed. Likewise general practitioners might expect the day hospital to accept daytime respon- sibility for some patients who are currently under their regular care.

Even the limited objective of reducing the waiting list for in- patient beds diversified and was interpreted in different ways. Some groups saw the day hospital as a possible 'half-way house' for discharging patients who could otherwise never be expected to vacate a permanent bed. An alternative view saw the day hospital as a 'half-way house' in the opposite direction, delaying the admission of patients who would otherwise become rapidly institutionalised. A further possibility saw the day hospital as an alternative to the use of emergency beds. No doubt there are other perceptions as well. The point that is being made here is simply to illustrate the way in which by starting with varying perceptions about the role of the day hospital in complimenting as well as replacing, both community and in-patient services, within the social work as well as the health services sector, we may begin to understand how patients move between the day hospital and other forms of care.

Informal discussions with relatives and participant observation at the meetings of the relatives' groups also suggested that the way in which 'senile dementia' is conceptualised might have a direct bearing upon the workings of the hospital. Many relatives are, at least initially, profoundly pessimistic and see the patient as going 'steadily downhill'. Some groups of staff, however, while expecting long term deterioration may describe to relatives how they hope to bring the patient up to a 'certain level' and 'maintain that level' of social competence.

These different views have different implications for discharge practices. Relatives may judge the services of the hospital by the degree to which it increases its services in line with what they see as a steadily growing burden. On the other hand staff may see a reduced number of day's attendance as a mark of success and actively work towards the patient's discharge, at least for a period of time, before readmission. Whether or not relatives accept and co-operate with this pattern of care may depend upon whether they come to accept a revised model of the patient's illness. In extreme cases relatives seem to have decided that their views were so at odds with those of the staff that they would be better withdrawing the patient entirely from the hospital and seeking alternative arrangements. From the point of view of staff such relatives seem to be 'manipulating the system'. In official statistics such a patient would appear as a 'discharged case'. In other instances relatives seem to have accepted a new view of the patient, and their attitudes towards them have apparently changed markedly, thus altering the nature of the problem with which staff are initially confronted.

Of course much remains to be done by exploring these perceptions in detailed interviews and in studying a larger sample of patients around admission and discharge in order to describe relatives' and staff groups' objectives and strategies. There are also many other aspects of the hospital which are equally significant - for example the relationship between health and social work services and the role of the social worker in the day hospital and in-patient wards. Again the point that is being made here is simply to illustrate the way in which, by focussing on varying perceptions of objectives and services, we gain a framework for describing how the service is developing. We also begin to lay bare some of the complications of evaluative research.

Plan of Investigation

A good deal of data collection was undertaken on this project before a final plan of investigation was drawn up. This procedure reflected the view that just as good research entails the free move-ment between theory and data so also good research design involves movement between data collection and the plan of investigation and

back again. During the early part of the research I collected
material through the following activities: a review of Health Board
papers on the design and planning of the hospital; attendance at
meetings of the hospital working party (initially responsible for the
planning process); observation at the weekly case conference/staff
meetings at the hospital; participant observation at the regular
meetings of the relatives' groups; a review of patients' case notes
with extraction of a set of information on patient characteristics,
prognosis, diagnosis, reason for admission as given in psychiatric
and social background reports, and other data, on the complete hospital
population at one point in time; more informal conversations with
staff, relatives and some patients; some limited observation of hospital routines, occupational therapy sessions and other activities;
visits to some other hospitals.

These data will be reported separately but in the present context
there were significant methodological achievements. I developed good
working relations with hospital staff and established the level of
trust and co-operation which the main study requires if it is to be
successful. I also explored the feasibility of a range of data
collecting techniques in the context of this hospital and established
that later plans were practicable.

One of the main difficulties in specifying a detailed plan of
investigation was the fact that since hospital policies and practices
were still evolving many aspects of the research procedure had to be
decided in the light of the hospital's development. This difficulty
reflected the view, discussed earlier in this paper, that it would be
an oversimplification to presume that the exact nature of the
hospital's policies and services (that is, what it was that was being
evaluated) could be known a priori. For example, during preliminary
work, data collected through the relatives' groups were amongst the
most useful although at the start of the project these groups did not
exist. Again, the working party disbanded on responsibility for the
new hospital passing from area to district level within the Health
Authority. It was not at first clear just how many steering groups
would operate within the district administration. Nevertheless some
general features of the planned final investigations are clear.

The two years planned for the study will be divided into separate
periods. Several months will be used to familiarise new staff with
the hospital, continue observation work, pilot interview schedules
prepared on the basis of preliminary data and analyse hospital records
for the period between the start of the hospital and the start of the
main phase of the research.

The research will then systematically monitor the activities of
the hospital over a set period. Thus for each new patient we shall
ask such questions as; How was the patient referred to the hospital
and why? On what basis were psychiatric and social background
assessments made and what reasons were given for admission or not?
What was the attitude of relatives towards admission? What was the
prognosis on admission? What other services were previously involved?

What nursing programme and other treatment did the patient receive?
If the patient was discharged what reasons were given? What was the
attitude of relatives towards discharge? What other forms of care did
the patient receive on discharge? How did doctors, nurses, social
workers, relatives and referral agents judge the success or otherwise
of the hospital in relation to this patient? Through the answers to
such questions we would hope to build up an overall picture of the
work of the hospital as it evolved through major groups pursuing what
they saw to be its main purposes. Whether or not it will be possible
to monitor all new cases in this way will depend upon the 'turnover'
that the hospital achieves. Initially it took up to 25 patients each
day with about 50 attending each week. It may be necessary to sample.

It is also an important feature of the study that it is planned
to use a team of fieldworkers. Although it will obviously be sensible
to maintain some flexibility, at this stage it is envisaged that one
will continue with observational work and records analysis, that the
second will be mainly responsible for interviewing (especially relatives and GP's) and the third will conduct the comparative studies
described below as well as undertaking fieldwork in connection with
the main case study. The use of a team of workers is also useful in
allowing data to be collected in different places at the same time
and in some particularly intensive kinds of observational work. It
will be possible to observe the hospital from the perspective of
separate observers.

Since the research will combine the collection and analysis of
both quantitative and qualitative material, it will also be possible
to observe the hospital from the perspective of separate data sources.
For instance, a statistical account of patient flow through the
hospital over a 12 month period will be set in the context of, for
example, an account of those varying conceptions of confusion amongst
the elderly that have influenced the decisions which produce this
flow pattern. Medical and social work records will be used as a
source of both statistical information and as indicators of those
notions of a successful service which are embodied in reporting
practices.

Thus, following the principles of methodological triangulation
it is planned to examine different facets of the hospital's services
from the standpoint of different sources of material - interview data,
records and direct observations. It is not unusual in studies of this
type to collect material of different kinds. But in this research it
is hoped to triangulate data with respect to the same sample of
patients, so that rather than comparing social workers general modes
of assessing patients with the way psychiatric diagnosis generally
occurs, we shall be comparing the rather specific assessments related
to particular clients. Likewise we will discuss relatives' attitudes
in relation to those particular clients also. In practice this may be
complicated but it will be much easier with a team of researchers.
If successful, it is a powerful way of exploring the relationships
between different groups' conceptions of the patients and hospital
and the service provision that ensues. In analysing the data it is

also planned to pursue those methods of quantifying qualitative
material which have been explored in some other studies. Certainly
the analysis of large volumes of observational data is often unsatisfactory at the present time.

Finally, it is planned to conduct comparative case studies of
some other psychogeriatric day hospitals in order to be able to set
the study of this one hospital in a broader context. In line with
the general approach of this research it is important to stress that
these comparisons will make no pretence to the tight control of
similarities and differences between hospitals in order to isolate
those causal factors that account for variations in the outcomes of
services. (Even leaving aside the problems of this mode of analysis
to which I have already referred, there would, anyway, be too many
variable factors and too few causes in the sample, to attempt such a
design). It is not essential to the underlying logic of this study
to conduct comparative work but it will considerably enhance the
policy implications of the research by ameliorating some of the
grosser defects of the single case study approach.

Given the way in which the aims of the project have been described the case study method does have many advantages. In particular
it fosters the very detailed and intensive fieldwork that is required
in the competent use of observational methods and in building up a
picture of the way in which varying conceptions of the hospital's
purposes interact to produce its services. But there is a major
weakness. Such research is always open to doubt that the particular
case may have been so unusual that it is misleading to draw any
general conclusions from it all. Several briefer (and necessarily
more superficial) comparisons will seek to allay these doubts by
providing some answer to the question, 'To what extent is this
hospital idiosyncratic or to what extent might we reasonably expect
conclusions drawn from a study of this hospital to apply to other
psychogeriatric day hospitals also?'

It is proposed to spend approximately four weeks in each of
several other hospitals and in each case the research will mirror the
work of the central case but, as it were, in miniature. Periods of
observation will be smaller and fewer professionals will be interviewed. However, these data will be adequate in indicating major
similarities and differences. Some of the differences will also
dictate variations in data collection. For example, relatively few
hospitals have formal relatives' groups. So it will be necessary to
maintain a flexible approach.

There will also be lessons to be learned from the comparative
studies as the research progresses. There is advantage to conducting
these studies towards the end of the research since by that time the
main pattern of investigation will be well established. On the other
hand comparisons conducted early may sensitise the team to features
which might otherwise have been neglected. It is therefore proposed
to conduct data collection for the comparative studies at different
points through the research.

Concluding Note

In summary, then, the centrepeice of this research will be an ethnography of one psychogeriatric day hospital set in the context of comparative case studies, and drawing upon direct participant observation of the day-to-day life of the hospital, observations of case conferences, staff meetings and the range of planning and administrative meetings connected with the running of the hospital, hospital records (especially case files and psychiatric and social background reports but also records of meetings and planning documents) and interviews (both formal and informal) with relatives, members of the major staff groups within the hospital and those groups of community based professionals whose activities have a direct bearing upon the work of the hospital.

In this paper I have been suggesting that these are the data required in the evaluation of a new psychogeriatric day hospital if we take seriously, the points, first, that a 'controlled experiment' is not possible (even if it were desirable), second, that there are a range of views about the right criteria of 'success' and, third, that the nature of the service that it is planned to evaluate often remains, initially, unestablished. I have described some of the problems of launching an evaluative study in health care consistent with these starting points.

As a final note, one further feature of setting up this study has seemed important to me. Although, as I have described, it was necessary to negotiate the nature of the evaluative exercise with professionals, administrators and others, seldom was any doubt expressed about the desirability of 'evaluation' of some kind as a basic feature of health service provision and seldom were either practical or ethical objections raised to data collection in spite of a certain amount of intrusion which some of the methods entail. Perhaps this respect for the activity of 'evaluation' makes it especially important that social scientists should be very clear indeed about the nature of the social process in which they are engaging when they undertake this kind of research.

<u>Annotated References</u>

All too often, the literative review section of a research report reads as something of an academic ritual. In this note I try to illustrate how I am seeking to use existing literature as a resource to solve the problems touched upon in this paper.

The following are references to some studies directly related to research on psychogeriatric day hospitals. The topics dealt with include:

(1) Problems of the excessive demand for hospital beds and the 'silting up' of day care facilities.

(2) The interrelationships between social and medical problems of patients admitted to psychogeriatric care.

(3) The comparison of community with hospital care as measured by follow-up studies.

(4) The interrelationship between services.

(5) Roles and attitudes of relatives towards the mentally disturbed elderly.

Berger, Milton M. and Berger, Lynne Flexner (1971), 'An Innovative Program for a Private Psychogeriatric Day Centre', <u>Journal of The American Geriatric Society</u>, Vol. 19, pp.332-36.

Cross, K.W., Hassall, Christine and Grath, G. (1972) 'Psychiatric Day-Care: The New Chronic Population?', <u>British Journal of Preventive and Social Medicine</u>, Vol. 26, pp.199-204.

Goldstein, S., Birnbom, F., and Miller, B. (1975), 'The Team Approach in a Psychogeriatric Unit', <u>Journal of the American Geriatric Society</u>, Vol. XXIII, pp.37-75.

Goldstein, S, Sevriuk, J., and Grauer, H. (1968), 'The Establishment of a Psychogeriatric Day Hospital', <u>Canadian Medical Association Journal</u>, Vol. 98, pp.955-59.

Goldstein, S.E. and Carlson, S. (1976), 'Evolution of an Active Psychogeriatric Day Hospital', CMA Journal, Vol. 115, pp.874-76.

Greene, J.G. and Timbury, G.C., (1979), 'A Geriatric Psychiatry Day Hospital Service: A Five-Year Review', <u>Age and Ageing</u>, Vol.8.

Greiff, Shirely, A. and McDonald, Robert, D. (1973) 'Roles of Staff i in a Psychogeriatric Day Care Centre', <u>The Gerontologist</u>, Vol. 13. pp.30-44.

Hassall, Christine, Gath, D., and Cross, K.W. (1972), 'Psychiatric Day-Care in Birmingham', <u>British Journal of Preventive and Social Medicine</u>, Vol. 26, pp.112-20.

214

Isaacs, Bernard (1971), 'Geriatric Patients: Do Their Families Care?', British Medical Journal, Vol. 4, pp.282-86 .

Kasius, Richard V. (1966), 'Some Aspects of Patient-Flow in the Dutchess County Unit, 1960-63', in Gruenberg, Ernest M. (Ed.). pp.194-213.

Lipscomb, Colin F. (1971), 'The Care of the Psychogeriatrically Disturbed Patient in the Community', American Journal of Psychiatry, Vol. 127, pp.107-15.

McDonald, Robert D., Meulander, Arthur, Hold, Olga and Holcomb, Nancy S. (1971), 'Description of a Non-Residential Psychogeriatric Day-Care Facility', The Gerontologist, Vol.II, pp.322-28.

Markson, Elizabeth, Kwoh, Ada. Cumming, John and Cumming, Elaine. (1971), 'Alternative to Hospitalization for Psychiatrically Ill Geriatric Patients', American Journal of Psychiatry, Vol.127, pp.95-102.

Martin, F.M. (1966) 'Trends in Psychogeriatric Care', Planning, Vol. XXXII, No. 467.

The problems of evaluation in the field of mental health are dealt with quite fully in:

Gruenberg, Ernest, M. (Ed.), (1966), Evaluating the Effectiveness of Mental Health Services, Proceedings of a round table at the Sixtieth Anniversary Conference of the Millbank Memorial Fund, April 5-7. 1965, published as Part 2 of the Millbank Memorial Fund Quarterly, January

A general discussion of evaluative research, pointing out many of the issues raised in this proposal, is:

Weiss, Carol, H. (1972), Evaluation Research: Methods of Assessing Program Effectiveness, Englewood Cliffs, New Jersey, Prentice-Hall.

Statements on an approach to evaluation quite different from the position adopted in this proposal are to be found, for example, in:

Cochrane, A.L. (1971), Effectiveness and Efficiency: Random Reflection on Health Services, The Nuffield Provincial Hospitals Trust.

Williams, Alan and Anderson, Robert (1975), Efficiency in the Social Services, Oxford, Blackwell; London, Martin Robertson.

In seeking guidance on particular methodological problems I propose to rely quite heavily upon:

Denzin, Norman K. (1970) The Research Act in Sociology, London, Butterworths.

215

Douglas, Jack D.(1976) <u>Investigative Social Research: Individual and</u> <u>Team Field Research</u>, London, Sage.

Useful comments on the particular difficulties of analysing qualitative data are contained in:

Blaxter, Mildred (Ed.) (1979) 'The Analysis of Qualitative Data: A Symposium', <u>The Sociological Review</u>, Vol. 27, No. 4 New Series.

The approach to the study of organisational goals and objectives within this proposal is consistent with, and influential by, the key discussions in:

Albrow, Martin (1968) 'The Study of Organisations - Objectivity or Bias?' in J. Gould <u>Penguin Social Science Survey</u>, Harmondsworth, Penguin.

Bittner, Egon (1965) 'The Concept of Organisation', reprinted in Graeme Salamen and Kenneth Thomson (Eds.) <u>People and Organisations</u>, London, Longman for the Open University Press.

Zimmerman, Don H. (1971) 'The Practicalities of Rule Use', in Jack D. Douglas (Ed.) <u>Understanding Everyday Life</u>, London, Routhledge and Kegan Paul.

A full (if now dated) review of research which illustrates the problems of studying goals and objectives of hospitals is:

Perrow, Charles (1965) 'Hospitals: Technology, Structure and Goals', in James G. March (Ed.) <u>Handbook of Organisations</u>, Chicago, McNally.

DISABILITY EVALUATION
Ronald Lyle

Planning a rational programme of rehabilitation for the disabled elderly person, involves not only a diagnostic assessment of the pathology present, but also a functional evaluation of the degree and type of disability present. The process of predicting likely difficulties, and of compensating for these, is likely to become even more necessary as increasingly, elderly patients are unable to be accommodated within hospitals. Until recently, only a few clinical psychologists took a particular interest in the problems of the elderly, but on closer examination, one can discern a number of areas in which their skills might be put to good use.

A prime skill of the psychologist lies in making a detailed behavioural and cognitive assessment of his patient, although in recent years, considerable energies have also been channelled into the conducting of treatments. The types of assessment in which the psychologist could play a part, fall naturally into two groupings. These consist of:

1. Functional assessments of behaviour and

2. Cognitive assessments predictive of coping behaviour.

Each of these will now be dealt with in turn.

A substantial proportion of occupational therapy time in physical rehabilitation is absorbed in testing competency in Activities of Daily Living. However, such tests are rarely standardised, in the sense of being administered in the same way, and at the same length, to each patient. In addition, some compromise is always required as between the time needed to conduct the test and the comprehensiveness of the assessment obtained. A further important distinction may be drawn between those tests of A.D.L. which are administered behaviourally in the presence of the examiner, and those which are scored simply from the rater's personal recollection of the patients general level of competence.

Most of the better known indices of A.D.L. e.g. the Barthel Index (Mahoney and Barthel (1965)), the Kenny Self-Care Evaluation (Schoening and Iversen, 1968) and the Katz Index of A.D.L. (1970) all provide for some criteria for determining the degree of dependence or otherwise on others in performance; the criteria frequently differing according to the activity assessed. Halstead and Hartley (1975) adopted the interesting approach of quantifying dependency by using a diary method to record the frequency and duration of acts of assistance to the patient by staff care. Hence the patient's needs, and their cost to others, might be evaluated. They cited the example of two patients, both incontinent, once per day in one case, and twelve times in the other: the latter posed a considerably greater demand on staff time. The importance of distinguishing capability from performance was illustrated by the findings of discrepancies in the same self-care skills as performed at different times of the day, due

in part to the effects of fatigue. They also argued that tests of
A.D.L. frequently elicited an atypically optimal performance from the
patient, because of a sense of occasion: hence observation over a
period of time was to be preferred. Halstead and Hartley, in a very
thorough paper, also investigated percent inter-rater agreement on
recorded time and frequency of assistive acts for various categories
of A.D.L., but found this to range between 37 and 80 per cent for the
former, and 51 and 97 per cent for the latter.

The present study reported here, sought to overcome some of the
difficulties inherent in previous work, and to develop a more rapid
and logical way of assessing A.D.L. Typically, A.D.L. assessments
group activities into categories such as Toilet, Feeding, Dressing,
Bathing etc. This may at first sight appear sensible enough, but on
further consideration, many of the activities which are thus grouped
together, do not necessarily involve the exercise of identical, or
even similar, motor functions. If it were possible to identify
groupings of items where certain movement patterns were perhaps shared,
then possibly competency on one item of the group might enable predictions to be made about competency in other items of the same group.
The present study describes an attempt to identify just such <u>functional</u>
groupings of items, and to arrange them into an hierarchial order of
difficulty. The study was undertaken as a prelude to a trial of the
effectiveness of treatment in the rehabilitation of stroke patients,
but the principles are potentially applicable to other types of
pathology.

Subjects

The subjects were twenty hemiplegic stroke patients attending the
Astley Ainslie Hospital. Patients exhibiting gross short-memory
impairment or having over-riding disability such as blindness, were
excluded. Degrees of dyspraxia and asphasia were not, however,
criteria for exclusion. The mean age was 63.6 years.

Materials

The Home Unit in the Astley Ainslie Hospital was equipped to
permit testing of the 109 A.D.L. items listed in Table 1.

Table 1   Full list of ADL items

ADL	1	Standing balance
ADL	2	Walk 20 metres
ADL	3	Propel wheelchair
ADL	4	Operate door lever
ADL	5	Operate light switch
ADL	6	Operate door knob and key
ADL	7	Wash, rinse and wring teatowel
ADL	8	Place on pulley and raise
ADL	9	Fetch and assemble ironing board
ADL	10	Iron towel
ADL	11	Sweep with long brush

ADL	12	Sweep with short brush and dustpan
ADL	13	Wet mop part floor
ADL	14	Move bin across floor
ADL	15	Operate coin meter
ADL	16	Ascend and descend 5 steps
ADL	17	Get on and off bus
ADL	18	Get into and out of car
ADL	19	Upper garment on and off over head
ADL	20	Upper garment on and off front opening
ADL	21	Lower garment on and off over feet
ADL	22	Fit and remove appliance
ADL	23	Shoes on and off
ADL	24	Dressing gown on and off
ADL	25	Stockings Tights or Socks on and off
ADL	26	Stockings Tights or Socks on and off
ADL	27	Menstrual hygiene
ADL	28	Empty and change catheter bag
ADL	29	(Standing) get stick from floor
ADL	30	On and off chair
ADL	31	Get up from floor
ADL	32	In and out of bed (taking down cover)
ADL	33	Tie shoelaces (using board)
ADL	34	Take gloves on and off
ADL	35	Fasten tie or scarf
ADL	36	Fasten tie or scarf
ADL	37	Fasten buttons on board
ADL	38	Fasten hooks on board
ADL	39	Fasten buckles on board
ADL	40	Fasten zip on board
ADL	41	Wind watch
ADL	42	Take money from purse
ADL	43	Produce coins to order
ADL	44	Operate telephone
ADL	45	Sign name
ADL	46	Sew button
ADL	47	Use scissors
ADL	48	Elecshave or lipstick
ADL	49	Elecshave or lipstick
ADL	50	Cut toe and finger nails
ADL	51	Brush and comb hair
ADL	52	Strip and make bed
ADL	53	Plug in to low point and switch on
ADL	54	Carry coal bucket
ADL	55	Prepare open fire
ADL	56	Strike match
ADL	57	Dust windowsill
ADL	58	Open window
ADL	59	Use carpet sweeper
ADL	60	Get on and off toilet
ADL	61	Use toilet paper
ADL	62	Flush toilet
ADL	63	Manage clothes at toilet
ADL	64	Feel hot and cold taps

```
ADL  65    Simulate wash and dry face
ADL  66    Simulate wash and dry neck
ADL  67    Simulate washing arms to nails
ADL  68    Simulate washing body and back
ADL  69    Simulate washing legs and feet
ADL  70    Simulate wash and dry hair
ADL  71    Brush teeth
ADL  72    In, out and soak dentures
ADL  73    Wet shave
ADL  74    In and out bath
ADL  75    Drink from mug or straw
ADL  76    Sup with spoon
ADL  77    Butter bread
ADL  78    Cut and eat bread (knife and fork)
ADL  79    Eat with fork
ADL  80    Eat boiled egg
ADL  81    Take plate from high press
ADL  82    Open jar
ADL  83    Lift bag of tine across room
ADL  84    Open tin
ADL  85    Turn gas hotplate on and off
ADL  86    Fill kettle
ADL  87    Put kettle on hotplate
ADL  88    Plug kettle in level socket
ADL  89    Pour hot water into teapot
ADL  90    Pour tea into cup
ADL  91    Carry laden tray to low top
ADL  92    Put cup and plates on trolley
ADL  93    Wheel trolley to sink
ADL  94    Turn taps on and off
ADL  95    Wash up crockery
ADL  96    Dry crockery
ADL  97    Take pan and dish from low press
ADL  98    Read recipe
ADL  99    Peel and cut potatoes
ADL  100   Grate and weigh cheese
ADL  101   Break eggs
ADL  102   Beat eggs
ADL  103   Drain potatoes
ADL  104   Beat all together
ADL  105   Light oven
ADL  106   Insert dish in oven
ADL  107   Take hot dish from oven
ADL  108   Serve onto plate
ADL  109   Clean utensils
```

Common brands of goods were used to allow replication elsewhere. The 109 items were drawn from a range of ADL protocols from a variety of centres, and were selected to cover in some depth, as wide a range of activities as possible. A system of scoring was devised as depicted in Table 2 on the basis of the degree of supervision which the patient required in performing the relevant task.

Table 2   Scoring Criteria

0 - Can perform no part of the test

1 - (If applicable) Performs test partially - can complete only with major assistance

2 - (If applicable) Completes test with slight help OR supervision recommended for safety

3 - (If applicable) Completes test with specified mechanical aid

4 - Completes test safely and independently but takes a longer time or has some difficulty

5 - Performs test normally.

The use of this relatively objective criterion, in addition to being more meaningful for discerning the patient's needs (e.g. self-sufficient, requires mechanical aids, home help) was intended to increase agreement on ratings.

Procedure

The patients were tested on each applicable item by one or two experienced Occupational Therapists. A correlation matrix was next computed on the data so obtained, to identify test items closely correlated across the patient population. Groups of items forming natural, _functional_ subscales, involving perhaps similar movements, were thus detected in place of the logical, _a priori_ scales (e.g. Dressing, Bathroom, etc.) which currently predominate.

With the aid of SPSS the groupings of correlated items were examined to determine whether they fulfilled the stringent criteria for Guttman scales. When the term cutting score is used, this means that a patient was deemed to have passed an item when his score equalled or exceeded that score. Since ability or otherwise to function independently is frequently a meaningful basis for classification of the disabled for the purposes of discharge, a minimum cutting score of 3 is appropriate, as it represents the minimum level of competence to perform and individual test item without assistance.

Results

Twenty-three items, listed in Table 3, were discarded as being insufficiently widely applicable or not suitably correlated for inclusion in a Guttman scale. Eight non-scale items (Table 4) were discarded since all patients scored at least 4 on them, and six items (Table 5) consisting of male and female variants of similar activities were condensed into three.

221

Table 3   Uncorrelated or insufficiently applicable items

ADL	4	Operate door level
ADL	5	Operate light switch
ADL	22	Fit and remove appliance
ADL	23	Shoes on and off
ADL	27	Menstrual hygiene
ADL	28	Empty and change catheter bag
ADL	32	In and out of bed
ADL	33	Tie shoelaces
ADL	34	Put gloves on and off
ADL	36	Fasten tie or scarf
ADL	38	Fasten clothing hooks
ADL	41	Wind watch
ADL	45	Sign name
ADL	46	Sew button
ADL	63	Manage clothes and toilet
ADL	68	Simulate washing body and neck
ADL	71	Brush teeth
ADL	73	Wet shave
ADL	74	In and out of bath
ADL	88	Plug kettle in level socket
ADL	93	Wheel trolley to sink
ADL	101	Break eggs
ADL	102	Beat eggs

Table 4   Non-scaleable items passed by all patients

ADL	58	Open window
ADL	61	Use toilet paper
ADL	64	Feel hot and cold taps
ADL	65	Simulate wash and dry face
ADL	66	Simulate wash and dry neck
ADL	75	Drink from mug or straw
ADL	76	Sup with spoon
ADL	94	Turn taps on and off

Table 5   Equivalent male and female items

ADL	25	Socks on and off (Men)
ADL	26	Stockings or Tights on and off (Women)
ADL	35	Fasten tie (Men)
ADL	36	Fasten scarf (Women)
ADL	48	Electric shave (Men)
ADL	49	Apply lipstick (Women)

The remaining 75 items were arranged into 12 Guttman scales, which follow in the body of the test. Within each scale, the number in brackets indicates the cutting score applied. The items in each scale are arranged in descending order of difficulty. For each scale, two statistics are quoted, namely the coefficient of reproducibility, which is a measure of the predictability of a respondent's response pattern on the basis of his total score on that scale; and secondly the coefficient of scalability. Nie et al. (1975) recommend that a coefficient of reproducibility of above 0.9 and a coefficient of scalability of well above 0.6, be taken to indicate that a Guttman scale is valid. Names were assigned to the scales following inspection of constituent items.

GUTTMAN SCALE: BALANCE

(Cutting Score in Brackets)

ADL	9	(4)	Fetch and assemble ironing
ADL	50	(4)	Cut toe and finger nails
ADL	2	(4)	Walk 20 metres
ADL	17	(4)	Get on and off bus
ADL	16	(4)	Ascend and descend 5 steps
ADL	16	(3)	Ascend and descend 5 steps
ADL	81	(4)	Take plate from high press
ADL	29	(4)	(Standing) Get stick from floor
ADL	1	(4)	Standing balance
ADL	2	(3)	Walk 20 metres
ADL	1	(3)	Standing balance

Coefficient of Reproducibility = 0.9234
Coefficient of Scalability = 0.6800

GUTTMAN SCALE: SHOULDERS

ADL	60	(4)	Get on and off toilet
ADL	31	(4)	Get up from floor
ADL	13	(4)	Wet mop part floor
ADL	11	(4)	Sweep with long brush
ADL	12	(4)	Sweep with short brush and dustpan
ADL	105	(4)	Light oven
ADL	60	(3)	Get on and off toilet

Coefficient of Reproducibility = 0.9000
Coefficient of Scalability = 0.7255

GUTTMAN SCALE: ARMS

ADL	8	(4)	Place on pulley and raise
ADL	14	(4)	Move bin across floor
ADL	24	(4)	Dressing gown on and off
ADL	19	(4)	Upper garment on and off over head
ADL	3	(4)	Propel wheelchair
ADL	42	(4)	Take money from purse

ADL	51	(4)	Brush and comb hair
ADL	86	(4)	Fill kettle
ADL	82	(4)	Open jar

Coefficient of Reproducibility = 0.9800
Coefficient of Scalability   = 0.8667

GUTTMAN SCALE: TWO WRISTS

ADL	99	(4)	Peel and cut potatoes
ADL	60	(4)	Get on and off toilet
ADL	7	(4)	Wash, rinse and wring teatowel
ADL	104	(4)	Beat all together
ADL	79	(4)	Eat with fork

Coefficient of Reproducibility = 0.9400
Coefficient of Scalability   = 0.7143

GUTTMAN SCALE: TWO HANDS

ADL	84	(4)	Open tin
ADL	91	(4)	Carry laden tray to low top
ADL	80	(4)	Eat boiled egg
ADL	107	(4)	Take hot dish from oven
ADL	39	(4)	Fasten buckle board
ADL	40	(4)	Fasten zip board

Coefficient of Reproducibility = 0.9333
Coefficient of Scalability   = 0.7419

GUTTMAN SCALE: ONE HAND

ADL	84	(3)	Open tin
ADL	10	(4)	Iron towel
ADL	20	(4)	Upper garment (front opening) on and off
ADL	21	(4)	Lower garment on and off over feet
ADL	15	(4)	Operate coin meter
ADL	30	(4)	On and off chair
ADL	37	(4)	Fasten buttons on board
ADL	79	(4)	Eat with fork
ADL	104	(3)	Beat all together
ADL	108	(3)	Serve onto plate

Coefficient of Reproducibility = 0.9789
Coefficient of Scalability   = 0.8261

GUTTMAN SCALE: GRIPFORCE

ADL	54	(4)	Carry coal bucket
ADL	83	(4)	Lift bag of tins across room
ADL	6	(4)	Operate door knob and key
ADL	59	(4)	Use carpet sweeper
ADL	83	(3)	Lift bag of tins across room
ADL	87	(4)	Put kettle on hotplate
ADL	106	(4)	Insert dish in oven
ADL	62	(4)	Flush toilet
ADL	85	(4)	Turn gas hotplate on and off
ADL	89	(4)	Pour hot water in teapot
ADL	57	(4)	Dust windowsill
ADL	90	(4)	Pour tea into cup

Coefficient of Reproducibility = 0.9333
Coefficient of Scalability = 0.6923

GUTTMAN SCALE: PINCH

ADL	78	(4)	Cut and eat bread (knife and fork)
ADL	78	(3)	Cut and eat bread (knife and fork)
ADL	77	(4)	Butter bread
ADL	100	(4)	Grate and weigh cheese
ADL	67	(4)	Simulate washing arms to nails
ADL	67	(3)	Simulate washing arms to nails
ADL	100	(3)	Grate and weigh cheese
ADL	77	(3)	Butter bread

Coefficient of Reproducibility = 0.9750
Coefficient of Scalability = 0.8857

GUTTMAN SCALE: ADROIT

ADL	26	(4)	Stockings tights or socks on and off
ADL	96	(4)	Dry crockery
ADL	44	(4)	Operate telephone
ADL	49	(4)	Elecshave or lipstick

Coefficient of Reproducibility = 1.000
Coefficient of Scalability = 1.000

GUTTMAN SCALE: COMPLEX 'A'

ADL	52	(4)	Strip and make bed
ADL	97	(4)	Take pan and dish from low press
ADL	109	(4)	Clean utensils
ADL	95	(4)	Wash up crockery

Coefficient of Reproducibility = 0.9750
Coefficient of Scalability = 0.7143

GUTTMAN SCALE: COMPLEX 'B'

ADL	70	(4)	Simulate wash and dry hair
ADL	72	(4)	In, out and soak dentures
ADL	53	(4)	Plug in to low point and switch on
ADL	103	(4)	Put cup and plates on trolley

Coefficient of Reproducibility   =   0.9692
Coefficient of Scalability   =   0.7778

GUTTMAN SCALE: PLAN

ADL	18	(4)	Get in and out of car
ADL	56	(3)	Strike match
ADL	98	(4)	Follow recipe
ADL	47	(4)	Use scissors
ADL	55	(4)	Prepare open fire
ADL	43	(4)	Produce coins to order

Coefficient of Reproducibility   =   0.9667
Coefficient of Scalability   =   0.8333

Discussion

It is worth noting that many of the Guttman scales appear to represent the use of a particular limb, or a particular pattern of movement or skill. These <u>functional</u> scales are contrasted with the grouping of items by location (bathroom, kitchen) or type of activity (cleaning, dressing) which appear to be the norm in current ADL tests.

A move towards functional groupings of items would offer some advantages. First, identification of particular defective patterns of movement may allow improvement on a wider number of ADL items by directing therapy at the defective pattern. Secondly, knowledge of performance on a handful of items may enable predictions to be made over a larger range of activities. Thirdly, there may be implications for the design and prescription of aids. On the basis of economy of effort, the case can readily be justified. Let us assume that a patient be first tested on the most difficult item within each scale, and if he passes that item, be credited with having passed the remaining items within that scale. Should he fail the most difficult by scoring below the specified cutting score, the least difficult item is next administered. Should he fail that, he is regarded as having failed all items contained in that scale. Should the individual pass the last difficult, the remaining items could be administered sequentially in increasing difficulty, until a failure occurred. Assuming this latter convention, a reworking of the data reveals that, on the patient sample studied, the Guttman scales would effect a saving of 53 per cent on the number of items which would require to be administered.

It must be admitted that the number of patients tested was relatively small (n = 20). This was because of the time required to administer all items to each patient. Replication on a further 20 hemiplegic patients is underway, although in further support of our findings, it must be stated that the criteria for Guttman scales are very strict, and that we expect our scales to survive cross-validation.

Although the new ADL test will have been validated on hemiplegics it is likely that other groups of physically disabled for whom a particular limb or pattern of movement is impaired, may produce Guttman-type scales of ADL too. Further studies are needed to ascertain this.

Cognitive assessments predictive of coping behaviour

In considering the application of psychology in making cognitive assessments of the elderly, one fairly quickly becomes aware that although cognitive testing is relatively well developed and established within clinical psychology, there has been little attempt systematically to use this information to predict the individual patient's ability to survive independently within society. Thus, although we might be able to say that a patient had an I.Q. at the 40th percentile, we would be unable to predict with any confidence whether he were able to use a bank account for instance, or to organise shopping and self-care activities. One of the best known memory tests, the Wechsler Memory Scale, for instance, simply allows us to compute a 'memory quotient' but leaves us in the dark as to how to use this in predicting the patient's ability to cope with everyday tasks. Just how much memory does a patient require in order to be able to cope with independent existence? And how can he be taught to compensate for this difficulty? For this reason I think it is necessary that we begin to develop measures of cognitive function which are more directly related to competence in Activities of Daily Living. Typical defects which we would wish to identify amongst the elderly, would be degrees of apraxia, and confusional states. Broadbent has made an important step in this direction with his Cognitive Difficulties Questionnaire (1979). This is basically a check-list of symptoms which the patient himself (perhaps rather ill-advisedly) is asked to complete as they describe his own difficulties. A complicating factor here, might be lack of insight, or even memory failure such that deficits in performance were not even recollected!! What is really required, I submit, is a memory or more general cognitive assessment, correlated with a measure of performance in Activities of Daily Living. Thus it would be possible to determine at what levels of cognitive impairment, various activities began to become impaired. Such knowledge might be useful, in deciding whether a patient were fit to return to live alone, or whether, and to what extent, the services of a home-help might be required. In a recent unpublished study (see Appendix) using Progress Assessment Charts to evaluate institutionalised male psychiatric patients, Lyle 1980, found some clusters of items which appeared to constitute Guttman scales identifying cognitive dimensions of everyday activities, e.g.

work performance, prudence, communication, and calculation. Similarly the three scales Complex A, Complex B and Plan identified in the earlier ADL investigation reported above, appeared to identify cognitive dimensions also.

All these approaches represent something of a departure from the almost pure science approach to cognitive testing which has tended to be the norm hitherto. It is obvious, however, that our ways of testing individuals will have to change in this direction if we wish to make predictions about their ability to cope with the demands of life.

REFERENCES

Broadbent, D.E. (1979), The Cognitive Difficulties Questionnaire. In preparation.

Halstead, L. and Hartley, R.B. (1975), Time Care Profile; An evaluation of a new method of assessing ADL dependence. Archives of Physical Medicine and Rehabilitation, 56, pp.110-115.

Katz, S., Downs, T.D., Cash, H.R., and Grotz, R.C. (1970), Progress in development of the Index of ADL. Gerontologist, 10, pp.20-30.

Lyle, R.C. (1980), Guttman structures in Gunzburg Progress Assessment Charts of institutionalised psychiatric patients. Unpublished study.

Mahoney, F.I., and Barthel, D.W. (1965), Functional evaluation: The Barthel Index. Maryland State Medical Journal, 14, pp.61-65.

Nie, N.H., Hull, C.H. Jenkins, J.G., Steinbrenner, K., and Bent, D.H. (1975) Statistical Package for the Social Sciences. (2nd edition). New York: McGraw Hill.

Schoening, H.A., and Iversen, I.A. (1968), Numerical scoring of self-care status. Archives of Physical Medicine and Rehabilitation, 49, pp.221-229.

GUTTMAN STRUCTURE IN P.A.C. ASSESSMENTS OF 38 CHRONICALLY INSTITUTIONALISED PSYCHIATRIC PATIENTS

Orientation

Finds way to six different neighbourhood places

Makes enquiries from strangers in unfamiliar places

Makes enquiries from police and passers-by

Makes enquiries for goods in shops

Remembers and delivers simple message after 10 minutes.

    Coefficient of Reproducibility: 0.9684
    Coefficient of Scalability: 0.8723

Time Orientation

Can write clock times to dictation

Understands time intervals e.g. 3.30 – 4.30 = 1 hour

Understands time equivalents e.g. $9.15 = \frac{1}{4}$ past 9

Can state correct time + 2 hours.

    Coefficient of Reproducibility: 0.9737
    Coefficient of Scalability: 0.8095

Calculation

Can add sums of £ p

Can add different coins up to £1

Can add coins up to 50p

Can add coins up to 10p

Understands time equivalents

    Coefficient of Reproducibility: 1.00
    Coefficient of Scalability: 1.00

Out and About

Uses public transport for unfamiliar journeys

Arranges for minor repairs (watch, shoe, radio)

Reads store guides, advertisements

Journeys by public transport, changing once

Purchases food from different sources

Use public transport for simple journeys

Adds simple sums, bus fares, lunches

Can address an envelope

Can write an acceptable signature

    Coefficient of Reproducibility: 0.9240
    Coefficient of Scalability: 0.7920

PRAXIA

Executes complex useful activities independently

Slightly less complex activities without supervision

Several simple tasks outside of routine

Manual dexterity fairly good: hammering, sewing.

    Coefficient of Reproducibility: 0.9605
    Coefficient of Scalability: 0.9048